# A Woman in the Great Outdoors

# A Woman in the Great Outdoors

Adventures in the
National Park Service

Melody Webb

UNIVERSITY OF NEW MEXICO PRESS ❧ ALBUQUERQUE

Library of Congress
Cataloging-in-Publication Data

Webb, Melody, 1946–
   A woman in the great outdoors : adventures in the
National Park Service / Melody Webb.— 1st ed.
        p. cm.
   ISBN 0-8263-3175-0 (cloth : alk. paper)
   1.  Webb, Melody, 1946– 2.  United States. National Park
Service—Officials and employees—Biography. 3.  United
States. National Park Service—History. 4.  National parks
and reserves—United States—Management. 5.  National
parks and reserves—Government policy—United States.
I. Title.
   SB481.6.W43 A3 2003
   333.78'3'092—dc21

                                           2003010131

1      2      3      4      5      6      7      8      9

Book Design Kathleen Sparkes
Cover Design Robyn Mundy
Index Andrew L. Christenson

Photo frontispiece Lake Clark National Park in 1978,
courtesy of M. Woodbridge Williams/
National Park Service, Harpers Ferry Center.

Text Typography Minion 11/14
Display Typography Capelli Ultra Plain and Oz Handicraft

Printed in the United States by Sheridan Books, Inc.

∾

To Jack Neckels, John Cook, and Zorro Bradley.
They believed in me.

∾

# Contents

# Preface

Although I am a historian, this book is not a history of national parks, nor is it a personal history or memoir. Instead, I have tried to meld the two genres in order to humanize an institutional study and to broaden an individual's parochial perspective. I use my career in the National Park Service to capture the intangible aspects of day-to-day life—its hassles, successes, and processes. While charting in some detail my career experiences, I also more generally provide context of other events occurring simultaneously or of similar experiences happening elsewhere. For example, my summer on the Yukon River in 1976 contrasted greatly with my peers' celebration of the bicentennial of American independence. On the other hand, my experiences with forest fires were comparable to those of others throughout the park system.

Because this is a chronicle of one person's career, it follows the typical trajectory of a public servant. The first half of the book is one of learning with hands-on experiences perceived with youthful idealism. As I became more removed from day-to-day operations, the second half is characterized by the pragmatism of policy and decision-making. The first half may have more personal adventures, the second half perhaps more enduring consequences.

America's national parks have often been referred to as paradise on earth. They are among the most beautiful places in the world. While older cultures often perceive our history as youthful, we have preserved significant places with as much objectivity as politically possible. Thus our natural and cultural treasures are the nation's crown jewels, entrusted to the National Park Service with political oversight and occasional interference from the Department of the Interior, whose secretary is a member of the president's cabinet.

The environmental perspective of the president of the United States and his designated Interior secretary determines policies and many practices within national parks. I began my career during President Gerald Ford's rather benign administration. Although Ford had once served as a seasonal park ranger, we felt no favoritism but enjoyed strong leadership from the assistant Interior secretary, a strong environmentalist. President Jimmy Carter saved Alaska from developers and forced Congress to pass appropriate legislation. Then President Ronald Reagan and Interior Secretary James Watt shocked the National Park Service with forceful policies favoring concessioners, business entrepreneurs, and recreational users. Most of my career reverberated with issues stemming from these anti-environmental policies. Only in 1997, during President Bill Clinton's second administration, did the pendulum begin its brief swing back toward conservation with a greater awareness of how threatened paradise had become.

Threats to national parks come from many sources. Many are politically inspired; others come from poor managerial judgment. Some threats come from expanding recreational uses, others from business opportunists, still others from visitors themselves. The greatest threat to national parks is ignorance of what is happening to them. It is my hope that this book, in some small way, will increase awareness that although national parks may not be endangered, they are clearly threatened.

National parks and history are my two dearest loves. While I studied one and hiked in the other, it never occurred to me that I could have them both together. Like most college students of the 1960s, rather than worrying about a career, I majored in what I loved, history. My only concern was that I didn't know what I would do with it. I did not want to be a university professor nor did I want to move into law, politics, or journalism. In 1966 the passage of the National Historic Preservation Act sparked the beginning of a new field known as public history. But when I joined the National Park Service and became a public historian, I also became a misfit historian. No one really understood what I did. National parks are associated with naturalists and rangers, not historians. I was neither a professor nor a ranger, so I didn't fit in anywhere. Moreover, I was a woman in a man's world.

Being a female historian in the National Park Service, however, did not keep me from loving mountains, wildlife, and wild places. I believed as ardently in their protection as any ranger or naturalist. I hiked, backpacked, and climbed, not realizing I was unusual. Since I had considered myself typical of my generation, it didn't occur to me that being a woman made any difference. It did. Often I found myself the only woman in a meeting, on a field trip, at a conference. As an eager novice wanting to learn, I unwittingly played to the male ego and solicited male attentions. As I aged, I acquired knowledge and abilities that challenged or confounded men's expectations. In short, I took getting used to.

The National Park Service embodied all that I loved. Its mission is to preserve unimpaired the nation's most beautiful and historical places. This mission also bonded disparate people—historians, rangers, scientists, laborers, bureaucrats—and created an exclusive elite, which one assistant secretary of the Interior compared to the Hitler youth movement. In this book I hoped to capture this unique ethos, this esprit de corps, this intangible sense of community, this collective idealism.

Integral to an understanding of my feelings toward the National Park Service is my relationship to Robert M. Utley. Not only did we share a love of history, the West, and the National Park Service, but our values and beliefs also coincided. To me, Bob merged all that I loved and longed to be. Initially, he helped me understand the arcane field of historic preservation, explained the significance of good bureaucrats, and taught me to write. When I deviated from his professional path into what most would consider the "real Park Service," he relished being a superintendent's spouse.

I never rose in the National Park Service to a high management position. I never became a superintendent of a large natural park nor an executive in a central office. But for twenty-five years my career involved me in a significant phase of National Park Service history. I was in Alaska as we struggled to establish a second park system, larger than that in all the Lower 48. From Santa Fe, I witnessed the abuses of politicization and its effect on strong managers. In my first superintendency, I found the joys of accomplishing goals of lasting consequence and of experiencing the brotherhood of superintendents. And in my last four years at Grand Teton National Park, I battled wildfire, fought irrational assaults on bison, celebrated the return of wolves to Yellowstone, tried to minimize the effects of development and overuse on a popular park, and toiled over the universal bane of employee discontent.

My experiences are not unique, only occasionally unusual. Through them, I try to examine a unique institution that has its own value system, worldview, and precise mission. There is a cliché in the National Park Service that we get paid in sunsets, meaning our work environment is among the most spectacular in the world and compensates for our lousy salaries. We take pride in that cliché. Our mission is more important than money.

I hope that I have captured a small element of that wonderful mystique and, at the same time, raised a consciousness of the dangers confronting our most treasured places. If I have, then the special efforts that Bob Utley, Jack Neckels, John Cook, and Zorro Bradley invested in me have paid off.

Others that I must acknowledge helped in the completion of this book. Faithfully, for six years, Russ Dickenson has sent me the news clippings compiled in the Washington office from various parks and newspapers around the nation. As a former director of the National Park Service he received these as a courtesy from the present director. After I retired, these news clips kept me informed of what was happening in national parks. No other source could have kept me as current and aware of park issues as the local newspapers. Mark Gardner also sent me clippings about national park issues from the *Rocky Mountain News* and the *Denver Post.*

After several years of hearing my stories about the various problems in national parks, a good friend, literary agent Carl Brandt, suggested that I write them in the form of a memoir. Because I was unaware of the genre, my late sister, Rita Scott, lent me some of her favorites. From Carl and Rita, I learned to appreciate a good memoir. Both of them read various versions and offered wise counsel: Carl urged greater context and Rita wanted more introspection. I doubt that I have provided enough of either for both of them. Of course my husband, Bob Utley, has read everything several times over, always encouraging, always supportive, always insistent that it be publishable. Hal Rothman, one of the best historians on national parks, gave me thoughtful criticism and enthusiastic encouragement. Clark Whitehorn, now of the Montana Historical Society, offered valued and constructive comment. My editor, David Holtby of the University of New Mexico Press, helped me shape one book from diverse and convoluting memories. My copyeditor, Jill Root, kept my style and word usage consistent and appropriate. Tom DuRant of the National Park Service's Harpers Ferry office responded with astonishing alacrity with photographs of me in Alaska. Finally, I thank Yale University in general and the Beinecke Library and the Howard R. Lamar Center in particular for providing a supportive and distraction-free environment in which I could work. Most of all, I thank my family and friends who have cheered me on in this unusual endeavor. I hope I have not disappointed them.

# A Woman in a Man's World

 was the only woman in the room. In 1975, at twenty-eight, I was also the youngest. Because I had just started my job with the National Park Service two months earlier, I was also the newest federal employee and, as I soon learned, the only federal historian in Alaska. Moreover, all the others in the room worked for the Bureau of Land Management, a sister agency in the Department of the Interior but nonetheless an ideological rival of the National Park Service. The meeting took place in Anchorage, Alaska's largest city, where most of the federal agencies had their headquarters. My office, however, was in Fairbanks, four hundred miles distant and, as the home of the University of Alaska, the state's undisputed academic and cultural center.

Had I known all this, I might have felt intimidated. Instead, what these men described excited me. The Bureau of Land Management wanted to restore five historic buildings at Fort Egbert, a turn-of-the-century army post near Eagle, on the Yukon River about twenty miles from the Canadian border. Through restoration and interpretation, they hoped to encourage tourism to the Yukon.

Their photographs showed structures in various stages of deterioration. One, the mule barn, was huge, nearly 150 feet long. Others were smaller and reflected some recent repair work. To the apparent cha-grin of the new BLM archeologist, Gary Matlock, construction crews had bulldozed debris and leveled the ground around four of the structures, irretrievably destroying significant archeological information.

"Unlike the National Park Service, which specializes in this sort of thing," one of BLM's managers said, "we have never done anything like it anywhere in the nation. We want to do it right." To help them, they had enticed Gary Matlock away from the National Park Service with a higher salary and the distinction of serving as BLM's first archeologist in Alaska. Bearded and longhaired, dressed in blue jeans and work shirt, Gary stuck out even in Alaska's casually dressed bureaucracy.

Right off he insisted on planning what to do before doing anything, even patching the roofs. Instead, the managers talked about finding uses for the structures, such as allowing the residents of Eagle to use them for community activities. Gary didn't argue, but on a bulletin board behind his head a bumper sticker, surely fixed there by him, proclaimed, "Preser-vation is a use." The slogan reflected Matlock's Park Service values, which contrasted with the pragmatic and utilitarian thinking of the BLM man-agers. I sensed that there had been philosophical disagreements in the past that might not have been completely resolved.

"Because we want to do things right," Gary said, turning the subject back to the current concern, "we need to know the history of Fort Egbert, how it related to the civilian gold-rush town of Eagle, who the major per-sonalities involved were, and how significant the site is." Turning to me, he said, "Here is where you enter the process. As the only federal historian, we hope you will work with us on this project."

His invitation thrilled me. Since childhood I had loved history. My father occasionally took our family of five girls to Indian ruins and dinosaur pits near our Arizona home. After receiving the owner's permission, Daddy let us dig until we became either bored or hungry. Daddy and my oldest sister had nice collections of arrowheads, but I found only pottery shards. Nevertheless, I enjoyed reading stories about Indians and looking through their cast-off wastes for something of value. Later, in high school, I saw a television show on the restoration of Williamsburg, Virginia. The role historians played in tracing the history of a structure fascinated me. Using history to recreate a historic past seemed the ideal job. Now, fifteen years later, BLM was offering me a dream.

Although I could hardly contain my excitement, I raised an issue. "I would love to work with you," I said, "but the National Park Service hired me to do specific projects. Since we are always short of funds, I think BLM should pay my salary while I work for you." Although new to the bureaucracy, I did know that BLM managed 90 percent of Alaska's land, including oil leases, and consequently had plenty of money.

All the men, including Gary, looked stunned. They began to argue that everyone was "bootlegging" the project. Congress hadn't specifically authorized the restoration. Instead, they were taking money from other projects and operations to do the job. "If we pay your salary," Gary pointed out, "we won't have enough money to do other requirements, such as archeology, interpretive planning, and architectural studies. We all need to stretch a bit to make the project work."

"I understand your concerns," I repeated, "but I don't think the National Park Service should pay for a BLM project."

We talked about the problem for a few more minutes. Then the most senior manager concluded, "We've gone as far as we can today. I've got other meetings to attend." We all shook hands, and I left feeling that, despite my youth, I had held my own.

The next day, when I got back to my basement office in Gruening Hall at the University of Alaska in Fairbanks, my boss, Zorro Bradley, met me at the door. "Good heavens," he said, "what kind of a hornet's nest did you stir up in Anchorage yesterday?" I didn't know what he was talking about. "Apparently the area manager of BLM's Fortymile Resource Area called our boss," he said, "and claimed you were impossible to work with. He said you were opinionated, dogmatic, adversarial, stubborn, and tactless."

I couldn't believe that Zorro was talking about the same meeting I had attended. When I described the meeting and my comments, he quietly said, "We all work for the same federal government. When we can, we ought to help each other out. Even if these men refuse to work with you, I think it might be good if you do the research and send it to them. Show them that you are above such pettiness." Still bewildered by the reaction my comments had aroused, I fumbled to explain myself. "Don't let them get to you," Zorro said, trying to reassure me, "just do the job and show them how wrong they were."

After nearly thirty years in the bureaucracy, Zorro knew how to roll with it. As much a maverick as his name, he had been exiled to Alaska from Washington, D.C., for marshaling the opposition of archeologists to the interdisciplinary approach of the National Historic Preservation Act of 1966. On his own, with almost no supervision or support, he had developed programs to assist Alaskan Natives in preserving their cultural traditions. On St. Lawrence Island, in the Bering Sea, he worked to educate the islanders to guard rather than rob their ancestors' graves. By accepting them and their culture, he won their respect and trust.

Maybe because of Zorro's training in anthropology, he did not dismiss my problem with BLM simply as a new employee's ignorance of interagency cooperation. Instead, from the men's comments, he feared there was either a personality or a gender problem. He foresaw the difficult road ahead for me and hoped to insulate me from further abusive confrontations.

Hours later, I still vibrated from the sting of their words and cringed from their unjust appraisal of me. I couldn't believe that I had been so obtuse and imperceptive as not to have picked up their negative vibes. Usually I related well to men. In fact, BLM's aversion to me contrasted starkly with how men had previously treated me.

I grew up a tomboy and was often more comfortable with boys than girls. Dolls bored me. Instead I preferred to ride stick horses, build forts, and explore the vast salt-grass pastures behind our home in northeastern Arizona. When I entered school, basketball and baseball filled my recesses rather than the hopscotch and jump-rope games of other girls. Because of my slight build, I was faster than any boy and usually won foot races. Although my mother worried about my boyish walk and my preference for sports and an outdoor life, I surprised her by liking fancy dresses, attending parties, and playing kissing games.

By high school we had moved from our small town to Tucson, the second largest city in Arizona. Here, with puberty approaching, girls and boys had separate gyms. Instead of applying myself to my studies—I had graduated valedictorian from the eighth grade—I talked and flirted with boys, played cards, enjoyed parties and dances, and generally frittered away my time. I saw myself conforming to the expectations of being a city girl. While never one of the most popular girls, I was well liked, served in student government, and starred in dramatic productions.

In college, boys finally discovered me. My skinny body had filled in and became willowy. I dated often and was frequently propositioned. Three men in one year even proposed marriage. Yet I still enjoyed outdoor activities, especially hiking and backpacking. These interests and my friends led me to join Tucson's Civil Defense search-and-rescue team. When hikers got lost in Tucson's mountains, the team tried to find them before the desert heat finished them. Because only a few women reveled in the hot, exhausting work, I found myself the focus of attention. Men sought me out to talk, seeking to demonstrate their skills and share their knowledge. Later, when I took up flying through the University of Arizona, all my classmates and instructors were men, but they rooted for me to gain the coveted private-pilot license.

In 1969 I married a physician with a strong ego and numerous hobbies. Although he had no interest in history, he was supportive of all my endeavors. One of my early frustrations was not being taken seriously as a historian. A graduate school colleague once said, "Melody, you are just a dilettante housewife dabbling in history."

Not until 1971, however, when I tested my stamina at Outward Bound, an outdoor wilderness school, did my personality collide with the male ego. By this time I was twenty-five years old, eager to climb mountains and learn survival techniques. Fearful of being left in the wake of younger, more fit bodies, each day I faithfully exercised, jogged, and hiked. Consequently, at Outward Bound I was among the few who had conditioned themselves. Within three days my outdoor skills and innate leadership threatened the younger men. One complained: "You are a girl, damn it. Why don't you act like one?"

For the first time in my life, I learned that men found me a strong personality. They thought I was too dominant, too quick to act, and too opinionated. "You're a machine, too efficient, with no emotions," said one young man. "You don't ever *not* come through. You always have to succeed." Another said, "You aren't a woman, soft and needing protection. Why can't you just let me take care of you!"

Now, just three years later, I confronted a similar scenario, not with nineteen-year-old boys but with mature men. Obviously I could not dismiss the problem as immature male egos. I was the problem, either because of my strong personality or because I was a woman or, more likely, because of both.

By 1975 the women's movement was still in its infancy. Only a couple of the Ivy League colleges and none of the military academies had opened their doors to women. As a result of the Civil Rights Act of 1964, women had begun to have more opportunities to advance into previously prohibited occupations. But few women had worked their way into the bureaucratic hierarchy. Consequently, I had no female role models, and men, especially Alaskans, had little experience with professional women.

Weighing only 105 pounds, I looked fragile and insignificant. But my body language, assertiveness, and personal beliefs deviated from societal norms of femininity. Moreover, I didn't properly recognize or defer to men's superiority in age, position, and seniority.

If I had played the role of novice, which I was, and sought advice on how to proceed, the men might have responded as positively as those on my search-and-rescue team and in my flying classes. Instead, I dared to consider myself their professional equal. I had broken the unspoken rules of conduct between a "girl" trainee and an experienced male manager. I wondered if they would have accepted a male historian taking the same stand.

Regardless of my bruised ego and belief that I had been unfairly treated, I could see only two ways to proceed. I could call each of the men in the meeting and apologize for my behavior and plead ignorance of interagency cooperation, thereby calling their bluff. Or I could proceed as Zorro suggested: Do my job, do it well, and let that speak for my professional capability, regardless of personality or gender. Because I didn't believe that my failure to cooperate was the real reason for their displeasure, the first avenue seemed dishonest and manipulative. The only way out of the mess, then, was Zorro's solution.

As I started to follow his advice, I realized that I didn't know how to begin. Although a charismatic high school history teacher had introduced me to historical writing in 1962, my subsequent training at the University of Arizona and San Francisco State College, which respectively earned me bachelor's and master's degrees in history, did not prepare me for anything larger than a seminar paper. Even my one published article in the West's leading popular magazine, *The American West,* was more limited in scope than the Fort Egbert study. I suddenly realized how poorly trained I was to plan, research, and write a long report.

Alaska's lack of appropriate secondary histories handicapped me further. I had to start with basic primary sources, travel narratives, memoirs, and government documents, then try to build an understanding of events and people throughout the Yukon. No wonder BLM wanted a professional historian to assist them. Eventually, I found my way to the basement of the University of Alaska Library, where the collections of unpublished manuscripts, correspondence, and diaries resided. A helpful archivist discovered an unused collection of letters from the commanding officer at Fort Egbert that gave me details of the everyday life and major events of the fort.

After six weeks I had drafted the rudiments of a historical study. It was seventy-five pages long—the longest paper I had ever written. It looked like a seminar paper, with endnotes and bibliography but no chapters. I had not comprehended the concept of chapters, so it was just one long chapter. But I was proud of my product and had found information that no one else had used. Zorro reviewed it and gave me some tips about writing on specific historic structures. Together we delivered the manuscript to Gary Matlock at BLM. He was surprised and not ungrateful.

Although I had written my first research study for the National Park Service, my dream of doing research in the field had not materialized. In fact, as Zorro later told me, his boss had instructed him to keep me out of

Eagle. White Alaskans resented and opposed carving additional national parks from Alaska's massive public lands. Hostility radiated from elected state officials, who decried the federal land grab before state lands had been selected, and from average citizens, who demanded their right to hunt, fish, mine, and develop anywhere in the state. Against this background, tensions between federal officials and Eagle's residents had grown so strained that no one wanted my opinionated presence feeding the flames. Zorro softened the blow with the announcement that the National Park Service had extended my appointment to a four-year assignment.

I was joining an organization in crisis. Prior to 1975, the National Park Service had been a tightly knit group of homogeneous white males. They focused on the large scenic parks of the West and believed that the park ranger was the building block for the service. Other disciplines served primarily to support the cadre of rangers, who protected natural resources and the middle-class American visitor. Their generalized skills in search and rescue, horseback riding, and diplomacy handled most park problems.

The inclusion of historical and recreational areas in the National Park System, in 1933 and 1947 respectively, confounded the purists and introduced new uses and users. Suddenly visitors wanted facts and stories about America's battlegrounds and archeological treasures as well as recreational opportunities such as boating, fishing, and swimming. Reluctantly, the rangers expanded their skills to protect the new visitor and the varied new resources, but still their joy remained the big natural parks.

By 1975, however, the National Park Service found itself undergoing an identity crisis. Three years earlier two urban parks near New York City and San Francisco had permanently altered the mission and future of the service. Purists believed that only sites with the most scenic, scientific, or historical values met criteria for national parks. Urban parks failed all criteria of national significance, they complained, consisting primarily of city playgrounds. Yet the service's most politically astute director, George B. Hartzog, Jr., saw urban parks as not only providing recreation for intercity people but also expanding his constituency exponentially and adding more voices and power to his congressional requests. Sharp divisions appeared between those who agreed with him and those who claimed that the new parks drained the older parks of money and people while diluting the national park concept. As Cleveland and Atlanta clamored for their urban parks, divisions grew wider.

Meanwhile, pressure came from the women's movement to integrate the white male organization. Although women had held positions as naturalists since the 1920s, more than 70 percent remained locked in the clerical ranks regardless of their qualifications. Moreover, only men could become rangers, reserving for their gender the unique hat and badge. Women were relegated to uniforms mimicking those of airline stewardesses, without identifying hat or badge. Responding to affirmative-action pressure, in 1971–72 Director Hartzog actively recruited female rangers, sent the first women to law-enforcement training, and appointed the first nonpolitical women superintendents.

At nearly the same time, Congress passed the Alaska Native Claims Settlement Act of 1971, with two small provisions that further stressed the National Park Service. One, known as d–2, authorized the Interior Department to study and set aside eighty million acres in Alaska for national parks, forests, and wildlife refuges. While no one questioned the national significance of the lands, eighty million acres was larger than the entire National Park System. Some worried that the tail would wag the dog. The other, even smaller section, 14(h), allowed Alaskan Natives to claim two million acres of historic sites and cemeteries from any public lands, even from the proposed parks. As the only federal historian in Alaska, my job description bridged both sections.

Shortly afterward two more blows traumatized the Park Service. First, President Richard Nixon fired the popular and dynamic Hartzog for inadvertently offending one of Nixon's confidants. Then, breaking a fifty-year tradition, the president did not select Hartzog's successor from the Service or the conservation community. Instead, he made the first purely political appointment the NPS had experienced. He chose Ronald Walker, the advance man for his trip to China. Although the young director tried hard, the Watergate scandal ended his regime. President Gerald Ford brought temporary stability with the appointment of a man who had spent his entire career in the Park Service.

By 1975, then, I joined a distressed organization, floundering to find its way. Shaken from its pedestal by nontraditional parks, noncareer appointments, women and minorities, and Alaskan responsibilities, the National Park Service turned for strength to its esprit de corps. Nearly from its beginning, the Park Service prided itself on its unique mission: to preserve national parks unimpaired for future generations. This pride inspired an intense loyalty to the agency and a bonding among employees, rivaling those of the U.S. Marine Corps. In 1963, a disgusted assistant secretary of the Interior had infuriated the Service by comparing the ranger mystique to that of the Nazi Youth Movement.

Ironically, despite all the crises that shook the agency, few within the Service attacked my gender or my personality. Rather, like Zorro, most people seemed to recognize my value and supported my retention. In one of the most macho of male-dominated cultures, I found tolerance, acceptance, and recognition. In other agencies and organizations lacking the traditions and strong identity of the National Park Service, I often encountered prejudice and scorn.

In contrast to other agencies and military cultures, the Park Service prized eccentric but competent individuals. Its first director was a self-made millionaire who often paid employees from his own pocket and once even purchased a park. Yet the political brilliance that ensured the success of the new agency had been offset by debilitating depression and irrational behavior embodied in a bipolar disorder. Nonetheless, a culture of acceptance welcomed creative but nonconforming mavericks.

One such maverick was William E. Brown. The short, sturdy, broad-shouldered man with brown hair and a full gray beard represented the best of the National Park Service. Unstinting in his commitment and idealism, he often worked himself into exhaustive collapses. At least three times he had quit the National Park Service in disgust with official policies only to come back when he found the profit-making world even worse. When the Alaska office sought park planners as key men for the proposed parks, he clamored to represent Yukon-Charley National Rivers, the area nearest Eagle–Fort Egbert. Because the proposed park contained historic sites from the Alaskan gold rush and the early development of the Yukon River, he argued that historic site preservation and interpretation would be more important than natural issues. As a historian, he believed he would make the best key man.

Within the first month after his move to Alaska in 1975, Bill Brown asked me to help identify historic sites in the Yukon-Charley area. My heart jumped. Here was my chance to try field research. He asked how much money I would need to complete a historic resource study of the area. From training in Washington, I knew that such a study included a narrative history and a description of the historic sites that could interpret that history. Naively, I thought I could do the whole project for $8,000, including $1,500 for the field inventory.

Shortly after meeting Bill Brown, we both attended the Alaska Historical Society meeting in Juneau in November 1975. We met for dinner with several other people from the National Park Service and the University of Alaska. Adjourning to the bar, we continued talking about a variety of topics. When Bill started telling about his great-grandparents being part of the Great Migration to Oregon, I teased him that his dates were wrong or his ancestors weren't part of the Great Migration. We bantered back and forth until I retired to my room.

Awakened by the telephone three hours later, I heard Bill Brown railing me abusively. After I left the bar, he had continued to drink and brood. What I had considered innocent bantering, he perceived as dogmatic arrogance. As he called me every name imaginable, I tried to recall what I had done to deserve such treatment. I heard how obstinate, opinionated, intolerant, aggressive, and egotistical I was. "You may be beautiful but you're a witch," he ranted. "I want you to stay out of my park. You will alienate everyone there." Resorting to tears, I finally got him calmed down, but I was too upset to sleep. The next morning at breakfast we smoothed over the crisis, but I could almost taste the tension between us.

I was still extremely distraught. For most of my life I had enjoyed sharing the male world. With the exception of Outward Bound, I got along well with masculine egos and even thrived under their attention. Suddenly, I had started to alienate men. Had I become obnoxiously opinionated or was I failing to conform to the expected image of a young attractive woman? Was my behavior that different from the behavior of the men themselves? Whatever, I was acutely traumatized and wary of my too-strong personality.

My first year in the National Park Service had not been happy. While Zorro seemed pleased with my performance, I had disrupted the status quo. Not only was I the only professional woman among the federal agencies, but I also failed to conform to expectations. My personal and professional insecurity was perceived as certitude and arrogance. As a woman pioneer in a man's world, I was not building a comfortable highway for subsequent professional women to follow. But now I had four more years to prove myself worthy of membership in that elite corps of men—the National Park Service.

# The Yukon

ollowing my harrowing experience at the Alaska Historical Society
meeting, I returned to Fairbanks and buried myself in research.
From November 1975 to May 1976 I researched the various archives
and libraries that contained Alaskan primary sources. In addition to
information for the narrative history, I collected a list of roadhouses,
mining towns, and trapper's cabins. By this time I was fairly comfortable with the researching and writing aspects of my job, but I was still
uncertain about how to begin the fieldwork. Barely on speaking terms,
Bill Brown told me that the people of Eagle still resented the "land grab"
of the National Park Service and suggested that I keep a low profile in
the community. I interpreted his comments to mean that he still found
me abrasive.

As I worked in my basement office at the University of Alaska, a
mature man of medium height with broad shoulders and a full brown
beard knocked on my open door. Dressed in clean but patched jeans and
a wool shirt, he looked like many Alaskans. He introduced himself as
Dave Evans, a trapper from Nation River. He had learned from some
University of Alaska archeologists that I was studying the Yukon River.

Because he had studied history in college, he came to find out what I knew about "his country." His voice was soft and hesitant, yet he obviously had a broad perspective of history. More important, he had personal experience with the Yukon River and a few of its tributaries.

As we talked, I made a impulsive offer: "Why don't you be my guide and help us both find historic sites. I can pay you $1,500 for the summer."

More cautious than I, he recommended that we think about it overnight. I invited him to dinner. He accepted and we talked some more. When I said something about the National Park Service, he looked oddly at me and said, "What do you mean, the National Park Service?" When I told him that I was a historian with the National Park Service, he stood up to leave. Breathing heavily, he said, "I thought you worked for the University of Alaska or I would never have stopped by. The National Park Service is trying to run me off my land. If Yukon-Charley becomes a park, I will lose my home, my livelihood, and my way of life."

I was floored. I knew that many Alaskans did not want to see national parks limit their hunting and mining practices, but I had never been exposed to such personal and visceral hatred. Using diplomatic skills I didn't know I possessed, I calmed some of his anger. By showing him some historic documents and maps that I had found, I diverted him. After a couple of hours of intense conversation, he said, "I like you and you seem a straight shooter. I will be your guide if you will agree to do it my way." I agreed without daring to ask him for details.

Later I learned his conditions. He wanted to use his own canoe with a nine-horsepower motor rather than the big power boats that most planners used on the Yukon. He detested freeze-dried food, the staple of all backpackers, and insisted that I purchase "real grub" from his grocery list. Finally, he planned to carry a gun and would shoot animals to provide fresh meat. He did not want my National Park Service ethic to impair him in any way. The area was not yet a national park, and he wanted to maintain his freedom as long as possible.

Summers are short in Alaska even though days are long. Dave wanted to get started within the week. As we studied the maps, we discussed strategy and logistics. We had less than three months to explore 250 miles of Yukon River, from Eagle on the Canadian border to Circle. These two towns provided the only road access to the Yukon, and fortunately for us the proposed Yukon-Charley park fell between them. We estimated that only the lower thirty miles of the Charley River, the Yukon's primary tributary in this section of the river, would be navigable. Thus we had nearly 300 miles to inventory in less than three months. Unless I knew of specific sites that we had to find, we agreed to examine only the mouths of the smaller tributaries. Given the limits of his small engine, he estimated it would take three trips of three weeks each to complete our work.

The next morning, before he left Fairbanks, Dave gave me his grocery list. It included potatoes, brown rice, lentils, cheese, lard, flour, baking powder, onions, tea, and brown sugar. He said we could take a dozen eggs and some slab bacon, but they would only last a day or two. I noticed no canned or processed foods on his list. It would be a different type of outdoor life for me.

As a child, I had always loved the outdoors. From childhood through college I hiked every chance I got. But when I moved to Alaska, my hiking days almost ended. Unlike in Arizona, Oregon, and California, I found few hiking trails. Instead, hiking involved cutting through brush, climbing over fallen trees, and sinking into spongelike muskeg or teetering for balance on tops of grass tufts called *tussocks*. It was not much fun. By the time Dave Evans and I planned our Yukon expedition, I was out of shape.

I also knew little about canoes, small engines, or rivers. I could swim, but none of my experiences had prepared me for one of the world's great rivers. Not only was it a mighty river, it was a wilderness. We would be solely dependent on each other—far more than I had been dependent in Outward Bound. I began to worry about my "strong" personality and how Dave would cope with it.

I worried about a lot of things in that last week before we left. My longest camping trip had been the three weeks of Outward Bound. This would be three times as long. Would my stamina hold? Had I done research thorough enough to find historic sites? Did I have the necessary skills to record these sites? I had spent a summer doing archeology on the Alaska Pipeline and knew the painstaking methods archeologists used to document and record sites. But I had never learned to use a transit or draft maps as they did. Moreover, I would not have time to provide that level of detail. I hoped that photographs and map documentation would be sufficient for this rough inventory. In truth, I really didn't know how to do a historic site survey.

Thus I met Dave Evans in Eagle besieged with doubts. I was so worried that I took little joy in seeing the town I had studied for nearly eighteen months. Perched on the high bank of the Yukon River only a few miles from the Canadian border, the small village looked much like I expected. With the exception of the white clapboard courthouse, presided over by Judge James Wickersham a century earlier, most of the fifty structures were of log construction.

I was relieved when we camped on a wooded island just offshore from Eagle. At least I would not have to confront the hostility of the town. Instead, Dave and his wife invited some river people in for dinner. It was hard to keep a low profile when you were going to spend a summer on the river with one of their friends. The river people, mostly aging hippies, were not shy in stating their feelings about federal agencies, especially the National Park Service. They all resented being in "trespass" on supposedly public lands. All they wanted was to live off the land as their forebears had done a hundred years earlier. To me it did not seem an unreasonable request.

As we pushed off the next morning, I wondered what I had gotten myself into. I hardly knew Dave, and here I was going to spend three months with him. I told myself that anyone who cared about books as much as he did couldn't be a bad person. Although we had met only once, we had long talks, and I thought we had similar values and interests. Nonetheless, I began to have second thoughts about my impulsive decision.

Even though I did not want to stick out as a government bureaucrat, my clothes and equipment were relatively new. I wore wool for warmth. Dave had recommended that I buy "Bean boots" from L. L. Bean. The rubber lowers kept the feet dry but the leather uppers allowed the feet and legs to breath. He, however, wore Nike track shoes. I also wore a drown-proof vest and sunglasses. Before we had gone an hour, Dave asked me not to wear sunglasses. When he talked to people, he wanted to see their eyes. Although the contact lenses I wore sensitized my eyes to light, I agreed.

Our first site was a hard one. We searched most of the first day for Montauk Roadhouse. There were no remains or even cleared areas where my documents said it should be. We climbed up and down bluffs, walked up one side of Montauk Creek and down the other, and moved in ever-widening circles. Finally we called it quits and motored out to an island.

"Mosquitoes are terrible on shore, but on islands there is usually a breeze to keep them at bay," Dave explained. He left me to empty the canoe and set up the tent. Without a word he disappeared into the woods. Later I heard a crash and went to investigate. He had toppled a standing dead tree and was sawing the six-inch-diameter spruce into fourteen-inch logs. These he carried back to the shore. Here he took an axe and rhythmically split each one into four pieces. Next he scooped the sand and piled it as a windbreak. With some kindling he started a fire, then added the split logs and finally a refrigerator rack that he used for a grill. I was fascinated. Each day he performed the same ritual, always leaving firewood for at least two additional fires. "You never know when you might be this way again and need a fire," he said.

Once more he stepped back into the woods, this time with his Browning .22 rifle. Hardly a moment had passed when I heard two shots. He came back to camp with two spruce grouse. "These are what we call bush chickens," he said, grinning with anticipation. He didn't bother with gutting or removing the feathers. He simply skinned the birds and removed the breasts and the little drumsticks. He said nothing else was worth the effort.

Meanwhile, because the tent belonged to me, I set it up without assistance from him. It was a mountain tent from North Face and was basically a small backpacking tent with a rain flap held in place with aluminum poles, guidelines, and stakes. It always seemed to take forty-five minutes to put up. While I struggled with the tent, Dave got water from the Yukon. "A little mud doesn't hurt anyone," he said. It never caused any problem with us, but most Yukon travelers don't drink the sediment-laden water.

Dave began to cook dinner. I peeled and chopped onions while he fried bacon and sautéed the grouse. Then, while he made hot tea, I scrambled the eggs into the onions. Everything tasted great. Dave didn't believe in eating lunch, so we were both ravenous. I had never skipped lunch and began to think that I didn't need it either.

The next morning Dave showed me how to make bannock over an open fire. Bannock is similar to biscuits, made with baking powder and flour. After it was half-done, he covered it with brown sugar and cinnamon and then folded it carefully in half, cooking one side and then the other. We fried up the last of the bacon, heated up last night's tea, and enjoyed the new morning. I had survived a full day.

By noon that day, I was not so sure I was going to survive until evening. Going without lunch with my metabolism was a dumb idea. We had set out to hike to a small gold-rush community about six miles away. Unfortunately, a forest fire had swept through the area, leaving downed trees to climb over or crawl under. It was slow going and hard work. The bannock quickly wore off, and I became hungrier and hungrier. By the time we reached the cabins, I was pretty weak. A handful of M&Ms gave me the energy to photograph and document the remnant buildings. Because of the modern cabin design and debris, Dave did not believe they were gold-rush era. They were more likely twentieth-century trapping cabins.

As we turned to go back, I knew I would have to go slowly. I had used up my carbohydrates and was now working on what little fat my body contained. I told Dave to go ahead and I'd follow the creek back to camp. He left me slowly putting one foot in front of the other. After a couple of hours I met him watching a tree.

"There's a yearling black bear up that tree," he said. "I've scared the mama bear away, and now I'm going to shoot the cub. I've waited for you to make sure mama doesn't attack you." Without another word, he shot the cub in the head and it tumbled out of the tree. Gutting the animal and cutting off its head made it more portable. I apologized to Dave for not being able to carry my share, but I doubted my own ability to get to camp. Burdened with the bulky animal, Dave's own pace slowed. It was nearly eleven that night when we stumbled into camp. Grateful that Dave had chopped plenty of firewood the night before, we were almost too tired to eat the bear steaks he cooked. "Sometimes a full-grown bear is tough with a strong flavor, but a yearling cub tastes a lot like beef," Dave said reassuringly. Never again, though, would I hike without something for lunch. I learned some limits to my stamina that I had not found in Outward Bound.

Each day followed in similar fashion. We floated or motored to a specific site or to the mouth of a creek or river, then looked for likely building sites. Dave's experience of living on the river proved invaluable. He pointed out that cabins usually were within walking distance of water, yet often on high ground to avoid floods and ice dams. His instinct led us to numerous cabin remnants and traces of trails. Few of the sites conformed to my list of sites derived from primary sources. Because I had no contacts in Eagle or Circle, I didn't know who would tell me the history of these nameless structures.

Once again Dave helped me out. "In Eagle lives one of the great fur trappers of the 1920s and 1930s—George Beck," he said. "If anyone knows this river, he does. I have wanted to talk with him and pump him for information but he won't talk with me. I have heard that he likes women." I filed that away. I didn't know how long Bill Brown and my friends in the Bureau of Land Management would keep me out of Eagle.

One achievement was the discovery of the gold-rush town of Seventy-Mile City, or Star City. We had not expected to find it so far from the mouth of Seventy-Mile River. There were ten cabins lined up like a town in three different rows. Each cabin had lost its roof, but the walls stood nearly six-feet high. The woods around the town had engulfed it, and the cabins were slowly moldering away. I measured each one, photographed each on four sides, drew a sketch map, and felt proud of myself.

Other gold-rush towns—there had been seven or eight between Eagle and Charley River—did not fare as well. A trapper burned Nation and Ivy City for firewood. The historic cabins gave him a convenient supply of wood that lasted several winters. During and after the gold rush, several hundred steamboats plied the Yukon. They also burned old cabins for firewood.

After nearly three weeks, our grub began to run out about the time our personalities started to clash. I couldn't do anything right. My directions would get screwed up, to Dave's irritation. Once I even had the Yukon flowing east. He never let me live that one down. The final straw came when I used his silver spoon to scoop lard to fry the potatoes. After he blew up and then cooled down, we both agreed it was time to head back to Eagle. For two days we motored against the flow of the Yukon. Both days it rained, and my mood mirrored the weather.

When I left Dave at Eagle and drove back to Fairbanks, I had one week to resupply our groceries and to do additional research on what we had already found and on what we might yet find. The week break was healthy for both of us.

The second trip down the Yukon I knew what to expect. We looked once again for Montauk Roadhouse, then moved on to spend the night with the oldest man on the river, Richard Cook, a thin, wiry, fifty-year-old man who lived solely off the land. Dave admired him even though he was prickly and alienated many of his colleagues. A well-educated engineer, he had found a young woman in Fairbanks who wanted to live in the bush. Shortly after we arrived, she took me to help pull in a gill net and remove the salmon. When we returned to shore, she must have forgotten to tie up the boat, and Dick discovered it gone. Dave and Dick motored downriver and found it several miles away, stuck in a logjam. It was nearly two in the morning when they returned, too tired to be angry. It helped my bruised ego to know that others could make mistakes too.

Years later, in June 2001, at the age of seventy, Dick Cook's body was found in a tributary of the Yukon River. After swamping his old canoe with its nine-horse motor (similar to Dave Evans's), he had tried to retrieve it. The river, swollen from the melting snowpack, was too wild for the tough, wily old trapper. He died as he would have wished—far away from an Anchorage hospital.

After Dave and I left Dick Cook in 1976, we motored to the ruins of

Nation City to hike up Fourth of July Creek. After the Klondike gold rush in the late 1890s, Americans left the Canadian gold fields to seek riches downstream in American territory. Feeling patriotic and happy to be on American soil, they often gave places nationalistic names. Thus such names as Eagle, Nation City, Fourth of July Creek, and American Creek abound.

Some of the most extensive early mining occurred on Fourth of July Creek. During the first thirty years of the twentieth century, the U.S. Geological Survey researched and published comprehensive reports on Alaskan mining. Here I gathered information about the value and extent of mining operations, but the reports documented cultural activities as well. Each year the USGS reports listed the number of mines on Fourth of July Creek, described the types of mining, and estimated the amount of gold collected. Thus I knew who lived on the creek and how successful they had been. I also knew that the mines of Fourth of July Creek traced the evolutionary history of mining from drift mines to open-cut mines to hydraulic mines. I hoped to see examples of each.

After hiking approximately eight miles along a good trail, we came to a wide, heavily graveled area. It looked like the descriptions of hydraulic tailings. I wanted to look around, but Dave had heard the mine had a caretaker and suggested we check in with him. We found Jack Wheeler in a log cabin whose interior walls had been painted bright yellow. A tall, thin, friendly, and talkative man, he proclaimed himself a modern-day prospector, but he'd made only one prospecting trip all summer. Although he dreamed of his personal bonanza—the elusive gold mine—he led a more mundane life. He operated the boilers for a convent in the Midwest and entertained the nuns with his Alaskan adventures.

For an Alaska prospector and adventurer, Wheeler was unusually afraid of bears. He admitted that his greatest fear was confronting a bear while out prospecting. This year, however, he thought he had the answer. "Bears don't like the smell of mothballs," he told us. "So I have scattered mothballs everywhere." His cabin did smell like the chest where my mother kept her wool blankets. After we sat talking awhile, I couldn't smell the odor as much. He had just started his meal of homemade pemmican—a concoction of dried beef, fruit, nuts, and lard—and invited us to share it with him. As I bit into the pemmican, it tasted like some petroleum product. Because he didn't say anything about the strange taste, I assumed it was rancid beef. As we cleared up the dishes, he confessed that he had accidentally packed his pemmican with his mothballs. Dave and I looked at each other and shook our heads in disbelief.

Wheeler walked us around the site. The mine owner had leveled the gravel tailings into a runway for his plane. "No one walks in this country any more," Wheeler said. "You are the only people who have walked in here during my time." One of the ruined houses actually furnished hot water. Water circulated from the hand pump through the cookstove to the faucet at the sink—a fascinating contraption. Most of one wall was missing. Jack acknowledged that he used the logs for firewood, but hastened to reassure me, "A propane stove will be flown in next week."

During the tour of the mine itself, he showed us an abandoned rocker, a hydraulic pump, and various piles of hydraulic pipe. At the creek he dug some gravel from bedrock and filled a gold pan. He showed us how to dip it into the creek, swish it round and round, and continue to rinse and swish it until only a few grains of black sand remained. Then with infinite care and a pair of tweezers, he extracted a tiny speck of gold. Dave and I tried our hands at gold panning. It was not as simple as it looked. The circular movement was unnatural, the heavy gold pan tired my shoulders and back, and stooping next to the stream stiffened my knees. After two hours the three of us had less than five dollars' worth of gold. Wheeler generously gave it to me in a small vial. As late afternoon approached, we decided not to spend a night with the mothballs. We said good-bye and continued on our way.

The next day, returning to camp from our search for historic cabins, Dave saw a beaver. He took aim but missed. He decided that juicy beaver meat was exactly what he wanted for dinner, so he sat down to wait. It began to rain. I told him that I'd go ahead and get a fire started, happy to get out of the rain. After two more hours I finally heard a shot. Sure enough, Dave came with the beaver. The meat was well marbled with fat and could be cooked on a stick over an open fire. It tasted much like pork and was worth the wait in the rain. Then he singed the tail. At last I was going to taste beaver tail—the delicacy that the old fur trappers of the past raved about. Yuck! Beaver tail is solid fat. I took one bite and that was enough. Even Dave agreed that he preferred it mixed with a little meat or vegetables.

For the rest of the summer, we followed similar patterns of long and hard days. When Dave found beaver or grouse, he did not hesitate to shoot. Although we floated on a river filled with salmon, we ate the fish only when his river friends shared theirs. Neither of us took the time to fish. After several days of hiking, my knees would begin to give me pain. I recognized the symptoms—my mother and sisters had arthritis. It was too much to ask that I would be spared. Because Dave thought I was a sissy anyway, I was careful not to let him see me limp.

Only two days really tested my ability to hike. The first time we hiked seven miles to Ben Creek, where we met Jim Layman. Jim immediately became one of my favorite people. He was a large, fat, jolly man who owned a motel in Seligman, Arizona. Each summer he flew into Ben Creek to do a little gold mining. He was shocked when he saw us walk into his cabin. "No one walks," he said. "You must be OK." When he learned that I was a historian, he took me all around his small mining operation. He had hydraulic pipe, a small dam for boom-and-sluice mining, and a steam boiler with some steam points to thaw the permafrost prior to sluicing or hydraulicking. I had read about all of these mining methods, but I had never seen them in reality.

During the evening he entertained us with stories about the Yukon. He told several colorful stories about Arthur "Cap" Reynolds, who owned a small steamboat; a transient murdered him for his money. As I had thought, Nation City, prior to being used for firewood, was the largest of the four mining camps dating from the turn of the century. Layman credited James Taylor with developing the area. Taylor consolidated the mining claims on Fourth of July Creek and later built his place across the Yukon from Nation City.

Layman warned us to stay away from Joe Vogler's place on Woodchopper Creek. I had heard about Joe Vogler's efforts to separate Alaska from the rest of the nation and regarded him as a crackpot. "Joe threatens to shoot any federal government bureaucrat that sets foot on his patented land," he said. "Of course, you walk, so he won't expect you to be government. They always come by helicopter."

The next morning Layman graciously cranked up his Willys Jeep and drove us as far as he could. My arthritic knees were immensely grateful.

The next time my knees were tested was the day that we trespassed on Joe Vogler's property. The two major mining camps of the Yukon-Charley area were on Coal and Woodchopper creeks. In the 1930s a former president of the University of Alaska, Ernest Patty, had consolidated the mining claims, drilled to test the richness of the ore, then constructed airstrips, mining dredges, and mining camps on both creeks. When gold mining became nonessential during the Second World War, Patty closed them and later sold them to different groups of miners. A series of owners tried to make Coal Creek pay. In fact, during the summer of 1976 a crew hoped to get Patty's old dredge working. While not really friendly, they were Alaskans. They fed us dinner and gave us a place to lay our bedrolls.

The next morning they gave us the good news that Joe Vogler had gone into Fairbanks. Relieved that we would not have to miss one of the major mining camps, we decided to hike over the divide along a road that connected the two camps. I knew that we would be trespassing on private land. Joe Vogler was one of very few Alaskans who had gone to the work of patenting his mining claim. Thus he owned some of the only private land in the proposed park. Yet at the same time his claim included some historically significant structures, ones with considerable documentation.

As usual, Dave set a fast pace. After a while my knees began to ache, so I slowed down. He continued and waited for me in the shade of a tree a couple of miles down the road. Eventually we came to the fork in the road. Left would take us to the mining camp and right would take us to the river. We decided to investigate the camp and get out before morning, when Vogler was due back.

When we were about half a mile from the camp, we heard the engine of a large truck. We looked at each other and our hearts sank. We could try and hide in the heavy brambles off the side of the road, but it would be embarrassing to get caught. Or we could try to brazen it out. Our decision was made for us when the truck rounded the curve and stopped beside us.

"Hey there," said a large-boned man with a cheerful smile. "Hop in and I'll take you to camp." We shrugged and got in. Knees notwithstanding, I would have preferred to hike back over the divide to Coal Creek. Dave introduced himself as a trapper from Nation River and simply said, "This is Melody Webb." Vogler asked no other questions, assuming I was Dave's woman and treating me as such. He gave me some hamburger and spaghetti sauce to make supper. I then dutifully washed the dishes and cleaned up.

Meanwhile, Vogler spouted off. Trained as a lawyer and well read in classical philosophy, he did not believe in the federal government. He wanted Alaska independent and free of federal entanglements. "Only three things can you trust—gold, land, and yellow Caterpillar metal," he expounded. "On the other hand, the federal government is corrupt, evil, and will rob you blind. It has no authority except intimidation. We should rise and overthrow it."

He had numerous original ideas. He believed that all of Alaska's forests should be burned to melt the permafrost. Then the whole state would bloom. Alaska should also become an independent nation and then keep out the "niggers" and Jews. Along with the federal government, "niggers" and Jews were the scourge of the world. To support his beliefs, he quoted Jefferson and Lincoln, as well as John Locke and others I had never heard of. There was no question of his hatred of federal bureaucrats. Apparently a helicopter filled with Park Service planners had set down on his landing strip. He told them to get out or he would blow up the helicopter. "The next time those Feds show up," he said. "I'll blast them without warning."

By eleven o'clock I was worn out, emotionally and physically. He showed us the bunkhouse where we threw down our sleeping bags. Dave's first comment was: "You can't tell him who you are. It would be holy hell." I disagreed. It would be dishonest and would simply reinforce his image of bureaucrats if he ever found out. I decided to tell him the next morning. Dave's last comment was: "He's a rogue, but I like him."

Tired as I was, I couldn't sleep. Eventually I heard Vogler chopping wood and went out to talk with him. "Joe," I said hesitantly, "before I break bread with you again, I have a confession to make. I work for the federal government."

"You do, eh?" he said looking up from the woodpile. "Who and what do you do?" When I told him, he simply said, "Well, you're young, you'll learn better." He then proceeded to start a fire and make coffee. I had to admit that he remained charming and cordial throughout the morning. Much of his bravado was tempered, and we actually conversed.

Later he told us that we could tour the remains of the mining camp and even the old mining dredge. I had never been on one of the floating monsters and knew only vaguely how they worked. The large arm with a series of scooped buckets dug into the soil and then dumped it on deck. Here the gold-bearing soil went through a series of strainers, being sprayed and shaken as it moved to the back of the dredge. In the stern the debris and waste rock found their way up a conveyer belt and fell on tailing piles via another long arm. The heavier gold continued down through a series of sluice boxes until it was eliminated from the heavy black sand by gold panning.

By late afternoon we decided to move on rather than partake of Vogler's hospitality for a second night. He drove us up over the road and down to Coal Creek, where we picked up our canoe and continued downriver a few miles before camping. As tense as the previous night had been, it was undoubtedly my most memorable experience.

Later Vogler ran for governor with the Alaska Independence Party and appeared on the television news program *Sixty Minutes*. In 1994 he mysteriously disappeared from his Fairbanks home. His fedora, gun, and dog were left at home. Friends searched the woods for days. Eventually a drifter admitted killing Vogler when he had tried to run him off his property.

After Woodchopper Creek, the historic sites became fewer. We did find an old cabin with numerous handmade tools and magazines dating from the 1940s. The place fascinated us, especially the wood craftsmanship. Whoever had lived there made a wheelbarrow and toboggan from native materials. Unlike most cabins that we had found, this one still had its roof. I hoped that I could find out the story behind the cabin.

Eventually we motored into Circle. It was late August, and we considered our summer's work essentially done. We had found 150 historic sites that needed more research and documentation. The Charley River proved relatively barren, except at its mouth. Elsewhere nearly every small stream had a remnant cabin that probably served as a trapping shelter. The mining areas that we found would be well recorded in the U.S. Geological Survey's bulletins, but the few attempts at farming might be harder to document. We had traced most of the old mail trail and found several roadhouses that served it. Our summer had been full, and we were tired and eager to get home. On the return trip to Eagle, Dave motored late each night.

When we finally reached the island where his wife had camped all summer, we found a message stating that she had caught a ride into Fairbanks. We fixed a simple supper and sat companionably by the campfire. For the first time we felt relaxed with each other. He told me about his father, a naval architect at the Massachusetts Institute of Technology who had designed the hull for the first nuclear-powered submarine. His father and he had been estranged for years. Dave resented being shunted aside as an adolescent and sent to live on a New Hampshire farm, then later to South Carolina. Instead of his own parents, he had adopted one of his teachers, who became "Ma." Despite his troubled youth, he graduated from a small college with a bachelor's degree in history—all because of Ma, he said. In the early 1970s he moved to Alaska to live off the land and along the way found a woman with comparable dreams.

I urged Dave to write his father and be receptive to any overtures. As he talked, I told him, I could tell that he wanted his parents to know him and his lifestyle. His nomadic life had made him want an anchor, some roots somewhere. He listened to me and nodded his head. He expressed surprise that I was as sensitive and savvy as he was beginning to see me. Then he admitted that Bill Brown and BLM employees had predisposed him to find me abrasive and overbearing. His instructions were to keep me from interacting in any way with the people of Eagle. I was not surprised or even hurt, but pleased that after three months Dave arrived at his own judgment.

The next morning we said good-bye and hugged for the first time. "You know last night was the first time that I really got to know you," he said. "I apologize for all the picky little bitches that I laid on you. You're one hell of a woman. I've begrudgingly grown to respect you. And I will write my father. I do want to see him before he dies." With considerably more satisfaction than at any other time that summer, I got in my truck and drove back to Fairbanks.

Ironically, considering Dave's initial hatred of federal agencies, less than two years later he joined the National Park Service, first seasonally, then permanently. Because of his skill with hand tools and building log cabins, Mount McKinley National Park hired him to rehabilitate its historic cabins in the backcountry. Later he moved to Arizona and continued applying his skills to historic structures throughout the Southwest. He did reach out to his parents, and they even visited him at his cabin on Nation River. Throughout the years Dave and I remained good friends and remember the summer of 1976 as a unique experience for both of us.

While I spent the summer of 1976 on the Yukon River, most Americans, especially those in the National Park Service, celebrated the bicentennial. In Alaska few of us felt the pressure of our colleagues in the Lower 48 to complete new visitor centers, develop fresh exhibits, and design costumes for living history programs depicting the Revolutionary War. Bicentennial fever stoked Congress to open its coffers and fund a multitude of construction projects in various congressional districts. Always short of funds, the National Park Service administrators used the event to acquire more positions, programs, and even research. Little of the largesse, however, found its way to Alaska.

As the culminating event approached, I caught snatches of a brewing controversy that tore my beloved agency in two. It seemed an insignificant issue to cause such turmoil: Should rangers at Independence Hall be allowed to wear guns? The National Park Service divided rangers into two groups: interpretive rangers who took visitors on tours and hikes, instructing them on the significance of the resource, and protection or law-enforcement rangers who protected the visitor and the resource from harm. Historically, protection rangers had been issued guns, but most kept them stashed in the glove compartment, preferring diplomatic and interpersonal skills for solving potentially explosive conflicts. The regional director for Independence Hall won the support and allegiance of "traditionalists" such as Bill Brown and Zorro, who opposed rangers' wearing of guns. Guns were not part of the ranger tradition—neither the interpretive nor the protection ranger ever wore guns in public. The tax-paying public should not be confronted with the insult of guns at a commemorative occasion.

The law-enforcement rangers, on the other hand, pointed to the disastrous riot in Yosemite on Independence Day weekend in 1970. Rangers and maintenance men armed with pickax handles and clubs stormed a crowd of unarmed hippies illegally camping and partying on the fragile meadows. The media escalated the scene into a public relations nightmare. As a result, Director Hartzog required comprehensive law-enforcement training for all protection rangers. Fortunately, rangers received their training just as more and more visitors brought urban crime to national parks. In the 1970s assaults, rapes, robberies, even murders occurred in greater and greater numbers. As trained police, rangers went nowhere without their guns—especially not to a major bicentennial jubilee. With the large number of dignitaries present, the director could not afford a riot and found a compromise with his regional director: Rangers in high-profile positions would not wear guns, but those on the barricades, where trouble could be anticipated, would and did.

Physically and intellectually removed from the gun debate, I focused on my historic site survey of the Yukon. In September I met with Bill Brown. I showed him the inventory of sites and some of the photographs. He was genuinely impressed with our summer's work and asked what I planned to do next. "The only way I know to find out the history of these properties," I said, "is to talk with people and collect oral history." He agreed immediately. He said that he had heard from several people that I had made a good impression on a few people, especially Jim Layman, who sang my praises.

Relieved, I wrote several letters to people Dave had suggested and asked if they would be willing to talk with me. I received enough responses to make the trip worthwhile, but I had not heard from George Beck.

Fall was definitely in the air as I drove into Eagle. Most of the summer visitors had left, except Jess and Cathryne Knight, who had managed the Northern Commercial Company store in Eagle for many years. They were warm and friendly people who welcomed me to their small cabin. Unlike nearly everyone else, they supported the proposed national park. While they had little information to help me identify the cabins on the river, their kindness soothed my self-esteem. Mrs. Knight advised me not to take the townspeople's hostility personally. "They're good people here, but sometimes they lose their perspective," she counseled. "Win over a few of the leaders and you will win over the town."

Next I interviewed Barney Hansen, who had mined Sam Creek. He told me a number of good stories but couldn't identify 95 percent of the historic cabins. After talking with three or four others and drawing blank looks, I had only one choice—George Beck.

Dave had shown me where George lived. Boldly I walked up to the door and knocked. A large man who reminded me of John Wayne answered the door. I used all my charm to persuade him to talk with me. "Hell, I don't have anything to say," he said gruffly. "That's why I didn't answer your letter, but come on in. I'd appreciate the company."

This man knew the river. He had built many of the small cabins we had found. He knew stories about nearly every cabin, who lived there, and what happened. In addition, he had married into the Ed Biederman family, which had run the mail between Eagle and Circle, so he had friends among the Native community at Eagle Village as well. Story after story flowed from his memory. I could hardly write fast enough.

I asked him about the cabin with the handmade tools. He told me Albert Hughes had built the cabin and tools. Then he gave me my first lost-mine story. Apparently Hughes wanted to test the prospects for gold on the north side of the Yukon. Despite the riches of strikes on the south, nothing worth mining had been found on the north. After trying several areas, he arrived at one outcropping where he picked off several specimens. Years later he came across the specimens and decided to have them assessed. The results came back with high gold potential. He boarded the next boat to Skagway, took the railroad to Whitehorse, then floated down the Yukon. He thought he had found the location but could not find the outcropping because of a landslide. Nonetheless, he decided to work the area and did for years without results.

George Beck told me other stories, some even risqué. He talked long into the night, often pulling out photographs to illustrate the Yukon characters he had known. In the early morning hours, fearing that I would wear out my welcome, I called a halt and suggested we pick it up again the next day.

Late the next morning I arrived and met a very different man. He was drinking and was not in a happy mood nor receptive to my charms. "You come in here and stir up memories that are better forgotten," he said. "I think you'd better leave." Disappointed, I left. The next day I tried again, but no one answered the door. Never again did I talk with him. He was a treasure trove of information, but he wanted no acknowledgment in my report. Less than a year later he died of a heart attack. I mourned his loss as a historian and a friend. I had liked him better than anyone else I had met.

Later I met Beck's brother-in-law, Charlie Biederman, who had lived on the Yukon until the 1950s. His father, Ed Biederman, ran the winter mail by dog team between Eagle and Circle. In 1918, approximately halfway between the two towns, Ed built a home. When he suffered frostbite and lost his toes, Charlie and his older brother took up their dad's route. As a result of running the mail, Charlie knew the Yukon almost as well as George Beck and helped fill in the gaps left by Beck.

During the summer of 1976, when Dave and I stumbled on Biederman's place, we thought we had stepped back in time to the 1930s. It looked as if Ed had just left. All buildings had roofs, and some of the buildings even had furniture. A blue-and-white oilcloth covered the kitchen table. A white pitcher and blue enamel washbowl rested on the chest of drawers in the bedroom. The iron cot had a red chenille bedspread. Old red linoleum, cracked and nailed in place, covered the floors. Plain white dishes filled the kitchen shelves. Yet none of the structures was locked, nor were there any signs of modern habitation or vandalism. No other structures on the Yukon retained such integrity and sense of place as Biederman's. Several years later I heard that an Alaskan Native had claimed the site and torn down some of the structures. I was glad that I experienced it when I did. It was a hauntingly memorable day.

Finally I had as much information as I needed to write my study. Within nine months I had drafted 550 pages of narrative and historic site descriptions. This time I had chapters and even developed a broader context to interpret Yukon history. I used Frederick Jackson Turner's thesis of successive frontiers to explain how history evolved on the Yukon. I thought most people would be able to relate to Alaskan history if it were developed within a context that they knew, such as the American West. At last I had fulfilled my dream of researching history, finding historic sites, and then writing about them.

Bill Brown praised my study enthusiastically and urged its publication. Despite our rocky start, we became good friends. He supported me in all my endeavors and often gave me small research projects. Never again did we discuss his explosion in Juneau. I just remained careful not to joke with him. I had learned the hard way that my bantering struck some people as strident and rigid.

It had been another tough year, one that I would not like to repeat. While I confronted the Yukon and survived, I had not enjoyed the summer any more than I had Outward Bound. Nonetheless, painful experiences make lasting memories. I grew more professionally and personally in that year than in all my college years. I had found my physical and maybe psychological limits as well. Although I had not realized it, life had been pretty easy for me. Belatedly I was getting tested. The irony of my summer was the slow realization that my Yukon experiences were unusual if not unique among historians. And I had thought I was neither prepared for nor capable of doing a routine assignment.

Regardless of my personal difficulties, I loved my job. The more I learned about the National Park Service the more I believed in its mission: "to conserve the scenery and the natural and historic objects and the wildlife therein and to provide for the enjoyment of the same in such manner and by such means as will leave them unimpaired for the enjoyment of future generations." My job satisfied my deep-seated idealistic need to do something good. It allowed me to use my professional training to preserve the outdoors that I loved so much. I could not imagine a more ideal job that combined everything that mattered to me.

# Alaska

At first, field research seemed the most exciting and challenging aspect of my job. As a child of the Sixties, I dreaded program management. Even the phrase reeked of red tape and jargon. It evoked images of an unfeeling government concerned with procedure rather than creativity.

Only eleven years earlier I had protested the evils of the Vietnam War. During my one college year at the University of California at Berkeley, 1965–66, I found myself caught up in a stimulating and passionate antiwar campaign. To learn the issues, I attended teach-ins. The more I heard, the more upset I became. By late fall, as President Lyndon Johnson ordered American soldiers to Vietnam through the ports of nearby Oakland, all of Berkeley—professors, students, and townspeople—rose in protest. Nearly everyone joined the first protest march of its kind. Swept up in the fervor, I walked with the crowd. At the Oakland city limits a phalanx of policemen, incongruously supported by a Hell's Angels motorcycle gang, stopped us. We didn't know what to do. Eventually the march broke up, and we all went home as peacefully as we had arrived—a marked contrast to later protests.

As the antiwar protests turned violent and hate-filled, I retreated from activism. Yet I still fervently believed the U.S. government wrong in forcing the Vietnamese into a government not of their choosing, all in the name of the war against Communism. Instead of marching, I refused to pay the telephone war tax. I lost that battle too.

With the wounds of Vietnam still open and painful in 1976, I did not relish being a part of the machinery of government. From my perception, researching and writing history did not contribute to those grinding gears I had protested. Program management, however, sounded like bureaucracy at its worst. Then, through the insights of one man, my aversion to government programs did an about-face.

Several years earlier, in 1973, I had met Robert M. Utley at a conference on writing the history and literature of the American West. He gave the keynote speech on particular people and particular places. Unlike academic historians at the conference, he worked for the National Park Service. First as chief historian and then as director of the Office of Archeology and Historic Preservation, he had risen nearly as high in the National Park Service as a historian could. A pioneer in the historic preservation movement, he was one of the promoters of the National Historic Preservation Act of 1966 and shaped its implementation throughout government and the fifty states. Despite the demands of a bureaucratic life, he still found time to write highly regarded scholarly books on Indians and the frontier military.

Utley's gray hair, distinguished reputation, gracious air, and hearing aid made him appear older than I later learned he was. But as he talked in his Arkansas drawl, I caught glimpses of what a Park Service historian did. At that time I had just completed graduate work for my master's degree and was unemployed. His job sounded even better than a job in Williamsburg. Unlike the professors, Utley did not hold the attendees at arm's length. He welcomed my questions about working for the Park Service and even invited me to dinner with the other dignitaries. When he offered to read and critique my manuscript on Russian women in Alaska, I realized that I had found a mentor, especially when he helped get it published in a popular magazine, *The American West.*

Over the next three years we corresponded frequently. Because of his position, he had professional responsibility for ensuring that the proposed Alaskan parks included historical and archeological resources as well as natural areas. As a result Zorro Bradley and I met with him in Alaska or Washington two or three times a year. Slowly I developed a different perspective on government and bureaucracy. Utley had a unique definition of a bureaucrat. "A bureaucrat," he repeatedly told me, "is someone who can make things happen that ought to happen and prevent things from happening that shouldn't happen." The way he talked about his job made it sound creative and positive. As he took more and more interest in the program management aspects of my job, I developed more interest in them myself.

In addition to doing historical research for proposed Alaskan parks, such as Yukon-Charley National Preserve, Zorro had hired me to help develop a program that would professionally certify Native historic sites selected as part of the two million acres that could be claimed under the Alaska Native Claims Settlement Act of 1971.

Fortunately for me, Zorro knew how to visualize a new program. I didn't have any idea how to start. We called our new program the Alaskan Native Historic Sites Project, or more simply 14(h), for the section of the law that authorized it. As early as March 1975, Zorro contracted with the University of Alaska at Fairbanks, and together we began recruiting and hiring graduate students in history, archeology, anthropology, and even biology from all over the United States. Several of our recruits had their doctorates, while others lacked only the dissertation. All had advanced degrees. Some had worked with Alaskan Natives, others with Indian groups outside Alaska, but all had field experience.

As they began to arrive, we had to find work for them. When we hired them, we had anticipated that the rules and regulations governing how we documented, evaluated, and certified historic sites would be approved for the summer field season of 1975. But interagency rivalry in Washington had snarled and delayed the rules. Four federal agencies and two different departments bickered over fine points that might hamper their land-management capability. Bob Utley, our representative on the task force, fought hard to keep our interests and concerns included in the final regulations.

When it became obvious that the regulations would not be finished for several months, Zorro decided to offer our services to the twelve Native Regional Corporations. Established under the Alaska Native Claims Settlement Act, these corporations would be selecting the historic sites. Zorro rightly believed that the Natives did not know how to begin to inventory their historic sites and offered professional assistance to each regional corporation. All but the one in southeastern Alaska accepted our help.

With little time for training, we sent eleven professionals to regions where their skills seemed best suited. We introduced them to the leaders of the corporation, gave them a few suggestions about working with the elders, and let them find their own individual approach to the unique problems of each corporation. Because these professionals had completed fieldwork in preparation for dissertations or had managed archeological projects, I thought they had more skills and knowledge than I. Later I learned they were scared, ignorant, and resentful of my abandoning them. Once again I had masked my insecurity with an aura of certitude. Coupled with an ability to adapt easily to new circumstances, I gave Natives and my staff the impression that I knew more than I did.

As the year progressed, the legislative deadline for submitting applications for specific historic sites approached. We turned up the pressure, and our staff began working nearly twenty-hour days. Most of them traveled to Native villages and collected the oldest elders in a room with a translator and numerous maps. Then they asked for specific sites that were part of the Native culture. Elders who could read maps pointed to areas of importance to them. Others simply told stories into a tape recorder of cultural memories and subsistence activities, which would be identified more precisely later. Lacking time to visit these sites on the ground, the professionals made a rough list of sites with a vague description of significance and location for each.

In December 1975 our staff returned to Fairbanks. Although exhausted and frustrated, in less than four months they had completed a basic inventory of seven thousand sites from which the corporations chose four thousand for applications. Many of the sites lacked tangible remains, making identification and significance difficult to define. Most of the sites consisted of sacred places, battlefields, locations of catastrophic events illustrated with stories or songs, sites associated with morality tales, and subsistence sites such as fish camps, hunting lookouts, navigational landmarks, trading places, and trails. My first staff filled me with pride for their hard work, long hours, and phenomenal accomplishments.

The immediate effect was twofold. First, the Natives came to trust us. When Congress passed the Alaska Native Claims Settlement Act, it gave the Alaskan Natives $963 million and forty-four million acres of land. It also established a system of checks and balances. Regional corporations, the profit-making organizations, carefully invested the funds and selected land for future economic potential. Village corporations represented the traditional arm and sought land and money to perpetuate cultural lifestyles. Both types of corporations found themselves bombarded with consultants from the Lower 48. A couple of regional corporations invested poorly and found themselves several million dollars in debt. As a result, Natives came to distrust whites. Our professional assistance without financial strings attached won their respect. Our staff's dedication, hard work, and idealism won their love.

The second effect of our first professional effort was the broadening of that trust to include the National Park Service. Because BLM, the Forest Service, and the Fish and Wildlife Service would lose land as a result of the claims settlement, they resisted and bureaucratically stalled any land transaction. Only the National Park Service had assisted and expedited Native land claims. As a result, Native corporations became the only Alaskan institution, besides environmental groups, to support the study and establishment of new parks.

For the next twenty-two months, we waited for Washington to complete the rules and regulations and to initiate other bureaucratic processes associated with Alaska land selection. With eleven hard-working professionals recently hired, Zorro did not want to lose their knowledge or their rapport with their respective corporations. He set them to work synthesizing their unique information about Alaskan Natives and how they used the land. The resultant summary, he surmised, would help provide context to certify the historic sites. Eventually most of the eleven regions had printed studies that listed the 14(h) sites and described their geographic setting, native peoples, previous archeological investigations, and relevant bibliography. These studies not only assisted the Native corporations but also contributed tremendous anthropological knowledge to the field.

With Zorro's assistance, our young people also advised the Native corporations on historic preservation matters. He urged them to begin planning for the eventual acquisition of the historic sites and their accompanying historical and anthropological information. Once stimulated, the corporations considered writing Native histories, establishing village or regional museums, and developing various forms of cultural interpretation. During the hiatus caused by lack of regulations, our professionals also worked on other projects for the National Park Service.

Although I provided some oversight to these projects, Zorro's expertise and imagination surpassed mine. Instead, I focused on my Yukon-Charley study. By September 1976, I had finished my Yukon field season and found my reputation within the National Park Service improved. I had spent three months living in a proposed national park. That was more than any key man had done. While one or two Eagle residents still shunned me, most of the town hated the Service more than they hated me. The employees of the Bureau of Land Management still kept their distance, but I had more than enough to do without helping them restore Fort Egbert.

As I struggled to write a narrative history based on my research, I received a phone call that elated me. Bob Utley asked me if I would like to visit a number of western historic sites. The American Heritage publishing company had contracted with him to write a history of the Indian Wars from 1850 to 1890. As part of the contract, he received $1,500 to visit Indian war battle sites.

Once during our various communications on the Alaska Native Historic Sites Project, I had confided to him that my dream vacation was to travel around the West and tour historic sites that I had read about but never seen. Living in Alaska limited my ability to travel and inhibited me from doing much more than dreaming. While Bob and I would not be able to see all of the West on this two-week tour, we would make a good start.

Because Bob had some official business in Yellowstone National Park, we met in Denver and drove to the park. The superintendent wanted to discuss keeping the park's historic archives in the park. National policy required parks to send historic documents to the National Archives for safekeeping. Bob did not believe that parks could or would maintain the proper conditions to preserve valuable documents. The superintendent, "Big John" Townsley, set high standards and hoped to convince Bob that Yellowstone, the first national park, was an exception. Townsley planned to dedicate one historic structure solely for the archives and agreed to rehabilitate and maintain it to the standards of the National Archives. Moreover, he offered to have an archivist inspect the facilities on an annual basis and agreed to hire a historian or archivist for his staff. Bob reluctantly gave in, although he feared that when Townsley moved on the next superintendent would abolish the archivist position and use the building for other purposes.

The next day we began our tour of the West. We tried to see more of Yellowstone, but an early winter storm limited our sightseeing. Over the next ten days we visited Sioux Indian battle sites, the Black Hills, Wounded Knee, and national parks. The national parks especially attracted me. For the first time I had the knowledge and training to assess how well they interpreted history to the public. I was also curious to compare them with our proposed parks.

The national park areas included Fort Laramie, Scotts Bluff, and Bent's Fort. To me Fort Laramie's significance arose from the fur trade period, but the National Park Service emphasized the frontier military story. I expressed my anger and disapproval to Bob and felt the public was not well served. Bob responded that all the structures dated from the military period, whereas nothing survived from the fur trade era. History in the National Park Service focuses on tangible remains. If an important event lacks a physical resource, the National Park Service doesn't tell much of its story. That is partially why there are many battlefields and forts as national parks but few representing the cultural, social, and intellectual aspects of American history.

At Scotts Bluff we ran into Merrill Mattes, an old friend of Bob's, who had once been superintendent of the area and was a longtime historian of the Platte River emigrant trails. He took great pleasure in showing us where the wagon wheels had carved a trail through the stone of Scotts Bluff. After having read many journals and diaries that mentioned Scotts Bluff, to stand there finally and imagine the hardships of the emigrants almost overwhelmed me.

From Scotts Bluff we drove to Bent's Fort on the Arkansas River. The Park Service had recently reconstructed it from the ground up on the original foundations. Bob admitted that early in his career he had supported the proposal to rebuild the famous adobe-walled trading post. Since then, he said, he had developed a more sophisticated understanding of historic preservation and opposed all reconstructions. Rebuilding a structure lost to history, however accurately done, does not restore its authenticity. Scarce funds had been spent to create a fake. Nothing historic had occurred in the new building. Even the superintendent called it an expensive sand castle that had to be repaired after each heavy rain. Nonetheless, as a stage set for living history, the building captivated visitors with the color and spirit of the old fur-trading post and way station on the Santa Fe Trail.

From Bent's Fort, we returned to Denver. We both hated to see an end to our magical trip. For me, it was a trip I had often dreamed of taking— seeing the West and its historic sites. For Bob, it allowed him to share his own love of the West and history with someone who valued them as much as he. For both of us, it was an opportunity to get to know each other better.

After two weeks "out of time," we entered "real time" again—the annual convention of the Western History Association. This conference was the forum for my first professional presentation outside Alaska. During 1975, along with my research on Fort Egbert, I had completed a smaller history on Kennecott's Alaskan copper mines in the proposed Wrangell-St. Elias

National Park. The great Kennecott copper corporation began at these almost unknown mines, whose copper ore was among the richest in the world. I summarized my conclusions for the paper I delivered in Denver. When the foremost historian of western mining commended me, the editor of the *Western Historical Quarterly* asked to consider it for publication. I felt that my writing career was moving nearly as fast as my Park Service career.

Following my idyllic vacation, I focused on writing my Yukon-Charley Historic Resource Study. By April 1977, I had completed my study, but Washington bureaucrats had failed to finalize the rules and regulations for 14(h). I needed a project. Fortunately for me, Stell Newman asked me to provide him a historical overview of the Seward Peninsula. Stell had a doctorate in anthropology and an interest in history, and was the most likeable of the planners for the proposed parks. He was key man for Bering Land Bridge, where the potential for early-man archeological sites fit his specialty. To show the continuum of human history, I focused on four historical periods: exploration, whaling, reindeer herding, and mining. Of the four, the whaling chapter captured my interest, and I read everything on the industry.

During the summer of 1977, I spent a couple of weeks on the Seward Peninsula, doing an abbreviated historic site survey. I visited Nome, a small railroad, several significant mining sites, and the largest gold-mining dredge in Alaska—all outside the park boundaries. Compared to my work in Yukon-Charley in 1976, it was indeed an overview, even superficial. Stell wanted to know the full historical context of the Seward Peninsula and how specific historic sites fit into the story. Each key man compiled relevant legislative support data for his proposed park. My study, along with archeological reports, documented extensive human activity in Bering Land Bridge. Congressional committees would study the data, consider the recommended boundaries, and include or exclude additional properties as political realities required. I finished writing my overview, accompanied with ample historical photographs, just in time for a late September congressional hearing.

That fall, Bob and I continued our tour of the West. Following the annual meeting of the Western History Association in Portland, we explored the Northwest. This time we seemed out of sync. Bob was preoccupied, distant, and hard to communicate with. Earlier in 1977 he had gone through a traumatic divorce. At the same chaotic time, he had left the National Park Service for the President's Advisory Council on Historic Preservation. He and the director of the National Park Service had not been able to agree on the preservation of historic buildings at Grand Canyon National Park. Because he could not loyally serve him, Bob accepted appointment as the council's deputy executive director, a position in the Senior Executive Service.

I too was preoccupied. As a result of the bicentennial, the National Park Service had gained extra permanent positions. Zorro was trying to make my position permanent and to give me a promotion at the same time. If a military veteran appeared on the list, Zorro would not be able to hire me. Veterans receive extra points and block non-veterans below them. More critical, because it was my position being advertised, I could lose my temporary job as well as the permanent job and promotion. Every couple of days I called Zorro to check on the progress. At Redlands, California, I stopped at a phone booth. I could hardly hear for the heavy truck traffic, but I heard that I had the job. We celebrated that night with a steak dinner.

We ended our week's tour in Portland. At last Bob tried to verbalize that he missed the National Park Service, its people, and its resources. He feared that he had made a mistake in leaving the service. Instead of managing real resources he found himself managing a process. While he had a higher profile, his job dropped him in the midst of the nation's biggest battles over historic properties. The additional stress and tension had fewer rewards. With each case, he was expected to find the compromise that would bridge warring factions and save the historic property.

At that time, I couldn't understand the loss he felt. He was still in history and preserving historic places, which I thought would be enough. But he was not part of the National Park Service. Only after several years could I understand the emotional bond that ties employees to that organization.

In Alaska, we in the National Park Service had a unique bonding. Nearly everyone else in the state hated us and wanted us gone. We found we could only be ourselves around other park people. Even my husband and friends made me defensive about our proposed parks. They all wanted to continue their lifestyle—hunting, mining, and doing whatever they wanted wherever they wanted. Whenever a group of park employees met, our shared values and goals united us. When we traveled, we often stayed in each other's homes rather than hotels. At the very least, we always got together for lunch or dinner. Each time a number of us would be in the same place at the same time, it was a stimulating and uplifting experience, one that we all cherished. Our camaraderie helped us cope with an all-encompassing hostile environment.

We also shared a vision. After learning from sixty years of mistakes in developing and managing national parks, we believed we had a chance to do things right. Early directors confronted building a constituency and focused on making parks accessible, enjoyable, and comfortable to visitors. Landscape architects designed parks with roads, trails, visitor centers, rest rooms, restaurants, lodgings, and viewing vistas. Some parks became too obsessed with visitor enjoyment, constructing swimming pools, golf courses, ski runs, even bars and liquor stores. The visitor often lost the beauty of nature as campgrounds and trailer parks swelled beyond capacity and traffic crawled bumper-to-bumper along narrow roads.

In Alaska we looked at such developments as distractions and intrusions. Alaskan parks could not be improved; they could only be perverted. Our ideal management plan was "leave it like it is." We saw no reason for the employee housing commonly constructed for isolated parks. Nor did we believe that visitors required lodgings with all the attendant water, sewage, and electrical systems unavailable in the Alaskan bush. All development should be confined to the small communities outside park boundaries. Campgrounds, trails, rest rooms, and roads within the parks seemed unnecessary. Finally, we believed that separate regulations should be written to manage Alaskan parks. They differed too much from those in the Lower 48 and necessitated sensitive and thoughtful management.

While we wanted minimum accommodations for visitors, we recognized the importance of allowing traditional uses, especially subsistence hunting by Alaskan Natives. While historical research and 14(h) occupied my time, Zorro put his effort into collecting subsistence data on all proposed parks. He sent anthropologists into the Native villages that used the parklands. They recorded where the Natives hunted, fished, trapped, and gathered berries and herbs. In addition, they collected Native place names, traced travel and subsistence patterns, and illustrated the material culture of subsistence. Most important, these anthropologists demonstrated how integrally subsistence and Native culture were entwined.

While we endorsed subsistence hunting, we did not condone sport hunting. We made a distinction between the rich doctor flying into a park to find trophies and only incidentally meat and the Native whose life and culture depended on the meat and the experience. Allowing any type of hunting, however, ran counter to national park philosophy. Our basic premise was to look at the Alaska parks with fresh eyes and to manage them differently from parks in the Lower 48. We recognized that the only alternative to subsistence use of national parks was welfare for the Native peoples. In promoting and marketing these parks, we tried to convince not only traditional park people but also environmentalists and members of Congress.

In planning our Alaskan parks, we turned for guidance to the Leopold Report. In 1962, Interior Secretary Stewart Udall asked a blue-ribbon committee of wildlife specialists to study the wildlife management policies of the National Park Service. He invited A. Starker Leopold, professor of biology at the University of California at Berkeley and son of ecologist Aldo Leopold, to chair the committee. When the highly publicized report appeared in 1963, it challenged current wildlife philosophies and practices. It emphasized ecological principles and biological diversity. Almost revolutionary in concept, it urged that scientific research serve as the basis for *all* management programs. It marked a clear departure from the emphasis on visitor comfort and enjoyment.

Bill Brown and the other key men tried to draw boundaries for the proposed parks that reflected ecosystem limits. For example, the Yukon-Charley

National Rivers proposal encompassed the entire Charley River basin. More dramatic, Noatak National Preserve in northwestern Alaska included a complete ecosystem of nearly seven million acres. Proposed Gates to the Arctic in the Brooks Range and Wrangell-St. Elias embraced eight and twelve million acres respectively. In addition, the proposals recommended that nearly all the new parks be designated wilderness. Our ideals and principles were as immense as the parks we dreamed of establishing.

Meanwhile, the rest of the National Park Service struggled with great difficulty to adapt to the Leopold Report. One of the first adjustments involved grizzly bears. Following Leopold's directive to reestablish natural conditions in parks, in 1970 the superintendent of Yellowstone National Park closed the park's garbage dumps, since the 1880s a source of food for the grizzlies and a spectacle for tourists. This action forced the bears to find natural food. World-renown grizzly bear experts John and Frank Craighead, who had researched Yellowstone bears since the 1950s, vehemently opposed the move. They claimed that closing the dumps would jeopardize grizzly bear survival. Sure enough, two years after the closure the park killed eighty-eight foraging grizzlies that threatened visitor safety. By 1975, the rangers had killed so many grizzlies that requirements of the Endangered Species Act placed the bear on the list of threatened species.

Applying Leopold's ecological principles to other aspects of park operations had less disastrous results. The National Park Service, nonetheless, took nearly ten years to stop using huge quantities of insecticides to control forest insects. The agency showed even more reluctance to accept the ecological value of fire. After researching fire in the sequoia forests, park foresters recognized that fire was critical to the germination of sequoia seeds. Foresters also observed that a hundred years of fire suppression had created thick underbrush that endangered the mighty sequoias with crown fires. Fighting years of tradition in stomping out fires, a few parks tried setting prescribed fires under carefully controlled conditions. In 1976 parks and forests in the Yellowstone area agreed to allow some naturally caused fires to burn. By 1978 the use of fire in perpetuating natural systems had become the new national policy.

Meanwhile, in November 1977 the Anchorage office of the Park Service sent me to Skagway to assess the significance of a cemetery. The Dyea River threatened to wash it away. Because it lay within Klondike Gold Rush National Historical Park, management wanted to know what to do about it.

At Skagway, I had my first experience with an established national park. Although only officially established the previous year, the contrast between it and the proposed parks where I had been working could not have been greater. For the first time, a park employee met me at the airstrip, welcomed me to the park, and showed me around. The superintendent invited me for dinner and treated me as his equal, admitting professional insecurities and fears. Instead of confronting hostile locals, I found that Skagwayites embraced the park. I found the change refreshing and satisfying. I liked being liked.

I visited the cemetery and found as many names as I could from the faded tombstones and wooden crosses. Most of the burials seemed to be Alaskan Natives. Next, I met with the Native leaders and the families of the deceased to learn what they wanted done. All but one family wanted the graves moved to another site. To develop the significance of the cemetery, I dug into the area's newspapers, explored some of the local document collections, and studied the Natives' culture, especially burial practices. Then I quickly drafted a report that provided a brief history with my recommendations. The accolades of praise from grateful managers in Anchorage startled me. This one week's work gave me a higher profile with them than all the substantive historical research I had done.

Still, historical research remained my first love. As a result of my work with Stell Newman and Bill Brown, two other key men for proposed parks wanted historical overviews of their proposed parks. During the winter of 1977–78, I started researching historic sites in Lake Clark and Wrangell-St. Elias. In late fall, however, the completion of the rules and regulations for 14(h), the Alaskan Native Historic Sites Project, brought my research to an immediate halt.

The regulations designated the Bureau of Indian Affairs as the lead agency with the National Park Service providing professional assistance.

Dutifully, we geared up for a summer field season of locating and evaluating Native historic sites. As we hired and trained a small group of archeologists, we wondered what the Bureau of Indian Affairs had in mind. Communication was minimal, even secret. When June 1978 arrived, BIA was not ready to go into the field. No one had been hired, money had been spent on strange types of field equipment, and the project manager was paralyzed with fear and panic.

Zorro and I decided to have our own field season on Hinchinbrook Island, just off Cordova in Prince William Sound. We decided to hire only archeologists to do the actual site work, reserving historians for archival research and anthropologists to collect associated oral traditions. This time we developed a structured training program for our new recruits, including historic preservation law, site mapping, wilderness awareness, and even the shooting and maintenance of shotguns.

The primary archeological site on Hinchinbrook Island covered several hundred acres. One set of archeologists sought the site's boundaries and significance while another surveyed the vicinity for additional sites described in the applications of the regional corporation. With the long summer days, the crews worked twelve-hour shifts, six days a week. Although they cooked, wrote reports, and visited with each other in large white-walled tents, they slept in small backpacking tents with better mosquito netting. Because salmon were spawning and large brown bears lined the creeks, each team of archeologists carried a shotgun for protection. Close quarters and constant company tested compatibility, but no real problems arose that crew captains couldn't resolve. By summer's end, besides the large Hinchinbrook site, they had investigated forty-two sites.

In between my travels to Hinchinbrook to supervise the archeological work, I also visited Lake Clark and Wrangell-St. Elias. I found Lake Clark the most beautiful of the proposed parks. The lake itself mirrored the fiords of Norway—steep cliffs dropping into the crystal blue water. Numerous other lakes and even some volcanoes dotted the park area. Staying with friends of my parents gave my visit a more personal and friendly aspect than my previous two site surveys. From Dick Bowman I learned much of the local history—its skeletons as well as its traditions. Dick did not pull back from telling me stories that rivaled Peyton Place. All towns have their hidden history, but rarely do locals trust historians enough to share it.

Later I visited the largest of the proposed parklands. Wrangell-St. Elias encompassed more than thirteen million acres of towering mountains in southeast Alaska—dwarfing Yellowstone's mere two million acres. After my preliminary flyover, I was able to drive to one of the last gold-rush boomtowns in Alaska. I found enough extant structures to interpret the gold rush for visitors. Weather, however, prevented a more thorough survey. Besides, most of what I located lay on private land.

As if I weren't busy enough planning and supervising our first 14(h) field season and researching and visiting two additional proposed parks, I also assisted the Skagway park in finding a historian to help write historic structure reports. These reports trace the history of a building through legal records, photographs, and public and private archives. Years earlier my dream job involved this type of research for Williamsburg. Now I had more than I could handle with my own research and the 14(h) project. The structural historian would work closely with the park's historical architect, who recorded the physical history of changes to the building. Because the historian reported to me, I made several trips to assess his progress.

On one of these trips, in July 1978, I decided to hike the Chilkoot Trail. During the Klondike Gold Rush, two overland trails from Alaska crossed the mountains to the Canadian gold fields. One from Skagway, the White Pass, eventually provided the route for the narrow-gauge Yukon and White Pass Railway. The other, the Chilkoot, left from Dyea, across the bay from Skagway. This trail was shorter but steeper than the White Pass Trail and thus captured most of the traffic until the railroad eclipsed it. During the winter of 1897, men cut nearly vertical stairsteps in the snow to climb over the pass, a scene depicted graphically in scores of photographs. During the spring I had taken the scenic train trip over White Pass; now I wanted to experience the rigors of the Chilkoot.

Not one to hike by myself, I had hoped that some of the Skagway staff might go with me. At the last minute my hiking partners had to cancel, and

I was on my own. A friend gave me a lift to the ghost town of Dyea, trail-head for the Chilkoot. During the Klondike Gold Rush, both Dyea and Skagway were boomtowns. Once the White Pass Railway pushed on to Whitehorse, however, Dyea fell into neglect. Now only one dilapidated building stood on the town site.

Because I would be backpacking, our Yukon grub would be too heavy. For lightness in weight and ease in preparation, freeze-dried food was the definite staple of choice. A tent made from a revolutionary new material, Gore-Tex, supposedly breathed yet kept out the rain without a rain fly and weighed only two pounds, a fraction of my North Face tent. At Sheep Camp, the historic first-night camping spot, it went together instantly, almost too good to be true.

Before sleeping I tried to see what existed of Sheep Camp. Unfortunately, not much remained of the small town that in 1897–98 provided bed and board for nearly thirty thousand Chilkooters. Only some debris, a few sill logs that marked foundations, and a largely unchanged natural environment characterized the rowdy, avalanche-prone community.

The next morning, the climb steepened and the trail narrowed. Old cans and bottles and even some old shoes, discarded by the Chilkooters, dotted the edge of the trail. In 1897, to prevent a shortage of food in the Klondike, the Canadian government required each person to bring a thousand pounds of food. Northwest Mounted Police checked the loads at the international boundary, just beyond the summit of the trail. A thousand pounds meant ten trips of a hundred pounds each. My load weighed only fifty pounds, and an improved hiking trail and modern backpack eased travel, but when my arthritic knees began to act up, even fifty pounds seemed too heavy.

As morning turned to afternoon, the sunny sky darkened and rain began to fall. The higher I climbed, the colder the rain and the colder the temperature. A curve in the trail opened the "Golden Stairs," looming ahead in the mist. Instead of stairs cut into the snow, boulders the size of houses littered the mountainside. All the old photographs of the Chilkoot Trail captured dramatic winter scenes, with no hint of what lay beneath the snow. Climbing up and around the boulders slowed my pace. The wet, slick surface of the rocks afforded few handholds or footholds. Fortunately, a steel cable, the remains of the historic tram of 1898, allowed me to pull myself wearily to the summit.

On top, the icy wind dropped my body temperature further. Wet and cold, I tried to walk fast enough to warm up, but my knees wouldn't support the pace. Slowing to accommodate the pain made me so cold that my whole body began to shake. Recognizing the symptoms of hypothermia and its lethal consequences, I knew I had to get warm—and soon. After shedding the backpack, my hands shook so hard that they could hardly pull out the Gore-Tex tent. My mind grew increasingly confused, and each movement required total concentration because even simple tasks seemed impossible to accomplish. Thankfully, the tent popped up without requiring guide poles or rain flaps, and I crawled inside with my pack. Getting out of the wind helped, but my body shook and my mind couldn't think. "Sugar gives heat," my crazed mind cried out, and into my mouth went several handfuls for a needed sugar rush. Believing that sugar gave me instant energy, I found the strength to pull out my sleeping bag. Careful to avoid getting the bag wet, I stripped off my dripping clothes and slid into its down warmth. Forcing myself to stay awake, I searched my pack for candy or anything to give me energy. All the freeze-dried food, unfortunately, required hot water to prepare. Finding one smashed granola bar, I ate it slowly, concentrating on each bite. Still shaking but no longer threatened with a confused mind, I set about to heat some water.

Outside the tent the wind howled. It blew more than sixty miles an hour, banging the tent walls and trying to sweep it away. Starting a fire out there would be impossible. Yet I had to have hot food at once. Knowing the risks, I set up my small backpacking stove inside the tent and carefully lit it with a waterproof match. Within three minutes water boiled for tea and freeze-dried stew. The tea warmed body and soul. I would not die.

By the next morning the storm had abated somewhat. I ate a big breakfast and resolved to push myself and to get out as quickly as possible. My knees screamed with each step. The continuing foul weather coupled with painful knees turned my pleasure hike into an endurance nightmare. Once, during a lull in the wind and rain, I stopped to rest and fell asleep in the middle of the trail. A hiker almost stepped on me. Getting up, I aimed for a cabin on the Canadian side for the night. Several people had already claimed it, but they cheerfully welcomed me to share the floor.

A happy and gregarious mixture of Canadians and Americans chattered about their hike. Most of them had saved their money for several years to tackle the trail. When they learned that the National Park Service paid me to hike it and even gave me extra to cover per diem, they gushed, "You must have the best job in the world." I needed that reminder. After only two and one-half years, I was already taking my job for granted.

The warmth of the cabin dried my wet gear and allowed me a good night's sleep. Before the sun I arose, started a fire, and heated water for tea and instant oatmeal. Without waiting for the others to awaken, I slipped out of the cabin and hobbled down the trail to Lake Bennett. From here, the noon train carried my weary body back to civilization. Instead of taking the usual five days to hike the thirty-three-mile Chilkoot, I had pushed my body to do it in three days. All in all, the miserable weather, the limitations of an aging body, and the difficulty of the terrain granted me a more realistic perception of the historic 1897 experience than I would have had with better weather and distracting companions.

When I finally finished my hectic summer season and returned to Fairbanks in September 1978, I immediately packed my bags for Washington, D.C. President Jimmy Carter and his boldly imaginative Interior secretary, Cecil Andrus, wanted to make conservation history. Because of congressional inaction, the protective provisions of d-2 ended in December. President Carter and Secretary Andrus planned to apply a little-used law, the Antiquities Act of 1906, to preserve the d-2 lands as national monuments until legislation could be passed. The Antiquities Act empowers the president to designate national monuments to preserve areas of historical and scientific interest. Thwarting the Congress and especially an Alaskan delegation bitterly opposed to more national parks, Carter knew his action would release a storm of congressional anger and

tumultuous litigation. We had to demonstrate that each monument embraced the smallest area necessary for management of ecological systems—
a new and controversial concept. With only three months to comply with
environmental law, the National Park Service embarked on environmental
impact statements assessing the effects of the action on communities, historic sites, and commercial activities, as well as on other environmental
aspects of the proposed monuments.

Most of the Alaska and Denver offices converged on Washington to
assist in the massive effort. Everyone worked hard, long, and fast. By the
time I left in mid-October, we had essentially completed the environmental documents. As I packed up my papers to leave, the work leader approached me and asked for my overtime hours. I said with some surprise:
"I'm a professional. I work as long as I am needed. I don't claim overtime."
Zorro refused as well. Considering the long hours my Alaskan staff contributed each year, I felt I'd be a hypocrite and a fraud to accept overtime.
Because we were the only task force members refusing overtime, we made
the others look bad. But I felt strongly that I was paid to do a job, not to
work forty-hour weeks.

Back in Alaska, the Alaska Native Historic Sites Project teetered on the
edge of oblivion. Because the first program director for the Bureau of
Indian Affairs had bombed out for gross incompetence, Zorro used all of
his bureaucratic skills to keep the whole project from collapsing. He found
a couple of capable people within the bureau who were chagrined at the
agency's disaster and wanted to work with us.

Fortunately for us, in March 1979 the National Park Service appointed
a new Alaska state director. This man came to have tremendous impact on
my career. He was one of the brightest and best managers the Park Service
had. Young, brash, aggressive, effective, and a third-generation Park Service
employee, John Cook had shot up the career ladder. By the time I met him,
he had been superintendent of Hubbell Trading Post and Canyon de Chelly
in Arizona, general superintendent over all southern Arizona parks, deputy
regional director in San Francisco, associate director in the Washington office,
and regional director of the Southwest Region. Part Cherokee Indian, he was

sensitive to Indian issues and values. As a result, he worked well with the Indian groups of the Southwest and was a natural choice for Alaska.

Almost immediately everyone experienced the sensation of leadership. No longer did anyone question who was boss. While Cook had a reputation for having killed a few careers, Zorro had known him for years and believed that he simply had no tolerance for poor performers or disloyalty. "John Cook wants things straight," he warned me. "From now on we keep him informed of all we do." Previously, no one in the Anchorage office knew, much less cared, what we did outside of research for the proposed parks. The Service's previous state director was grateful for the results of our 14(h) work but did not really understand the program. Within a month we had briefed Cook and his deputy on the program, and they flew off to meet their counterparts in the Bureau of Indian Affairs.

The next day we received a call from Cook in Juneau at the headquarters of the Bureau of Indian Affairs. "BIA is devastated with last year's debacle," he reported. "We can get the lead agency designation if we want it." Zorro and I discussed it and, surprising everyone, decided to be team players. We called Cook and told him that we would work with the bureau's Larry Cooper if he would head the program. We would live to regret that decision.

For the summer of 1979 the Bureau of Indian Affairs threw everything at the Alaska Native Historic Sites Project. Cooper became program manager and had the resources of the agency behind him. Within weeks he had contracts for helicopters, two base camps under construction in Prince William Sound and the Seward Peninsula, a twelve-person boat chartered for southeast Alaska, and authority to hire realty specialists. Cooper decided to salvage the field season with four projects: one in Prince William Sound, one in southeast Alaska, one on the Seward Peninsula, and one in the Brooks Range. We put four archeologists and four assistants in each field camp. I spent my summer rotating tours among the four projects, visiting each camp at least twice.

Like the last group of "Fourteen H'ers," our young archeologists put in long, hard hours. They loved their work and wanted to do a good job.

Once in the field, their dedication to thoroughness and quality often conflicted with BIA's emphasis on speed. Frictions developed between individuals, then spread to camp bosses and research leaders. Eventually the frictions rose to the level of Larry Cooper and Zorro.

Despite the tensions, the summer proved productive. We established excellent rapport with the Native corporations and villagers and instilled in them an awareness of the value of preserving historic sites. In addition, we acquired a huge collection of ethnographic and historical materials, as well as many published works. As one Washington authority claimed, our "work pushed back the frontiers of Alaska history."

Although we had investigated more than 150 sites, at the rate we were progressing it would take nearly thirty years to certify 4,000 sites scattered throughout Alaska. Consequently BIA wanted to dispense with certification and simply turn the sites over to the Natives. Eventually, in the early 1980s after I had left, the bureau won its case, and our 14(h) program ceased to exist.

Until BIA succeeded in this intent, however, we still had a winter's work to do. Deadlines for the National Register forms loomed while artifacts and field notes had to be catalogued, conserved, and integrated with oral history. Not infrequently I would arrive at my office at five o'clock in the morning to find my staff already at work. Several kept a bedroll by their desks and spent the night in the office, showering at the university gym and continuing to work. I had never known harder workers. Their lives were their jobs. They lived, breathed, and slept with their assignment. Their hard labor, dedication, and belief in their work matched my own values and idealism. As a result, my staff and I related more as friends and colleagues than as supervisor and subordinates.

With all of my flying around Alaska during the summer of 1979, I often stopped at the regional office in Anchorage. Here I learned that the rest of the National Park Service had finally become obsessed with Alaska. On December 1, 1978, after Congress had allowed its self-imposed deadline for establishing parklands to expire, President Jimmy Carter followed through on our environmental impact documents and created thirteen national monuments. Now an area larger than the entire National Park System came under traditional park regulations.

Because Carter wanted to force Congress to pass legislation, the monuments protected every acre of land under consideration by Congress with strict and inflexible preservation authority. The monument proclamations allowed no traditional use except subsistence. Unfortunately for the National Park Service, neither the president nor Congress provided funding or staffing to enforce the rigid tenets. Even without funds, John Cook requested a ranger force to provide a Park Service presence for the summer of 1979. Twenty-one handpicked rangers from throughout the system arrived to patrol forty-one million acres—averaging one ranger for an area the size of Yellowstone National Park.

Although Zorro expressed disgust with rangers carrying guns in Anchorage, the ranger contingent had a rough summer. Several were evicted from their houses. Others were refused service at restaurants and gas stations. One dentist in Anchorage declined to medicate a ranger's impacted tooth. At Glenallen, near Wrangell-St. Elias National Monument, vandals burned the plane that rangers used to patrol the huge park. Still the rangers continued with their jobs—answering hundreds of questions, searching for downed aircraft, and issuing citations for illegal hunting. They made a clear statement that the resource values of the monuments would be protected, and at the same time absorbed and dissipated extraordinary hostility. Near the end of summer, when the rangers quickly responded to an emergency call for a rescue on Mount McKinley, hostility eased a bit.

Previously we had coped with animosity, but it had rarely flared into outright hatred. With the coming of the monuments, one hateful act fueled another. Among the most frightening to our personal safety was the day John Cook found his office window shot with five bullet holes.

Fortunately for Zorro and me, our offices at the University of Alaska in Fairbanks limited displays of overt anger. But our relationship with the university created its own tension. Neither Zorro nor I had the "terminal degree"—the Ph.D. We had contracts with the university totaling more than a million and a half dollars, we hired university students and professors for projects, and with our offices at the university we had daily contact with professors who looked on us as less than their equals. As long as we worked as closely as we did with a university, we believed that we would have greater credibility within the university and the professions if one of us attained the exalted terminal degree. We discussed with John Cook my returning to graduate school. He was supportive, provided I agreed to stay with the Park Service twice as long as I attended school. Because I never intended to leave until retirement, I had no trouble with these terms. Thus, I took leave-without-out-pay for my first semester at the University of New Mexico, which supposedly had the best department for studying the history of the American West. I had every intention of returning to Alaska in December.

By this time I had completed nearly five years with the National Park Service. After my difficult first two years, I slowly gained self-confidence. Yet every day the job stretched and tested me. Routinely, I spent nearly every summer living out of a backpack, traveling throughout the immense state and visiting Native communities, our archeological work camps, and proposed parks. Even during the fall and winter I seldom got home before seven o'clock. Never did I feel that I was on top of my job—too much to do and too little time and too few people to do it all.

My experience, however, did not differ from that of any other National Park Service employee in Alaska. Everyone worked hard, often overwhelmed with the workload. Never before had the National Park Service tried to add forty million acres of parkland to the system at one time. Yet the work was gratifying. Few places of the world are as beautiful. We enjoyed collecting basic data, photographing pristine beauty, and marveling at the wildness still existing in the late twentieth century. Our single focus became: These parklands will be preserved.

What made our task unpleasant, often ugly, were Alaskans. Only the Alaskan Natives and a few environmentalists applauded our efforts. The rest of the people and their political leaders railed against us in the media, at public meetings, even in our neighborhoods. Alaskans are a proud, independent, and unforgiving people. They pride themselves on their stamina to withstand minus-fifty-degree temperatures, long winter nights, and heavy snow. No one is automatically an Alaskan; one must earn the title. Thus they regarded "instant park" experts with disdain and alarm. Fearing federal restrictions in national parks drove Alaskans into a frenzy of hate. As the new parks progressed toward reality, anger and hostility became the norm. No one, including employees of the National Park Service, wanted to create national parks just like they were in the Lower 48. Idealistic and optimistic, we believed we would make Alaskan parks special and unique.

In addition to Alaskans, the National Park Service bureaucracy created unnecessary hardships for us. The existing parks in Alaska reported to the regional director in Seattle, while those of us working on the proposed parks answered to an assistant director in Washington. Because personalities at the top clashed, orders went out instructing park superintendents to minimize their cooperation with us—even though their own parks were designated for expansion. Consequently, outside of the relatively new park in Skagway, I had essentially no experience or knowledge of how "real" parks operated.

After nearly five years, I was as ignorant of the duties of protection rangers and resource managers as park managers were of the Alaska Native Historic Sites Project. I learned early in my career that if you were not in park operations—protection, interpretation, maintenance, resource management— you were not part of the "real" National Park Service. Prior to John Cook's advent, only one supervisor ever visited our Fairbanks office. Zorro had more bureaucratic freedom than nearly any other employee, but it was a two-edged sword—he lacked management support until Cook arrived.

Professionally, in those five years I learned more than how to conduct historic site surveys. I also grasped and manipulated the concepts of program management. Surprising myself, I discovered that I enjoyed the bureaucracy. I matched wits with other bureaucrats and pioneered routes through red tape. I found program management as creative as writing history. Developing new programs that worked took imagination but also pragmatism. It also demanded a resiliency and adaptability to changing circumstances. Ironically, I found I relished the power that came with effective bureaucratic skills. The ability to find program funds, the recruitment and supervision of hardworking and productive staffs, and the opportunities to achieve nearly unlimited goals tantalized me. Tasting the gratification that came with success in a bureaucratic program, I knew I would never be content as a solitary historian. I loved the energy, synergy, and results of working with a team.

As Bob taught me the value of making the bureaucracy work, Zorro imparted his knowledge on getting the most out of each employee. By trusting me to develop and manage a new program and staff, he made me a creative supervisor. While my employees may have wanted more guidance and direction, I gave them the opportunity to grow and contribute as much as they wanted. In return, despite their insecurity, they beat all odds and delivered high-quality products and services that established their names and reputations.

In addition to becoming a supervisor who encouraged creativity and energy, my five years of hell and hard work had matured me into a team player. By the time I left Alaska, I worked well with everyone in all agencies—even the Bureau of Land Management. Although I had learned some valuable lessons, I knew that the issues of my gender and personality had not been fully resolved. Nonetheless, I believed I had something to contribute to history, the National Park Service, and Alaska. I looked forward to my return.

# Santa Fe

n 1973, at the same conference where I had met Bob Utley, I also met Richard Ellis, a history professor from the University of New Mexico. At that time Ellis argued that the University of New Mexico had the best graduate program on the American West. Where most universities only had one professor to teach the subject, New Mexico had four, all publishing authors. Consequently, large numbers of graduate students came from across the nation to study with them. Convinced that New Mexico appeared the best program, I did no more research and, in 1979, applied to the graduate school.

I alerted Dick Ellis that I was following through on his recommendation, and he ensured my acceptance. Once there, I contrasted sharply with the average graduate student. First, I already had a job and did not want to compete for the highly valued teaching assistant positions. That allowed me to take three courses for credit, audit three more, and study for my Spanish language exam. Second, I had little desire to kill time over coffee with other grads, arguing the finer points of history. Third, I focused solely on completing my studies in two fall semesters, the minimum time required. Most students spent two to three years collecting classes and rubbing shoulders with senior scholars. Although I enjoyed my colleagues, I had little in common with them or my professors.

For the most part, I found my professors parochial and unable to comprehend a historian outside academia. Although my job paid more than most of them were earning, they assumed that I would eventually want to teach at the college level. Thus some of them fought to keep me from taking courses that would be useful to my current job, such as computer programming and American literature. Fortunately, Ellis and the department chair knew Bob Utley and respected his government work. They supported me in my specialized program.

Shortly after I got launched at the University of New Mexico, Bob called to tell me that the most coveted historian position in the National Park Service was vacant. Both Bob and Bill Brown had served as regional historian of the Southwest Region, based in Santa Fe. "The position is wired for someone else, which means that someone else has been secretly chosen, but you should apply simply to show your credentials," he said. Dutifully I completed the dreadfully long and complicated federal application.

In early October Bob called again, "I just heard that the person who was hired for the Santa Fe job has turned it down," he said. "You are next on the list." I panicked. I was not ready to leave Alaska and had applied only because it was a safe way to let the National Park Service learn of my abilities.

Immediately I called my husband. Although we had grown apart during the past five years, we still communicated well. "My practice is here," he said, "so I can't go with you. But your career is important to you now, and you need to go. If you don't, you could lose your chance to advance in the Park Service."

Almost as soon as I had hung up the phone, Richard Sellars called to offer me the job. He headed the Southwest Cultural Resources Center in Santa Fe and would be my boss. I asked for a day to think about it. Next I called Zorro, who advised me to take the job and suggested that I call John Cook, who had once been regional director of the Southwest Region.

Cook leveled with me. "This is the best job for a historian we have," he said. "The Alaska Native Historic Sites Project has delivered all the pay-load it can for me, and I am not going to continue to battle the Bureau of Indian Affairs for it. While I will try to find you another job in Alaska, I can't promise you that I will succeed. This is a golden opportunity to move up the professional ladder. Take it!"

Although I was scared to leave colleagues who had learned to accept my personality, I knew that I needed the experience with "real" national parks. The change would undoubtedly be uncomfortable, but I decided to take the risk and grow professionally and personally. Thus, in January 1980 I became the new regional historian based in Santa Fe, New Mexico.

The entire Park Service envied the work environment of the Santa Fe regional office. Headquarters occupied the largest adobe office building in the world, a distinguished Pueblo design constructed as a relief project in 1939 by the Civilian Conservation Corps. The offices opened on a large grassy patio with trees, flowers, and a fish pond. Vigas supported the ceilings and projected, Pueblo style, from the roofline. The site nestled at the base of the Sangre de Cristos in the hills southeast of Santa Fe and commanded a sweeping view of deserts and plains rimmed by a mountainous horizon.

Bob had worked in this beautiful building in 1957–64, but it no longer housed the historians, archeologists, and architects. Instead, the Southwest Cultural Resources Center, home to all three disciplines, leased nearby space in Los Llanos, a large adobe home that later belonged to artist Georgia O'Keeffe. Each division chief, of whom I was one, had a private office with a fireplace. The building dated from the 1920s and had walls nearly two feet thick. Architects and archeologists had offices in various outbuildings. There was even a swimming pool, used by the underwater archeologists to test equipment. The beautiful home rested on nearly twenty acres dappled with juniper and piñon trees. A transplanted Alaskan could not have asked for a more serene and congenial environment as an introduction to Santa Fe culture.

The history division was the smallest in the center. I supervised two less-than-full-time employees—an architectural historian and a secretary—plus had oversight of one contract for $15,000. I couldn't help but compare this with my Alaskan responsibilities, where I supervised more than thirty people and a million-dollar contract with the University of Alaska. Yet my new job was a promotion and carried greater prestige.

Moreover, I would be working for the first and until then the only woman regional director, Lorraine Mintzmyer. I had followed her career with awe and admiration. Starting as a lowly secretary and working long, hard hours, she made herself invaluable as a budget manager to the regional director of the Midwest Region. In 1973, recognizing her innate leadership skill and under pressure from Director Hartzog to promote more women, the regional director took a chance and appointed her superintendent of Herbert Hoover National Historic Site in Iowa. Among the first women managers, Lorraine moved on to Buffalo National River in northwestern Arkansas, where homeowners resisting the new park sent her death threats and forced her to attend public meetings with armed rangers at her side. John Cook valued her courage, stamina, and will and hired her as his deputy regional director. In 1979, after Cook had moved to Alaska, the director named Lorraine as Cook's successor—only six years after she had been first appointed to a superintendency.

Lorraine Mintzmyer's bright career ended unhappily. In 1990, as regional director for the Rocky Mountain Region, she helped ignite a political storm. She and her peers in the U.S. Forest Service drafted a plan to manage the entire Yellowstone ecosystem as a collaborative undertaking between the two agencies. Called *Vision for the Future: A Framework for Coordination in the Yellowstone Area,* it angered the mining, grazing, and timber interests. They forged alliances with powerful senators and with President George H. W. Bush's Interior Department to thwart the plan. In a series of secret meetings, the administration watered down the plan, reversed action on all major issues, and transferred Lorraine to the East Coast. Six months later, in 1992, she resigned, claiming sexual discrimination and political harassment. The courts dealt with those issues, but politics had destroyed her promising career as well as an enlightened approach to the management of the Yellowstone ecosystem.

Before I had the privilege of working with Lorraine Mintzmyer, however, Bob learned that one of the congressional committees did not believe the small Advisory Council needed a deputy director. "If my position is abolished," he said, "government rules allow me to retire five years early, at the age of fifty." Rather than simply restructuring his job, he convinced his boss to abolish his job altogether, thus meeting the spirit and the letter of the congressional directive. This action allowed him to retire and immediately receive a reduced annuity.

Although we had known each other for nearly seven years, we had almost given up hope of getting together. Because of the sixteen-year difference in our ages and our diverse backgrounds, we agreed that we needed a neutral location where we could start life together on equal footing. Such a location must allow each of us to pursue our professional careers. Santa Fe was an ideal place to launch a relationship. I had a new job in the Southwest Region, and he now had an opportunity to write history full time.

While I waited for Bob to join me, I had much to learn about historic preservation. I knew the philosophy, laws, and principles, but I had never made operational decisions. Suddenly superintendents of small historic sites were calling to ask if they could put a sign on a historic house, paint a room a color not historically valid, or construct a new road. I had no background or knowledge on such issues.

I turned for guidance to Dave Battle, the region's chief historical architect. Dave had his architectural license, had worked in private practice, and had mastered many of the crafts necessary in restoring historic structures. His judgment always proved sound, and he explained patiently why some park actions might cause permanent harm to historic sites or buildings.

When Bob had the regional historian's title in 1957–64, he researched the history and significance of proposed new additions to the National Park System. In contrast, my job was more that of an adviser and occasionally a cop. I advised the park staffs in the Southwest Region (New Mexico, Texas, Oklahoma, Arkansas, Louisiana, and the Navajo Indian Reservation of Arizona) on historical matters. Mostly I counseled them on compliance with the National Historic Preservation Act of 1966, which contained provisions designed to guard historic properties against harm by federal undertakings. The law did not require that every historic place be saved, but it did force all federal managers, including park managers, to follow a process that compelled full consideration of alternatives to damage or destruction. When superintendents failed to follow the process, I had to be a cop with the support of the regional director and force compliance. The most important part of my advisory job was providing the regional director with the historical perspective to make planning and operational decisions affecting historic properties.

One of my first field trips was to Big Bend National Park, a jumble of deserts, mountains, and canyons cut by the southward sweep of the Rio Grande. The river marked the boundary between Texas and Mexico, and the park retained many vestiges of both the Mexican and the Anglo heritage. A proposed plan for Castelon, a historic district perched on the river between two plunging canyons, would demolish several historic buildings and damage the largely Mexican historic ambience. The assistant superintendent, Russ Berry, himself once a historian, seemed receptive to dropping the planned paving of the gravel parking lot. He even agreed to forego new buildings that could not be funded for many years in favor of adapting historic structures for use as park housing, a ranger station, and a museum. Dave sweetened the deal by offering some of his preservation funds to convert the buildings. Over the next week, we worked out a series of compromises that met management purposes while giving the historic buildings functional uses and retaining the integrity of the historic scene. This was my first planning exercise, and I marveled at how well, given a spirit of compromise, the needs of a park could be meshed with the requirements of law. But I had to admit that the exercise was less exciting than the work I did in Alaska.

For the next three months Dave and I traveled throughout the Southwest Region, I for familiarity and he to advise parks on maintenance of historic structures. He had worked in the region for more than ten years and knew it well. He had personally helped to restore many of the historic structures.

Of all the historical areas, Dave's favorite was the Lyndon B. Johnson National Historical Park in Texas. Because I was a child of the 1960s and had no use for LBJ, I couldn't imagine ranking the site so highly. Dave admitted that he had felt the same until he undertook to restore the historic structures of the new park as the former president himself kept close watch.

Dave Battle introduced me not only to the LBJ park but to the Texas Hill Country as well. "This is the only park where I would want to be superintendent," he told me. Dave's love for the area rubbed off on me. I enjoyed visiting it because the superintendent and the staff always extended a warm welcome. As I observed the coming and going of superintendents, I wondered if I too could be a superintendent there. Each time a vacancy occurred in the top slot, however, I had other pressures that kept me from applying. At that time I hadn't realized that regional directors rarely select historians to be superintendents.

Although my job lacked large challenges, I enjoyed the collegial environment of the Southwest Cultural Resources Center. I found the different disciplines supportive of each other and of me, but I missed the bonding I had experienced with my peers in Alaska. Here, without the adverse climate and social environment, relationships seemed more superficial and less binding.

Then, out of the blue, six months after I arrived, Sellars called me to his office. As a new supervisor, he took his counseling duties seriously. "Melody," he said, "I have complaints that you 'come on too strong.'" I disagreed until he pointed out two planning issues where I had "aggressively" pushed my concerns for historical integrity. I countered that I was no more aggressive about my programs than any man. He responded, "But Melody, you aren't any man. Most men don't expect women to be aggressive. Just soften up. Lower your profile. Try to get along instead of winning every battle."

While I knew that my personality had caused lots of problems in the past, I felt Sellars was overreacting. But I accepted his criticism and resolved to charm the two men who had made the comment. Nonetheless, the criticism stung. I had tried hard to work with everyone in a nonthreatening manner. I refused to lower my profile, but I did clean up my 1970s language. That alone improved my professional image with those two men, who later worked closely with me on a number of complicated planning issues.

Meanwhile my husband and I reached an amicable divorce, in which we remained good friends. When Bob joined me, we were able to settle down to a glorious married life. From the beginning our lives moved more smoothly than we ever believed possible. We shared household chores and history, basking in the compatibility of our personalities, interests, and values. To complete our idyllic life, we bought a small house in the rural subdivision of Eldorado, thirteen miles outside of Santa Fe.

At the same time, I continued to work on my doctorate. During the fall of 1980, I finished my second and last semester of course work. I had only my comprehensive exams and the dissertation to complete. Rather than take the usual eight to ten months to read and prepare for the exams, I decided to take them in the spring of 1981, only three months away. If I failed, I would take more time to study before the next exam. I didn't fail; I passed with honors—a designation last given by the department in 1969. I was flabbergasted. I had crammed only to pass the exam, not to excel. Consistently through my life, I feared failure and seemed to overcompensate and overachieve.

After my exams, when I was no longer trying to handle both school and a job, I became less intense and driven. I finally had enough time and energy to invest in the activities of the Eldorado Volunteer Fire Department. Shortly after we had moved to Eldorado, I declared it my civic duty to join the organization, not unlike the search-and-rescue team I had belonged to in Tucson. Although becoming a firefighter was the farthest thing from Bob's mind, he wanted to share my life in all its aspects.

Unlike most blue-collar volunteer departments, professionals and managers comprised ours. Unsurprisingly, more than half the department consisted of National Park Service employees and their spouses. Most Service employees are idealistic and civic-minded. In addition, being a firefighter is similar to being a park ranger. Even the deputy regional director joined as a firefighter. For once in a traditional male organization, I was not the only woman; we had almost as many women as men. As a result, we were short on mechanical knowledge and long on managerial ability.

The fire chief knew volunteer fire fighting better than nearly anyone in the nation, and he let everyone know it. John Liebson had an independent income that allowed him to work full time for the department. In addition, he taught courses in fire fighting around the country and was a leader in national organizations. Liebson was in his forties, with a master's degree in medieval studies and the maturity and sense of humor of a teenager, but he won the loyalty of every member of the department. He drilled us ruthlessly in the basics of catching a hydrant, stretching hoses, and squirting water. Using his knowledge of small departments, he found funds to purchase pagers and breathing apparatus. Our fire engine, a 1947 International, roared along at forty-five miles an hour. Our "bunker gear" or "turn-out gear" dated to the late fifties. Fortunately for us, while the pager went off frequently, most of the calls were false alarms or small brush fires.

In September 1981 one call came about three o'clock in the afternoon. A head-on collision between two cars had left one woman dead. Bob and one other firefighter responded to provide traffic control and wash away gasoline and glass. At that time we lacked emergency medical capability. Bob directed traffic around the car with the fatality without feeling any stress except sadness. On the way back to the station, however, he became dizzy, then couldn't speak. The driver of the fire engine took him directly to the hospital. When I arrived home, the driver called me to say he was with Bob at the hospital and asked if he had any heart conditions.

I tore to the hospital, fearing the worst. In the emergency room, I could hear Bob gasping and groaning. The doctors gave him a CAT scan, spinal tap, cardiogram, and other tests. They found nothing. One doctor concluded he had hyperventilated at the accident, but admitted the symptoms were extreme. Bob spent the night in the Intensive Care Unit and was ready to go home the next morning. While he admitted that he had once hyperventilated during the painful passage of a kidney stone, he said that he had no sense of a comparable experience at the accident scene.

One month later the symptoms returned, but less severely. He assured me that he was not hyperventilating and even breathed in a paper bag. Once again the neurologist ran him through a battery of tests, including an arteriogram of the arteries to the brain. Still they found nothing and offered no solution. An internist, however, believed that Bob suffered from a migraine variant and prescribed a beta-blocker, which he said would also lower his high blood pressure. Although the medication reduced the intensity of Bob's "episodes," he suffered dizzy spells several times a year. Because the internist had warned me that Bob could be having a series of small strokes, I watched carefully for signs of mental deterioration. I observed nothing and hoped the diagnosis of migraine variant was correct.

Shortly afterward, on Halloween, the pager woke us at 5:30 A.M. A chimney fire in the small town of Lamy, ten miles south of us, had inflamed a large house. By the time we reached the scene, fire flared throughout the house. Liebson broke us into two teams: one to perform search and rescue to ensure everyone was out of the house (the team released a dog) and the second to set up a portable tank out of which we pumped water. Lamy, unlike Eldorado, lacked hydrants or an immediate water supply. Liebson called other departments to assist us and set about to prevent the spread of the fire. With his minimal resources, he did not try to put out the fire, but rather protected "exposures" of nearby threatened property. Combating high winds and downed power lines, for six hours we battled the fire. Because of Liebson's calm and sound judgment, we saved the town and its church with no injuries to ourselves.

That fire cemented a bond among the Eldorado firefighters. I had not felt so strongly about such a disparate group of people since Alaska. Bob said the camaraderie was similar to his military experience. We traded off dinner parties, raised funds through a barbecue, and cared about the personal lives of each member. The fire department fulfilled my idealistic need to do good that was missing in my job. I came to feel as deeply for the fire department as I did for the National Park Service.

During the next five years, our experience grew, and our relationship with the department became the second most important relationship in our lives. Liebson built the department from eight people to nearly twenty, including an auxiliary of older individuals who helped maintain equipment and hydrants and assisted with the computerized paperwork. In addition, he built one fire station with a substation in the plan. We acquired a new fire engine and programmed another. Along the way the department voted me assistant fire chief with Bob as my first lieutenant. Every year we had at least one major fire, but only once did we confront fatalities.

In the spring of 1984 we received a call for mutual aid for a fire in La Cañada de los Alamos—a village in the Sangre de Cristo Mountains east of Eldorado. When we arrived, fire blazed out of windows, and the chief wanted to launch an interior attack. He had heard that two people might still be inside. He ordered the roof ventilated. This required two or more firefighters to climb up on the roof and cut a hole, letting the smoke and hot air escape and supposedly allowing firefighters to enter the building. I set up our ladder and proceeded to climb to the roof. A firefighter from the neighboring department was already on the roof. He shouted, "Not you, I want someone who can pull me out if I fall in." Although I had no doubt of my ability to pull him out, he was not comfortable with me. I backed down and let a colleague climb up.

I followed with an attack hose to protect them. Before they could cut a hole, the fire ventilated itself and began burning the roof beneath our feet. Despite Liebson's instructions that firefighters should never spray water on a ventilating fire, I sprayed. I didn't know that the other firefighters had already left the roof. Television cameras and newspaper photographers captured the image of me with one sole colleague engulfed in flames on top of a roof. It was a dramatic shot.

Later, after we had contained the fire, one of the firefighters pointed out the bodies. They were charred beyond recognition of anything human. Fire investigators surmised that the two people had been drinking and tried to start a fire in the wood stove with kerosene. Then both fell asleep. When the fire exploded and ignited other flammable materials, they were too drunk to respond. One never got out of bed. The other was kneeling beside the bed when overcome by flames. The woman had a six-year-old son at school who was suddenly without a mother and a home. The fire saddened us all.

Some time later, Liebson continued to pontificate about the county fire program and alienated the county fire marshal. Stretching his powers, the fire marshal removed Liebson as Eldorado's fire chief. Aghast at this audacity, our entire department quit. Because we put our lives on the line every time we reported to a fire, we argued, we ought to be able to choose our own fire chief—one whose judgment we trusted. As one firefighter put it, "It isn't a crime to be obnoxious." Eventually about half the department rejoined, but none of the National Park Service employees did. Bob and I regretted sorrowfully the demise of an important part of our lives.

Meanwhile, until July 1983 I spent nearly every weekend writing my dissertation. I took my "Yukon Frontiers" study and expanded it to a history of the entire Yukon Basin in Canada and Alaska. It was a big project, larger than most dissertations, but I wanted a publishable book. Even though Bob edited my work, I worried that it would not measure up to the work of my peers. I had spent less time researching and writing it than most graduate students.

My dissertation committee, however, quickly approved it and cheered me through my oral defense. In addition, I won the Popejoy Award. Named for a former president of the University of New Mexico, the award gave a thousand dollars every three years to the best dissertation and recommended it for publication. Promptly the University of New Mexico Press accepted my dissertation for publication, suggesting only a few minor revisions. Published in 1985 as *The Last Frontier: A History of the Yukon River of Canada and Alaska,* my first book filled me with as much pride as my first article. Generous book reviews in academic journals assured me that I could write history.

With my schooling behind me, I focused on my job. It had some rewards, but I was essentially a bureaucrat, and I couldn't get excited about program management of ongoing programs. Managing historic preservation compliance lacked the imagination and excitement of starting totally new programs. I remembered how Bob felt in 1977 after he left the National Park Service for the Advisory Council on Historic Preservation, and I could now understand his feeling of loss. Working with process was not as satisfying as working with park resources.

When the National Park Service leased a new office building, we moved from Los Llanos and joined with other divisions in a more effective but less appealing administrative environment. I also often served on servicewide task forces and came to be recognized as one of the best regional historians in the service. Having money to allocate for research also made me reasonably popular with university professors looking for extra income for themselves or their students. The most satisfying part of my job, however, was working on problems with superintendents. Here we actually dealt with historic resources and tried to preserve and interpret them more effectively.

My first few years in Santa Fe I spent working with the staffs of new or developing national parks. Jean Lafitte National Historical Park in New Orleans traced ethnic diversity throughout the Mississippi Delta. I commissioned studies to help us understand the Delta's ethnohistory and find the best sites to interpret the various cultures. Jim Isenogle was an open-minded, hard-working, pragmatic, and moody superintendent whom I came to value. We worked well together, and I gained insight into managing parks and dealing with advisory commissions, local communities, and politicians.

In 1983 Isenogle wanted something special for the visitors to the 1984 New Orleans World Fair. With funding from a supportive senator, Isenogle decided to build a new visitor center for the site of the Battle of New Orleans, where Andrew Jackson defeated the British in 1814. I offered to help expedite the compliance process and sent an archeologist to ensure that construction would not damage buried resources. Ted Birkedal, an articulate and thoughtful Norwegian immigrant with a doctorate in archeology, enjoyed history as an avocation. When he tested the site for the visitor center, he found garbage from the early 1800s. Not content to dismiss it, he read all he could find on the battlefield.

"Melody," he said a week later, "I think I've found the site of the Rodriguez house, Andrew Jackson's headquarters." I told him that the Mississippi River had eroded nearly two-thirds of the battlefield, taking with it the Rodriguez house. But he was ahead of me and pointed to aerial photographs that showed the river had not eroded two feet in the last thirty years. Moreover, he believed that first the army and then the National Park Service had accepted the erroneous survey of an amateur historian. We both studied all the documents and concluded we had to excavate to prove his theory.

Initially, when I discussed the possibility of finding the Rodriguez house with Isenogle, he grew impatient with delays for his visitor center but agreed to allow Ted two weeks before he would start construction. Working nearly eighteen-hour days, Ted and two other historical archeologists found three of the four corners of the house. Isenogle recognized the value of the find and moved the construction site. Once again Ted tested and found two outbuildings belonging to the Rodriguez house. In frustration Isenogle moved the site to a small island in the entrance road whose construction would have obliterated all archeological evidence.

With Ted's discovery, the National Park Service had a totally different park with everything interpreted wrongly. Instead of only one-third of the battlefield, we had nearly an intact site. But the tour road, the reconstructed ramparts, the interpretive brochure, and all interpretive signs were wrong. We had a major job overhauling a park that was already more than fifty years old. In addition, Ted proved the value of clearance archeology even to those superintendents who had viewed it as wasteful of time and money.

Another park that absorbed my attention was Hot Springs National Park in Arkansas. Here six empty bathhouses from the early twentieth century had become ugly eyesores and the Service's whitest elephants outside Ellis Island. Americans during the 1920s sought bathhouses for health reasons, but by the 1970s modern spas attracted the clientele. It was my job to help find uses for the beautiful but deteriorating structures. A new program allowed the private sector to lease historic park structures and adapt them to profitable enterprises. All profits arising from leasing the structures stayed in the park to maintain historic resources.

After several years of investigative architectural work and a few coats of paint, we fielded a prospectus requesting proposed uses. A wealthy Arkansan, Melvin Bell, wanted to lease all of them. He put together a team of architects that included some of the best in the state. His early reports and plans would protect the structures, allow the public to visit them, and yet make money. Then the 1987 Wall Street crash sent him reeling. He never recovered sufficiently to rehabilitate the bathhouses. After more than five years of work, we had to start over.

About this time, Pecos National Monument drew my attention. Surrounded by piñon-covered hills at the foot of the mountains thirty miles east of Santa Fe, Pecos preserved the ruins of prehistoric multistoried Indian pueblos and the associated ruins of a seventeenth-century Spanish mission. Friends and benevolent neighbors of the park were movie star Greer Garson and her oilman husband, Buddy Fogelson, who had donated some tracts of their ranch to the park and had long wanted to pay for a new visitor center to help visitors gain a better understanding of its significance. A young, ambitious superintendent, John Bezy, won their confidence and cleared away the bureaucratic obstacles. Dave Battle designed the building, and his preservation crew constructed it. Battle's masterpiece won acclaim as among the most beautiful and functional visitor centers in the entire Park Service.

Not content with this accomplishment, Superintendent Bezy strove to add a large wing to the building. Organizing a group of wealthy Santa Feans as the "Friends of Pecos," he raised the money. I looked on this expansion as an example of escalating ego and opposed it with all the other professionals in the Southwest Cultural Resource Center. We perceived the addition as an intrusion on the ruins the park was established to protect. Bezy claimed he needed space to interpret the Anglo period of history, a minor theme in a park whose major significance lay in the Indian and Spanish colonial story. Despite the opposition from his own regional director, Bezy went straight to National Park Service director William Penn Mott and convinced him of the importance of the project.

Next Bezy moved to other "improvements." In concert with Director Mott, he began planning the reconstruction of one of the Indian pueblos. Although National Park Service policy essentially prohibited reconstructions, Director Mott liked them and believed they helped the public visualize and experience a lost resource. He even pointed to how effectively Disneyland recreated historic sites.

Ever since the 1930s, however, historic preservation professionals excoriated reconstructions. In order to build reconstructions on the original site, most original architectural fabric and archeological resources are destroyed. Yet to make the new structures as accurate as possible requires extensive historical, archeological, and architectural research—all of which cost money. Then, constructing a new building is also expensive, typically costing several million dollars. Preservationists argue that those millions would be better spent preserving the original fabric. In contrast to the original structure or ruins where a historic event or culture occurred, the new reconstruction is essentially a fake, a Disney-like structure that detracts the public's attention from the real resource. Moreover, the new structure will also require more funds for operation, maintenance, and interpretation— all for a structure that has no history and is basically a stage set. Nonetheless, Bezy began raising money for the reconstruction.

One of Bezy's fund-raising events used the park as the set for a made-for-television movie, *Blue Cadillac*. Dismissing his protection rangers, he provided the sole oversight to the filming of a rock concert in the ruins. When I watched the video, I became upset. The movie company, unaware of the fragility of historic structures, hammered spikes into the adobe walls to hang heavy speakers and other equipment. These spikes not only weakened the adobe but opened holes for rain to erode the structure from the inside. Then winter snows could fill the holes, melt during the day, and freeze and crack the adobe at night. Dave Battle tried to educate all historical park superintendents to avoid hammering anything into original fabric, but his lessons did not always fall on listening ears. Moreover, the loud, vibrating rock music resonated through the structures at frequencies acoustical experts had shown contributed to the deterioration of structures made from native materials.

Of course, to me the most egregious insult was the inappropriate use of a historic Spanish Colonial church and prehistoric Indian pueblos in a rock concert. National parks are set aside to commemorate significant historic events and to educate and inspire the visiting public. To profanely exhibit historic resources as a setting for debauchery and licentiousness screamed of mismanagement and distorted values.

Outraged, I wrote a scathing memo to the regional director, documenting Bezy's insensitivities. Because Bezy had the ear of the director and claimed powerful friends, the regional director had no desire to take him on.

Not so John Cook, my old regional director from Alaska, who within a matter of months returned to Santa Fe. He had lost his Alaska position after taking a stand against cruise ships harming the humpback whales ply-ing Glacier Bay, a national monument. The shipowners complained to Interior Secretary James Watt, who wanted to fire Cook. National Park Service Director Russ Dickenson stepped in and convinced Watt that a "demotion" to the superintendency of Great Smoky Mountains National Park was punishment enough. After Watt resigned, the Service returned Cook to the position of Southwest regional director, which he had held before his Alaska assignment.

John Bezy's actions at Pecos appalled Cook. At once Cook quizzed me about my memorandum on the rock-concert movie. Even though he acknowledged that some damage might have been done to park resources, he did not deem it sufficient to warrant action against the superintendent. The matter was especially delicate because Bezy had allied himself with Greer Garson's secretary to play on old Hollywood relationships with President Ronald Reagan to get Bezy a hearing in the highest levels of gov-ernment. Whether or not Greer Garson actually knew of it, her name was used to support a demand for the removal of John Cook for interfering with a conscientious superintendent who was doing no more than responding to her wishes.

The Interior Department in these years was fertile ground for such charges, especially against one who had already offended corporate pow-ers. Agents of the department's Inspector General's Office descended on Santa Fe to investigate the charges. They interviewed me, and I called the shots as I saw them, typically blunt and undiplomatic. Bezy, I told them, had caused much harm to the park's resources and staff. While I could see that the investigators did not share my sensitivity to historic resources nor truly accept my professional assessment of damage wrought, I sincerely thought that they wanted honesty.

Later I saw their report. They praised Bezy for his achievements, recom-mended that Cook be dismissed from the National Park Service, and con-cluded that I should receive a reprimand for maligning an outstanding superintendent. Even so, Cook removed Bezy for numerous personnel viola-tions. His action, of course, set off a storm in the Interior Department. For eighteen months, Cook's termination papers lay on the desk of Interior Secretary Donald Hodel awaiting his signature. The advent of the George H. W. Bush administration in 1989 freed Cook from the threat, for the time being.

During the 1980s, the Reagan administration dramatically changed the National Park Service. Previously, political leaders had tried to shape park policy through their choice in a director and other Washington office appointments. With Reagan, the power tentacles stretched down to the regional director and senior superintendent levels. Cook became an example of what happened if park managers tried to do what they believed was right. First, he was exiled from Alaska for preserving whales rather than cruise ship profits. Then, in protecting historic properties and federal employees from a rogue superintendent, he nearly lost his job. As a result, managers throughout the Service hunkered down and tried to keep local communities and private corporations happy. As feelings of suppression filtered down to the lowest levels of government, morale plunged to all-time lows. My own idealism and belief in government suffered nearly as much as Cook's career.

The Reagan administration also perceived that the National Park Service had grown too big too fast. With the environmentalists exhausted after the Alaska fight, the administration halted the use of federal funds for additional parklands, especially the purchase of private lands within national park boundaries. With the appointment of controversial and colorful James Watt as secretary of the Interior, the administration basically declared war on conservation. Watt authorized jet airliners into Jackson Hole Airport within Grand Teton National Park, allowed engines to power float trips on Grand Canyon's Colorado River, and increased the number of cruise ships to Glacier Bay. But he also focused on improving the deteriorating visitor facilities in national parks. In four years he spent more than a billion dollars rehabilitating sewer systems, replacing water lines, and even preserving historic structures. With his flamboyant rhetoric more than his actions, Jim Watt revitalized the environmental movement as thousands of shocked park constituents joined the effort to stop him. His reign proved short. He put his foot in his mouth one too many times, and

Reagan replaced him with men who continued Watt's policies but with lower profiles and less controversy.

As we all despaired, one person gave us hope: Director Russ Dickenson. A man of medium height with graceful carriage, a ruddy complexion, and white hair, he brought elegance to the directorship. His suave appearance, however, belied his background and training. He had been a combat marine and a ranger, chief ranger, superintendent, and regional director. He had served in wilderness parks and urban slums. No director had had more experience with parks and park staffs. A Democratic appointee, he survived the Republican takeover of 1981. Watt fired all the other Interior bureau chiefs but kept Dickenson. With an honesty softened by diplomacy, Dickenson found that he could reason with Watt and minimize the damage inflicted by Republican policies. For three years he salvaged careers, diverted corporate demands, protected resources, and retained pride in the service. After Watt left, Dickenson's prestige diminished, and he suffered one humiliating setback after another until he retired in 1985.

Meanwhile, other issues affected me less directly. First, in December 1980, Congress passed the Alaska National Interest Lands Conservation Act, which transformed Carter's national monuments into national parks and preserves. The act and Alaskan state policies, however, deviated from our idealistic hopes. The act authorized sport hunting and trapping in national preserves and allowed mechanized access to wilderness areas. Although the act specifically defined subsistence as traditional uses by rural Alaskan residents, in 1989 the Alaska Supreme Court ruled the limitation to rural residents as discriminatory and in conflict with the state constitution. Nonetheless, for ten more years, under an annual congressional authorization, the state managed the subsistence program and allowed any state resident to claim subsistence rights, even wealthy hunters from Anchorage. Finally, after the Ninth Circuit Court of Appeals ruled that the federal government had the obligation to manage subsistence and Congress became disgusted with the Alaska legislature's refusal to amend the state constitution, in October 1999 the federal government took over the management of subsistence and limited the program to rural residents. Whatever the corruption of our ideals, 43.6 million acres of beautiful parklands officially became part of the National Park System.

I also gained a closer view of how established national parks grappled with the Leopold Report. The report recommended that parks eliminate nonnative plants and animals. In Bandelier National Monument, only fifty miles from Santa Fe, scientists documented the damage nonnative burros caused to soils, vegetation, and archeological ruins. As removal of the burros began, the Fund for Animals filed suit to block it, but the court ruled that the park had a legal mandate to rid itself of exotic animals. When Grand Canyon began its removal of nonnative burros, the Fund for Animals sued again and this time won the right to trap and transplant them. Tremendous logistical problems limited the number of burros removed, and park rangers resorted to shooting the burros to minimize the problem.

Sometimes scientists' efforts to eliminate exotic species conflicted with my own programs. Gardens and orchards associated with historic sites within natural parks often contained exotic plants. When well-meaning resource managers tried to remove them, I fought for their preservation and usually won.

By 1988 I was getting very bored. The fire department had collapsed, and nothing but my job held us in Santa Fe. Then John Cook asked if I would like to serve as interim superintendent of Chickasaw National Recreational Area in Oklahoma. It had no significant historic resources, so I had never been there. I had heard that it was a beautiful "city park" with a federal reservoir that attracted boaters, swimmers, and anglers. While I had little desire to be a superintendent, except maybe of LBJ, I felt that the experience would broaden my perspective.

Fortunately for me, the former superintendent, Jack Linahan, stayed an extra week to introduce me to the park and town. Jack was an old-line ranger, steady, conservative, and sound. He gave me some of the best advice I ever had. "Try to visit each work site at least once a week," he counseled. "The employees like to know you care, and you stay on top of the issues." With introductions to the community on the local television station and meetings with the mayor and city council, I was prepared for my month's assignment.

With a staff doing all the work, I was largely a figurehead, but I enjoyed the change of duties. I attended the luncheons of the different civic organizations and found them not as onerous as my 1960s background prepared me to expect. The park staff welcomed me and helped me learn what I needed to know. In return, I pulled the division chiefs together to work as a team.

One of the highlights of my month's assignment was riding weekend night patrol. Each summer the park hired three seasonal protection rangers to patrol the campgrounds and take care of emergencies. For more than twenty years, the same three rangers had returned. Unlike most seasonal rangers, whose law-enforcement training totaled a brief six weeks, these three had attended the same fourteen-week course required of permanent rangers. Moreover, because they worked weekends and nights, when most incidents occurred, they had more experience and probably better judgment than the permanents. Although they taught school during the winter, they remained committed to their summer law-enforcement work—at the cost of their marriages.

I met the three rangers as they compared notes at the local pizza parlor. From seven o'clock in the evening to two in the morning for the next two nights, we patrolled campgrounds, enforced curfews, and broke up fights. In between we talked. I had never realized how the National Park Service treated its seasonals. After twenty years of long hours and dangerous duty, they had the same grade and salary level as when they signed on. Moreover, they had no benefits—no retirement, no health or life insurance, no career status.

When I tried to address their concerns the next day, I met incredulity from the administrative officer and the chief ranger. First, one park alone could do nothing; it was a government-wide problem with no resolution. Besides, the seasonals knew the conditions when they signed on. Second, these seasonals were too gung-ho. They enjoyed being cops rather than rangers, gave too many tickets, and forgot the service aspect of rangering. I hadn't noticed anything but extreme professionalism and said so. But my opinion didn't carry much weight.

As I got to know the park better, I realized that it was a cultural landscape, created by President Franklin Roosevelt's Civilian Conservation Corps. Prior to the 1930s, it was hardly of national caliber. After the CCC planted nearly one million trees and shrubs and constructed miles of trails with rustic stone bridges, picnic pavilions, and retaining walls, the park could measure up to most others in an urban setting. Halfway between Oklahoma City and Dallas, Chickasaw fulfilled a recreational need. The campgrounds filled each night, and thousands played on Arbuckle Lake each summer day.

One Saturday as I toured the park, I heard the radio report a possible drowning. I sped to the scene to see if I could assist. The rangers were just loading a victim in the ambulance and asked me to take his wife and daughters to the hospital. On the way the wife tried to console one of the daughters. Earlier in the day her father had been playing with her by pretending to drown. Later, when he swam out to get a drifting water ski and started to sink, she thought he was joking again. She didn't call for help until he failed to come to the surface. At the hospital we learned that, despite continuous mouth-to-mouth resuscitation by the rangers, he was pronounced dead. I spent that time with the family, trying to help them through the experience. Finally their clergyman arrived and I left.

When I called the regional director to report the drowning, I was told to conduct a board of inquiry. The board would determine if there was anything that the park could have done better to prevent the death. I didn't have the slightest idea where to start. The chief ranger found reports from earlier drownings to guide me. I started interviewing people and gathering data. It had been a church group, and no alcohol was involved. Apparently the victim had eaten a large lunch and drunk several glasses of iced tea. Experts surmised that his stomach, in digesting the heavy meal, pulled oxygen from his extremities. When he pushed his body to swim, the lack of oxygen in his arms and legs made them cramp, and he sank. I concluded that the park responded remarkably well and that only a stronger warning in the brochure might have helped. During the crisis, I discovered that my years with the fire department kept me from panicking and allowed me to relinquish authority to the responding rangers.

As my month wound down, I found myself reluctant to say good-bye. I enjoyed being an interim superintendent and liked the staff. They gave me three farewell parties. The seasonals alone gave me one, where I was the only permanent employee invited. I regretted that I had been unable to bridge the gap between permanent and seasonal employees.

When I returned to Santa Fe, I resigned myself to an indefinite stay. In January 1989, John Cook volunteered me to chair the observance of the fiftieth anniversary of the Southwest Regional Office Building, the sprawling adobe palace that earned so much envy throughout the Service. I decided that all employees should be involved and struggled to kindle excitement. We even had a Santa Fe artist paint a canvas of the building from which we made a poster to sell. With those funds we were able to rent a tent, cater refreshments, and send out engraved invitations.

As I sweated through my first commemorative occasion, I heard that the superintendent at LBJ was retiring. Although I had said for years that I did not want to be a superintendent, I thought twice about it now. For hours one night Bob and I discussed it. The next day I went in and told John Cook that I would like the job. Surprised, he simply said, "You can apply when I advertise it." Because it was the same grade level as my current job, he could have given it to me without advertisement. I accepted his comment as a dismissal.

The fiftieth-anniversary celebration culminated in a program beneath a huge red-striped tent pitched in the parking lot of the regional office building. I presided at the lectern, set on an elevated platform seating Senator Jeff Bingaman, Congressman Bill Richardson, Park Service Director James Ridenour, John Cook, and other dignitaries. After I introduced Director Ridenour, he stepped to the lectern and said, "My job often gives me the pleasure of announcing new positions for superintendents. This one in particular pleases me because she is so pretty. Melody Webb is the next superintendent of LBJ." I was stunned and blushed as red as the dress I was wearing. Seated on the podium, I went forward to receive a kiss and a handshake. From the corner of my eye, I saw Cook grinning like the Cheshire cat.

After nine years as regional historian in Santa Fe, I was ready to leave. I felt I was losing my idealism in daily bureaucratic battles and saw myself sinking in a morass of process and paper. Moreover, I found that as a historian I didn't fit any better into the National Park Service of the Lower 48 than I did in Alaska or as a public historian among academic historians. But I was not alone. Historians as a whole don't feel the same intensity or have the loyalty to the agency of the rangers, who claim they bleed green blood. Because of my experiences in Alaska and Bob's feelings gained from an earlier Park Service, I felt differently. Nonetheless, I was a historian in a world focused on park operations. Rangers, maintenance foremen, scientists, and interpreters had the money, profile, and access to power that I needed to do my job right. But for some reason, historians and archeologists were never regarded as highly as those involved with nature. I yearned to be accepted.

Although those long years in Santa Fe were professionally less satisfying than my Alaskan years, they were valuable in other ways. They gave me time to know my new husband. If my job had been as challenging as my work in Alaska, I could not have had the time to spend building a highly compatible marriage. Nor would I have had time to work on my doctorate. While in Alaska, I lacked time to take even a college course, let alone complete a graduate program. There, I was pushed to the limits of my abilities all the time. In Santa Fe I experienced only occasional stress or tension when my advice to superintendents or regional directors was not accepted. Most often, however, I was well respected and regarded as a principled professional with high standards but willing to find win-win solutions to problems. Although I enjoyed my colleagues at work, we seldom met outside of the office. Instead, the fire department fulfilled that social role. Once it disintegrated, Santa Fe seemed empty of meaning. We had many acquaintances but few real friends.

Initially, Bob and I loved Santa Fe. We enjoyed the opera and other cultural activities. Then we began to observe that newcomers had taken over Santa Fe. Operagoers, artists, art collectors, boutique shoppers, and second-home owners exploited the ancient city. Hispanics, who once had dominated the population, slowly lost their political power and even their prevailing culture, which had given Santa Fe much of its charm and popularity. Resentful of their loss, they displayed their displeasure with passive-aggressive behavior—slowness in responding to service requests, surly attitudes, frequent use of Spanish to isolate and irritate Anglos, smoldering anger. As land prices and accompanying taxes escalated, many Hispanics found themselves "land poor" and frightened.

The changes made us uncomfortable. Although we understood the rationale behind the behavior of many Hispanics, the injection of race into the mix of culture, politics, and business made life outside of Eldorado and the National Park Service unpleasant. On the other hand, the rich newcomers affected a Santa Fe dress and patronized burgeoning boutiques to the exclusion of ordinary stores. Restaurants, museums, art studios, curio shops, and art galleries attracted more and more tourists, making parking and even driving an ordeal. As Santa Fe became the "in" place, we wanted out.

Disenchanted with Santa Fe and with managing bureaucratic history, I wanted something different. As early as 1984, we had fantasized my quitting the National Park Service and writing full time. With insufficient savings, however, we knew it would remain a long-term dream. Now, with a superintendency, I joined the National Park Service elite. I hoped it would provide the stimulation and satisfaction that I craved.

# Texas

Lyndon B. Johnson National Historical Park is the largest presidential site in the National Park System and the fourth largest national park in the Southwest Region. Divided between two units thirteen miles apart, the park tells two discrete stories. The Johnson City unit, comprised of Johnson's boyhood home and grandfather's log cabin from the 1850s, handles the early years of the president and his legacy as the "last frontier president." The Ranch unit in Stonewall, thirteen miles west, captures the complexity and power of a remote presidential White House. Here on LBJ's ranch is the Texas White House, Secret Service headquarters, aircraft runway and hangar, Johnson's first schoolhouse, the Johnson cemetery, and his own reconstructed birthplace.

In all, in 1989 the park contained more than eighty-five historic structures and 500 acres of cultural landscape with twenty-three miles of fences, eleven miles of roads, and thirty-four utility systems. The park's budget in 1989 was nearly two million dollars, with forty-five permanent and eight temporary employees. The park hosted almost 200,000 visitors per year. Its magnitude always surprised visitors. Even those who disliked Lyndon Johnson found it educational and seldom left without new insights to a complex president.

In August 1989, all this became my responsibility.

My first night in Johnson City I ate quickly and then walked around the boyhood home of Lyndon Johnson. The park staff kept the structure and its grounds in good condition. Illuminated by floodlights, it seemed to glow. I don't believe I had ever felt so happy with a job. It was *my* park! Its well-being depended on me. I knew the park staff felt neglected, leaderless, and divided among themselves. For once I did not feel inadequate or unprepared. I had no doubt that I could turn the park around and make it the shining star it had once been. As I stared at Johnson's old home, I realized that I too had found a home.

Two division chiefs helped ease my transition into management. Buddy Hodges, chief of maintenance, was neighbor to Mrs. Lyndon Johnson and had grown up in Stonewall. Tall, well built, with salt-and-pepper hair, Buddy's good looks and charm had made him a regional office favorite. In many ways he personified all that was good about the LBJ staff: warm, friendly, hardworking, and dedicated to Lyndon B. Johnson National Historical Park. Like all the local employees, his loyalty was attached to this one park, not to the National Park Service as a whole. Initially, because he was local and would stay in the same job for years, the regional office opposed his appointment as division chief. But he quickly learned his programs and became a key maintenance leader for the entire region.

Jack Bixby, chief ranger, contrasted sharply with Buddy. Jack's experience in some of the biggest parks in the system led him to the "Yosemite Mafia," an elite corps of rangers hand-picked to "clean up" after the 1970 Yosemite riot. Sometime later, however, Jack had lost his ambition or peaked out as chief ranger of trouble-fraught Big Thicket National Preserve, Texas. After several years, Cook ordered him to LBJ. Here he went along with whatever the superintendent wanted, never questioning or challenging any decision. While he did not assert much leadership, his experience and perspective often proved helpful.

Because of dwindling budgets, several parts of the park had been closed. The Johnson Settlement, consisting of the 1850s log cabin of Johnson's grandfather and several stone buildings from a later period, had no interpretation. The historic structures were locked securely, but sand daubers flew between the logs and boards to make nests among the furnishings. The locale once hosted costumed interpreters who cooked, gardened, and portrayed a frontier life for visitors. Now it lay forlorn and forbidding.

Interpreters had also once greeted visitors in LBJ's reconstructed birthplace at the LBJ Ranch. Now it too was locked and only the exterior visible from the passing tour buses. As a historic preservationist, I found the birthplace fascinating. While president, LBJ decided to reconstruct his birthplace, which had fallen into a ruin. His architect salvaged some lumber from the original structure and designed a replica on the original site. Too practical to reconstruct a building without modern plumbing and a kitchen, however, LBJ had it designed as a guesthouse, not a museum. In fact, the pretty little house with manicured lawn and flower gardens portrayed LBJ's history as he wanted posterity to remember it. Its closure denied visitors valuable insights into the thirty-sixth president's ego, his effort to revise history, his pragmatism, and his interest in local and personal history.

The bus tour of the LBJ Ranch also suffered from lack of funds. Although LBJ had donated the ranch to the American people, Mrs. Johnson had life estate and occasionally lived at the ranch. The Secret Service, still guarding the former first lady, limited visitor access. A National Park Service bus tour offered the only way people could see this portion of the park. Unable to hire seasonal interpreters, the park ran less than half the number of tours the public demanded. Moreover, because the buses lacked air-conditioning, the supervisor did not want to stress the drivers with additional tours or overtime.

My second day on the job, we had an all-employee staff meeting to introduce me to those I had not met. In the hanger at the LBJ Ranch, the park curator, Libby Hulett, provided homemade refreshments served on a cloth-covered billiard table with live plants as centerpieces. "One sure way to get maintenance workers here," Libby said, "is to promise food." I was impressed with the thoughtful ensemble of good taste in contrast to the makeshift arrangements of most parks.

I spoke briefly: "As you all know, this is my first superintendency and my first park assignment. I am excited to have the chance to learn from the best park staff in the region. I hope y'all [in Texas, one learns that usage quickly] will be patient with me and help me rebuild the team that this park is known for." While I could sense some skepticism from a few old-timers, most of the staff responded to my heartfelt remarks with enthusiasm.

Afterward, as I socialized with the staff, Libby pulled me aside. "Mrs. Johnson is here at the ranch," she said, "and wants to meet you now." Never in my nine years with the regional office had I even been inside the Texas White House, let alone met the most admired woman in Texas. Libby took me to the west room, previously LBJ's office, later remodeled by Mrs. Johnson as her primary reception room. Here Libby introduced me to Mrs. Johnson and her daughter Luci Johnson, then quietly and appropriately left.

Mrs. Johnson looked much like her photographs but more animated. Too often her photos looked strained and posed. At home she radiated warmth and welcome. Her strong Texas drawl inquired where I was living, when my husband would join me, and other nonthreatening questions to help me relax. "Gracious" became the word that best characterized the former first lady. I could easily see why everyone in the park adored her.

Luci, on the other hand, bubbled with curiosity. In the process of moving back to Texas from Canada, she looked forward to being more involved with the park. "What do you see as your three most important goals?" she suddenly asked, unrelated to anything her mother and I had been discussing. Caught by surprise, I told her the first things that popped into my mind based on nine years of dealing with the park: "I would like to reopen the Johnson Settlement and the birthplace, buy new buses, and build a new visitor center." Like a corporate executive, she dissected each goal. Applauding my first goal, she probed the reasons for the other two.

"The eight buses that carry visitors throughout the LBJ Ranch," I told her, "are nearly twenty years old." I described the hardship that, in hot and humid central Texas, lack of air-conditioning laid on visitors and employees alike. Designed before handicapped accessibility became law, they had no wheelchair lifts. The biggest problem, however, was their age. As they aged, they required more and more maintenance. Parts and supplies were becoming harder and harder to find. Eventually, I said, the park itself will have to make parts that are no longer available.

"You make a convincing argument, but tell me why you need a visitor center," Luci quizzed. "I thought Daddy wanted the state park, which is just across the river, to be the park's visitor center." She brought up a valid point, but I told her that most visitors were unable to visit both units. It was unfair to visitors at Johnson City not to have a decent interpretive experience.

"It has been nearly twenty years since your father was president," I said. "Since then people have forgotten his contributions, and most lack an understanding of the issues of his time." In addition, I told her that the park staff was crammed into tiny offices in the Johnson City post office that limited their efficiency and effectiveness. I reminded her that my predecessor had suggested converting the long-vacant hospital into a visitor center, perpetuating the use of a handsome and historic structure.

Concerned that I might already have said more than I should, I decided it was time to leave. Mrs. Johnson suggested dinner some night when my husband arrived. I agreed to let her know and thanked her for her hospitality. As I walked out the door and let my breath out, I realized I had been holding it. Obviously I was more tense and anxious than I had thought. Establishing rapport with Mrs. Johnson was essential to my success.

When I arrived back at headquarters, Sandy Hodges walked into my office. "The townspeople want to meet you," she said. "Would you mind if we held a get-acquainted reception for you?" Sandy, supervisor of the Johnson City interpretive unit, had recently married Buddy. I knew her less well than Buddy, but liked her for her candor and straight-arrow values. "I want it to be a class act," she said. "All I need is your approval to use about $60 from the Southwest Parks and Monuments fund." SPMA, a nonprofit organization, sold books and interpretive material in park visitor centers and in return supported various park projects and activities denied federal funds. First I asked if the event would be closed to the public. "Of course not," she responded, "but special invitations will go to the movers and shakers of Blanco, Fredericksburg, and Johnson City. We also ought to invite some politicians." I authorized the reception.

The quality of the reception surprised me. At the Johnson Settlement interpretive center, Sandy had set up four tables with red-and-white-checked tablecloths. Using fresh flowers as centerpieces, she had baskets of homemade bread and platters of dried beef and cheese. She left no detail to chance. To minimize the effects of the late summer heat, a bus from the ranch drove the guests from the boyhood home to the settlement. Buddy served as master of ceremonies and introduced me to every dignitary. His brief remarks described my doctorate, book, articles, and other achievements. He told me later that he wanted everyone to know that I had credentials beyond those of the usual superintendent. Everyone who spoke with me congratulated me on sponsoring such a splendid reception. Sandy had succeeded beyond my wildest expectations. The afternoon established the perfect tone for my inauguration as superintendent.

Meanwhile Bob and I bought our dream house near Dripping Springs, thirty miles east of Johnson City and eighteen miles from Austin. Constructed of limestone with contrasting orange paint, the house was only one part of an ensemble of matching outbuildings—a barn, goat shed, and pool house. Not only did it have an ideal space for Bob's study, but it also had a swimming pool, verandahs and porches, a Hill Country vista of more than fifteen miles, and eighteen acres of beautiful groves of live oak. With a house designed for entertaining, we committed ourselves to the values of an older National Park Service: entertaining Park Service officials whenever they visited the park. During the next three years, we hosted two park picnics, three large dinner parties, and countless smaller gatherings.

One of my first official tasks was to hire an administrative officer. I chose Reba Hyatt from Cumberland Island National Seashore, Georgia. She too fell in love with the Hill Country and became a valuable member of my management team. After only a short time on the job, she came into my office. "Melody," she said, "I think the administrative division has a disproportionate amount of funds, especially when half the park is closed." I was speechless. Never before had division chiefs put the park ahead of their divisions. She recommended an exercise in which supervisors described their programs from the ground up. Then, as a team the division chiefs would decide which would be funded. The process worked remarkably well, mostly because Reba's honesty and generosity set an example for others. As a result, I accomplished my first goal. We hired more seasonal interpreters and opened both the Johnson Settlement and the birthplace.

This budget exercise made supervisors more aware of all activities in the park and forced them to evaluate their own for the greater good of the park. Slowly I saw a team forming. To help the process along, I suggested that we celebrate the twentieth anniversary of the establishment of the park. With committee members from all divisions, I charged Sandy Hodges with the responsibility to decide how to celebrate the anniversary. To my surprise and delight, the committee recommended celebrating it throughout the year, with a special activity every month.

Because the whole park supported the yearlong celebration, all worked well together. We built a park float for use in four local parades. To educate and inspire the park staff, we had six all-employee staff meetings with outside speakers. Most important of all, Mrs. Johnson agreed to sit with the staff for a formal park portrait. While the park hosted an essay contest for the local high schools, interpretive programs went out to nursing homes and elementary schools. For the visitors we had special daylong programs such as Pioneer Crafts Day, Founders Day (on December 2, when the park was signed into law), and LBJ's birthday party.

The year's highlight occurred in April 1990 with a free barbecue at the LBJ Ranch. Sandy sought donations from local businesses and collected four thousand dollars to offset the costs. More than five hundred people attended, including Mrs. Johnson, John Cook, superintendents of national parks in Texas, former superintendents and employees of the LBJ park, contributing businesses, and local political figures. Because of Sandy's good taste and attention to detail, the day could not have gone better. Everyone in the park felt proud of their achievements.

While the park busied itself with the twentieth anniversary, I found myself bogged down in paperwork. The previous superintendent had tried to transfer the vacant hospital behind the boyhood home, federally funded so still in federal ownership, to the National Park Service for use as a visitor center. In the process he had alienated Congressman J. J. "Jake" Pickle, an LBJ protégé who occupied LBJ's old seat in the House of Representatives. I tried to mend the fences with his congressional staff. Then one morning a call came from the congressman himself. "What has happened with the hospital?" he demanded. I tried to tell him that the Department of Housing and Urban Development would not transfer the building unless the Interior Department paid the remaining $500,000 debt. "That's ridiculous," he said. "It is just moving money from one part of government to another. Let me see what I can do."

Congressman Pickle stirred the pot. I found myself writing and rewriting justifications and explanations to the National Park Service in Washington, the Interior Department, and the Office of Management and Budget. No one wanted to make the transfer. Pickle rattled my cage again. "Who determines what projects get funding and in what priority?" he demanded. I tried to describe the complicated construction program of the Service. He lacked the patience to hear me out. "What is the name and telephone number of your boss?" I gave him John Cook's name, then hurriedly called Cook to warn him of the congressman's impending call.

Later I learned that Pickle wanted Cook to establish a priority for converting the hospital into a visitor center. Cook simply told him that he would do what he could to get the building transferred and converted. Pickle leaned on him hard, but Cook had learned to handle pressure. Nonetheless, Cook made the LBJ visitor center the Southwest Region's number-one construction priority—above the needs of all the other parks under his jurisdiction. As a result, when the Park Service director chose the most important projects for the nation, the visitor center for LBJ ranked twelfth.

With a commitment from the National Park Service to convert the building, a national priority ranking, and a construction date, Pickle went to Congress and acquired planning money for the first year. Next, he twisted the arm of the secretary of Housing and Urban Development and succeeded in getting the structure transferred without cost to the National Park Service. Once again we had a special ceremony. This time Jake Pickle gave the keynote address.

Although approaching eighty, Jake Pickle had more energy than a man half his age. He ran everywhere he went, and all the rest of us trailed several steps behind. Well known and beloved for his thirty years in Congress, he believed in hard work, keeping in touch with his constituents, and honest politics. A wonderful storyteller, he charmed everyone with his modesty and effectiveness. Over four years, through his congressional seniority and the power of his personality, he obtained appropriations to fund the new visitor center. Although the estimate for converting the hospital to a visitor center ballooned from two million to more than nine million dollars, he gave the project credibility. Without his hard work, determination, and reputation, I could not have met my second goal.

At the conclusion of my first year as superintendent, Bob and I paid for a chile dinner for all park employees and their families. Because John Cook could not attend, I invited the deputy regional director, my immediate supervisor, Dick Marks. He had arrived in Santa Fe before I left and was very supportive of my superintendency. As Cook's hatchet man, he forced a number of nonperformers to retire. Consequently, he and Cook became mired in Equal Opportunity complaints filed by white males over the age of forty.

We held the appreciation party at the ranch in the aircraft hangar, appropriately decorated in a Mexican theme. The red-and-white-checked tablecloths held centerpieces of horseshoes welded into the initials *LBJ*. A country-western band got everyone in a festive mood. After the meal, I got up to introduce Dick Marks and thank everyone for a year's hard work. As I said, "I think this is the best park in the region," the outside door opened and in marched the biggest man in the park dressed in a pink rabbit suit and banging a brass drum. Everyone in the hangar erupted in laughter. Laughing so hard that tears streamed down my face, I tried once again to thank the park. Just as I said, "This is the best park . . ." the pink bunny entered again, banging the drum even harder. Once again he brought the house down. This time, however, I didn't bother to open my mouth. I just pointed to my deputy regional director and said, "It's your turn."

The Energizer Bunny, star of television ads promoting batteries, wonderfully symbolized what had happened in the park during that first year.

After the party, Dick Marks helped Bob and me transfer the leftovers into smaller containers for freezing. "Have you thought about where you want to go next?" he asked.

Shocked, I said, "I have a visitor center to build and hadn't planned to move for a while."

"Well, you aren't going to stay here long enough to build it," he said. "I've had a couple of superintendents ask me about you as potential assistant superintendent material. If you don't make your own choice, someone else may make it for you."

Bob and I were numb. Bob had bluntly told Cook, an old colleague and friend, that we did not intend to leave our idyllic home near Dripping Springs. I interpreted Marks's comments as speaking for Cook as he pushed an unwelcome move. I knew that my time at LBJ would be limited. Either I would have to move or be forced to resign. On the other hand, I was flattered that big-park superintendents had asked about me. Maybe I owed it to the National Park Service to be more flexible than I wanted to be.

A few months later I attended a superintendents' conference for the Southwest Region in Santa Fe. Park Service Director James Ridenour spoke about ongoing operational matters to an unenthusiastic group of superintendents. Although he had announced my appointment as superintendent and even kissed me, now he didn't recognize me. Only 10 percent of the two hundred superintendents were women, and I was one of the highest ranking. If it had mattered or if he had cared, I reasoned, he would have remembered me.

Although I had been to many superintendents' conferences while I worked in the regional office, I found it difficult to make the transition. The superintendents still considered me part of the regional office, while the regional office now considered me part of management. As a result, I didn't fit in. Many of the superintendents sat around and complained about regional office staff who would not let them do what they wanted. Although Cook held the meeting in Santa Fe to let more regional office employees attend, few did. Overall, spirits were low and speakers prattled about topics irrelevant to park policy or operations.

I turned my attention back to the park. I started nominating employees for recognition awards. Sandy and a maintenance foreman won Outstanding Employees of the region and attended the celebration in Washington, D.C., commemorating the seventy-fifth anniversary of the National Park Service. Only three were awarded in each region. Then the safety committee chair won the regional director's Safety Achievement Award for 1991. Buddy's hard work won the region's Maintenance Management Award for large parks. In 1990 the park won the Garrison Gold Award for best interpretive program with the twentieth-anniversary activities and placed second in 1991. In addition, I sought and received promotions for several undergraded employees.

Slowly I began to feel I had a real team. The employees responded to praise, handwritten notes, and challenges. They welcomed new program thrusts, and each tried to do better than the last. As a result, the profile of the park rose to among the highest in the region. Other superintendents asked me to send employees to train theirs or to bail them out of some problem. Employees from other parks always wanted to visit LBJ, and, accommodating demand, we hosted several regionwide and Servicewide meetings and training courses.

By June 1991 I felt good about being the superintendent of Lyndon B. Johnson National Historical Park. Dick Marks's comments, however, continued to haunt me and to undermine my confidence. Bob had a board meeting in Yellowstone with Eastern National, a nonprofit cooperating association that managed the bookstores in eastern parks. I decided to go along and see more of Yellowstone. From Salt Lake City we drove to Jackson Lake Lodge in Grand Teton National Park. Even though I had not been impressed when we visited the area in 1976, the park was Bob's favorite, so I reserved a room with a view of the mountains.

It was a warm day without a cloud in the sky. The mountains jumped out and into my heart. I couldn't believe that I had been so jaded in 1976 that I had not recognized their magnificence. From our room we stared at the mountains, then at the mountains mirrored in Jackson Lake, then again at the mountains. I could not get enough of them. While I was disappointed in the interpretive programs, I felt that the mountains spoke for themselves. Maintenance of the park was abominable. Paint peeled off the park residences, which were located too close to the park entrance station. Rest rooms leaked and smelled. Plainly the park needed new leadership. While we toured, we heard that the longtime superintendent had retired and that his replacement had decided not to take the assignment. I told Bob, "This is the park where I want to retire. I can imagine no more beautiful assignment in the entire National Park System."

Two days later, at Yellowstone, I spoke with Bob Deskins, one of the superintendents at the Eastern National board meeting. When I told this old-line ranger and superintendent that someday I wanted to be superintendent at Grand Teton, he said, "You should be superintendent now. You are better qualified than anyone else that I can think of." I was speechless. Although Deskins had worked mostly in the Southeast Region, it was the largest region, and he had seen many managers come and go.

After a delightful visit to Yellowstone, we returned to Texas. I called Dick Marks immediately and mentioned that Deskins thought I was qualified for superintendent of Grand Teton. "That's a moot issue," he said. "Jack Neckels is going to get it." Neckels had been assistant superintendent of Grand Teton before he moved to Santa Fe as one of the associate regional directors. I liked and admired him, but I was disappointed. Even though I didn't want to leave LBJ, to become superintendent of Grand Teton National Park would have been a tremendous incentive.

While superintendent of LBJ, one of the thankless tasks I agreed to do was revise the National Park Service's policies on historic preservation. Given a committee of the best specialists in the Service, I pushed them along on a tight deadline. When we had a draft, I suggested bringing some superintendents to review and critique it. They shot us out of the water, claiming it read like a college text and contained too much repetition. They sent us back to the drawing board to begin all over again.

From my Alaska days I knew one of the superintendents, Dave Mihalic of Mammoth Cave National Park. He was one of the recreational planners with the Bureau of Land Management whom I had supposedly upset back in 1975. I hadn't seen much of him in the intervening sixteen years. He had left his high-paying job with BLM to take a demotion for his ideal job, back-country ranger at Glacier National Park. Soon, however, his talents and ambitions pushed him up the ladder to his first superintendency, at Yukon-Charley National Preserve in Alaska, then as Cook's assistant superintendent at Great Smoky Mountains, and on to Mammoth Cave.

That evening Dave invited me to have dinner with him and the other superintendents. We had a great time discussing issues and trying to solve long-term leadership problems within the National Park Service. When I described some of my problems, I received support, suggestions, and even some envy. For the first time, I was one of the guys. Now I understood the special camaraderie and unique fraternity of superintendents. It didn't matter if you had little in common with them. What mattered was that you were one of them. They closed ranks around you. It was a great feeling.

After that positive experience, I looked forward to August 1991, when I would meet all the superintendents at the gathering in Vail, Colorado, to mark the seventy-fifth anniversary of the National Park Service. Held in a glitzy ski resort during the off-season, the event attracted the attention of the media and environmental groups. For more than a year, the deputy regional director of the Pacific Northwest Region, Bill Briggle, had working groups analyzing the biggest problems afflicting the National Park Service. These four groups focused on organizational renewal, interpretation, environmental leadership, and cultural and natural resource stewardship. The weeklong conference had keynote addresses by the nation's environmental and political leaders. But it also included work sessions on the four major topics. Few agencies care enough to examine themselves critically, admit problems, and develop strategies to improve. As we probed and analyzed the Service's weaknesses, the esprit de corps, long absent, returned in force. The conference was an inspiring and uplifting experience. I hadn't felt such unity since my Alaska days.

In the elevator one morning, I met Tom Kenworthy, a *Washington Post* correspondent. From my nametag he noticed that I was superintendent at LBJ and started talking about a recent documentary on LBJ. We conversed through breakfast. He asked me what I thought about the conference. I spoke without thinking, about the Service's lack of leadership, the bunker mentality among superintendents, and the fear of risk-taking—nearly all the result of former Interior Secretary Jim Watt's anti-environment campaign. When he whipped out his notebook and began taking notes, I groaned internally. Once again I had spouted off without concern for the consequences. Despite my training and experience with the media, I had forgotten to request "not for attribution."

After I returned to LBJ, I waited for the bombshell article. Friends in Washington, D.C., called first. "I'm glad that someone had the guts to say what needed to be said," declared one. Another chimed in, "It took a historian to call a spade a spade." Finally someone faxed me the article. While my comments were accurate, they were taken out of context and made me look disloyal. I called Cook and alerted him to my indiscretion. Without lecturing me, he simply said he'd cover for me and take the heat.

Although somewhat relieved, I still felt badly. To cushion the impact of my comments, I wrote confidential notes to the director and deputy director, explaining the context for my remarks. Cook later told me that the notes helped immensely. When I saw the two leaders in October, Ridenour didn't recognize or remember me, but the deputy director, a career professional, hit me on the shoulder and said, "You didn't need to send that note. We all get misquoted by the press, but thank you."

Although my years at LBJ seemed like a continuous party, we grappled with some tough issues. Most absorbing was the planning and designing of the visitor center. The old hospital contained more than thirty-five thousand square feet that could be used for exhibits, curatorial storage, and administrative offices. Because LBJ funded the hospital before he left office and its architectural design met established aesthetic criteria, the structure qualified for the National Register of Historic Places, triggering all the historic preservation processes. To ensure that the interpretation focused on LBJ's contributions rather than merely his retirement or Johnson City years, I asked my old Alaska friend Bill Brown to help with the interpretive planning and the orientation movie.

Meanwhile, Pickle and I worked to keep appropriations flowing. Once at a dinner party Bob and I had for Mrs. Johnson and the Pickles, Jake said, "Lady Bird, I'm going to Houston for prostate surgery and won't be in Washington to marshal the last funding cycle through Congress. You must write Lloyd [Senator Lloyd Bentsen] and ask him to help." I gulped out loud. One of the long-standing rules was never to ask Mrs. Johnson for political favors. As I held my breath, she turned and asked me to draft a note for her. I could have hugged them both.

Besides the visitor center, my other major goal was new buses. Although several parks had similar transportation systems, the National Park Service did not have funds for replacing them. Visitors and employees alike complained. Although I gave personal tours to several Democratic congressmen and pointed out the age of the buses, there was no political return in funding new buses. Then the brakes of an ailing bus failed as a mechanic drove it back to the bus barn, and it sailed through the Secret Service gate. Fortunately, no visitors were on board nor was anyone hurt. Immediately all buses underwent intensive inspections, and we even brought in consultants from the Texas Department of Transportation.

Despite these precautions, several months later the brakes of another bus failed. This time it occurred on a tour just as the bus descended from the highest point on the ranch. The driver/interpreter skillfully negotiated it down the hill and around a curve until it coasted to a stop. Then she calmly radioed the mechanics for another bus and driver. Waiting for the replacement, she continued her interpretive stories. After transferring her passengers, she collapsed, drained emotionally and physically from the near-disaster.

When Cook heard about the brake failure, he pulled out all stops to get funding for new buses. No one in the National Park Service wanted to be charged with negligence or involuntary manslaughter. Within a matter of weeks, the park received emergency funding for five new buses. Almost literally by accident, I had fulfilled my third major goal.

Another major park issue was Mrs. Johnson. The most immediate concern was her mortality. Although healthy and active, she was seventy-eight years old. Jim Hardin, the Secret Service agent-in-charge, cautioned me on our first meeting, "The day Mrs. Johnson dies is the last day of our responsibility." He recommended that we develop a plan to provide immediate protection for government property. Because of Mrs. Johnson's popularity, he expected mourners to pick up small mementos as they circulated through the house. The plan took nearly two years to be approved by the family, Secret Service, and National Park Service.

A less pressing but no less troubling concern was an assessment of Mrs. Johnson's contributions to history. Most historians would agree that she and Eleanor Roosevelt were the most active and effective first ladies in the twentieth century. But because we all loved her so much, I feared that our perspective might be skewed. I kept cautioning my staff that we needed time and distance to assess objectively her role in the Johnson administration and later with the National Wildflower Research Center.

Her significance would determine how the National Park Service eventually interprets the Texas White House. Unlike Bess Truman, who lived in the same unchanged house for twenty years, Mrs. Johnson remodeled LBJ's office, removed "ugly shag carpets," and added modern technology such as fax machines, microwave ovens, and a heated swimming pool and spa. The issue of how much restoration should be done was a thorny topic that I felt should not be tackled until we had several years to contemplate her significance. At the moment what existed was original fabric created by the first lady herself. If the National Park Service went in and restored the house to its 1960s appearance, it would lack authenticity but would allow the visitor to visualize how the thirty-sixth president lived.

Less philosophical and more operational issues also occupied the park staff. Overhead lawn-sprinkler systems sprayed water on the wooden components of the Texas White House, birthplace, and boyhood home, accelerating rot, decay, and loss of original fabric. In the cemetery, the sprinkler system sprayed hard water on the tombstones, leaving white deposits and contributing to rapid deterioration. Buddy believed the answer lay in an expensive, labor-intensive, underground leaky-pipe system. A low level of water would continuously leak into the ground, keeping the grass watered without affecting the historic structures.

Providing fire protection to the Texas White House was another headache. Initially, the park invested hundreds of thousands of dollars in developing halon fire-suppression systems. Halon, a hydrocarbon gas, removed oxygen from a fire environment and suppressed fires without causing the damages that water or solid suppressants did. Then the National Park Service became aware of the environmental harm that hydrocarbons caused to the ozone layer, and directives followed that not only banned but also required the removal of all halon systems. Our only solution was a dry-pipe sprinkler system. While we researched the problem, we installed temporary sprinklers in the attic and furnace rooms.

One other ongoing issue was the Hereford cattle herd. When LBJ was alive, he bought registered bulls and cows, constructed a show barn, and entered cattle shows. The market dictated the characteristics bred into the herds. In the 1960s people preferred well-marbled, tender beef, so ranchers bred short, squat, fatty Herefords. By the 1980s, however, the dangers of saturated fat to personal health became known, and breeders developed Herefords that were tall and rangy. Initially, park management followed the evolution of the breed, competed in cattle shows, and sold surplus cows as registered cattle.

Then purists raised the issue of historical authenticity. They believed that the park, instead of keeping pace with the market, should raise only cattle that looked like those LBJ raised. As regional historian I had felt that the purists were being too precious and that the average visitor didn't care what LBJ's cattle really looked like, especially as maintaining a genetic bloodline would become increasingly expensive. I lost the battle, and now as superintendent I had an archaic herd. No breeder wanted our registered cattle, so we sold surplus cows on the commercial meat market for a fraction of their true value. Moreover, to prevent inbreeding we had to find additional bulls with the LBJ bloodlines to expand the gene pool.

Finding registered bulls with the proper bloodline became increasingly difficult. Somehow a reporter for the *Austin American-Statesman* heard about our search and drafted a cute article that the Associated Press circulated throughout the nation. Suddenly, calls came from breeders as far away as Hawaii. A dentist in Montana donated "Mr. Rust" to our cause. His bloodlines matched our need, and we dispatched the ranch crew to get him. Accustomed to a cooler climate and vastly overweight, Mr. Rust had difficulty performing his role. The one time he attempted it, he damaged himself irreparably. No matter how I asked the question, I could not get the ranch foreman to explain the problem. Finally I read the veterinarian's report. Mr. Rust suffered a corkscrew penis and would never be able to service cows again. Without fanfare, we bought a younger bull, which served the herd quite well.

Concurrent with my superintendency was my election as president of the George Wright Society. Named for the biologist whose private fortune in 1929 paid for the first scientific survey of wildlife in national parks, the professional society promoted the preservation of natural and cultural resources through research and education. Just prior to our triannual conference in 1990, the daughter of George Wright, Sherry Brichetto, decided to donate nearly $250,000 to our humble organization. Run on a shoe-string as a labor of love by a former chief scientist of the National Park Service, the society lacked the organization to handle such a bequest. With help from the president of Eastern National, I reorganized the society, placing power and accountability with the board of directors.

With a strategic plan that focused our interests and concerns, we took a leading role in the National Park Service's seventy-fifth anniversary and published several significant monographs. Then we heard about the Fourth World Congress on National Parks, to be held in Caracas, Venezuela, in February 1992. The World Congress met only once every ten years and represented an important opportunity for the George Wright Society to gain international recognition. When we learned that only a small contingent of scientists would represent the National Park Service, the society decided to send four board members, including me. We sponsored a session on research in protected areas, wrote and delivered papers, and eventually published an international monograph on coordinating research and management to enhance the protection of national parks.

The World Congress was an eye-opener for me. At all previous congresses, the United States had played a leading role—Yellowstone even hosted the congress in 1972 as part of its centennial celebrations. In Caracas in 1992, however, Director Ridenour gave a speech that lectured other countries and insulted the Third World. Then, during the plenary sessions on Third World problems, Ridenour, bored with translations, hosted a party for select participants. Newspapers headlined his disparaging speech coupled with photographs of frolicking partygoers. Almost as bad, the United States never asserted leadership or even support for major initiatives. I was embarrassed to be affiliated with the National Park Service and took refuge in my George Wright Society identification.

Ridenour was a do-nothing director. Even his memoir, *The National Parks Compromised: Pork Barrel Politics and America's Treasures,* is filled with his official travel but handles no controversy and offers no insights or even personal observations. When he was hired, he was instructed to keep the Service and parks out of the news. He succeeded. No issue or controversy broke the tranquil surface. In fairness to Ridenour, however, he did believe that protection came before enjoyment of the resources and emphasized scientific research. Of course, his employees still trembled from the trauma of the Watt years, and few were willing to fall on their swords.

In the treatment of federal employees, President George H. W. Bush contrasted strongly with Ronald Reagan and Jimmy Carter. Because Bush himself was a longtime government servant, he believed that hardworking career professionals created good government programs. For a brief period we weren't lambasted with rhetoric about our worthlessness.

After the World Congress, I returned to the United States just in time to learn that Grand Teton National Park was recruiting an assistant superintendent. Hearing Dick Marks's warning echo in my mind, I talked with Bob about applying. "It would be hard to go from being a superintendent and the boss to being an assistant superintendent who has all the crappy jobs," I said to Bob.

"But if you don't choose where we go," he reminded me, "we may wind up where neither of us wants to live."

"If I do have to be an assistant superintendent," I said, "Jack Neckels is one of only three senior superintendents for whom I would work."

The following evening Bob called from an Eastern National board meeting in Boston. He had just finished dining with Russ Dickenson, the last career director of the National Park Service. Russ had served as Grand Teton's chief ranger in the 1960s. We both had tremendous respect and affection for this man, who had come up through the ranger ranks and had served in nearly every major position and in a variety of parks. He was articulate, smooth, politically pragmatic, but dedicated to the inviolate mission of the National Park Service.

"Russ says that you absolutely have to apply for Grand Teton's assistant superintendency," Bob said. "He says there is no better park to learn the myriad issues that you will confront as you move forward in your career." I agreed to apply.

To keep morale high, I did not tell anyone at the park that I had applied for Grand Teton. Nothing is more unsettling, I believed, than uncertainty. I had also made a big deal over staying at LBJ until my career ended and was embarrassed to admit I was ambitious. Although going from a superintendent to an assistant superintendent sounded like a demotion, it was actually a promotion. If I got the job, I would be on a fast track for a big-park superintendency. I would have "paid my dues."

As Jack Neckels began to call my references, rumors swept the park. I had been foolish to try and keep my application a secret. Buddy felt that I hadn't trusted him. The subordinate staff couldn't believe that I would willingly leave them. A bigger concern for them became my replacement. Several people were rumored to be in the running, and they were not people the staff wanted as boss. Meanwhile, the Grand Teton selection process stretched on for three months.

At a planning meeting on our visitor center, I talked with Cook about my application. He admitted that Neckels had called him. "Somehow I don't think Neckels will give me the job," I confided in him. "He has worked for a strong woman [Lorraine Mintzmyer] for nearly nine years. I can't see him taking on a strong woman as his deputy." Cook agreed.

Two days later Jack Neckels offered me the job. He liked what I had done at LBJ, especially the building of a team. "I would like to build a team here at Grand Teton," he told me. "Each division chief does his own thing." He also wanted my experience in historic preservation. "The park is constantly being hammered by the Wyoming state historic preservation officer and the local historical society," he said. "I want you to get them off my back." He asked me to come for a two-week orientation so that I could experience the chaos of summer.

Meanwhile I heard that Cook was in political trouble again. This time the Interior Department had sent a handpicked team of professionals to investigate the large number of Equal Opportunity complaints and employee grievances that had been filed against him. At the same time, the regional office offered a training course in quality management to bring in superintendents for Dick Marks's retirement party. Before flying to Santa Fe, I called the two most senior superintendents in the region to enlist their support in "saving Cook." They were appalled that he was being investigated for disciplining nonperformers. We agreed to meet and plot strategy before we met with the investigators.

In Santa Fe, we decided that the best course was to request a meeting between the investigators and all the region's superintendents. Together we worked out a scenario dividing the points that had to be brought up. We also agreed that the meeting would be with only the supportive superintendents. The negativists could seek their own meeting.

At the end of the quality-management course, we outlined our strategy to the superintendents. While not all liked Cook, they all supported his stand on nonperformers. Not one superintendent went on record to bad-mouth him. During the meeting with the investigators, my role was to keep all strong egos focused on the same issue. Occasionally the senior superintendents ruffled a few feathers, and I had to smooth them out—I who once alienated everyone. In the end, we convinced the investigators that if they crucified Cook, no manager would ever be able to discipline nonperformers again.

I left Santa Fe and flew directly to Grand Teton for my two-week orientation. When I returned, a special note from Cook awaited me. "I want to take a moment and say a special thanks to you," it read. "What you and the others did for me on August 7th is beyond words. And I know of your leadership role in it. Caring can cause pain but any pain in doing what is right is well worth it when I see how you and others care too. To you, Lady. Thanks from one of your solid supporters."

Before I left LBJ, I had one major task: survive an operations evaluation. Every four years the regional office sent a team of specialists to each park to evaluate every aspect of park operations. This included personnel practices, budget management, maintenance programs, interpretive activities, and resource management. The team interviewed both supervisors and employees to seek out problems or issues not being handled and then to offer solutions. In the past, these teams dug out dirt and tried to make superintendents squirm. The new team leader, however, wanted to help parks and in some instances even compliment them.

In preparation, we had spent several months answering standardized questions and addressing long-standing issues. The team put us through the wringer for a full week. In return, we hosted them to a typical LBJ barbeque where we socialized together. In the end, the evaluation stated unequivocally that the park was among the best managed in the region. They had only a few recommendations to improve our interpretive programs. Everything else received rave reviews.

After Cook was briefed on the operations evaluation, he sent me the following congratulations: "Way to Go!! A good team evaluated a good team. But a good team to survive such an evaluation must not only be good in and of themselves but also be well led. Share my congratulations and thanks." As a result, I felt I was leaving LBJ on a high-flying cloud.

The park held my farewell party in the show barn. It had been scoured clean, and computer-generated graphics and crepe-paper streamers hung from the rafters. In one skit Sandy Hodges mimicked me so perfectly that she brought roars of laughter and tears to my eyes. Mrs. Johnson, who hated to give speeches, said how much she had enjoyed Bob and me and how pleased she was with my achievements. Cook gave me a miniature pin of the National Park Service badge and said, "I had these made in limited quantities to give to unique and special leaders. One day I expect to see Melody as regional director."

Then it was my turn. "I hope I can get through this without breaking down," I began. "This was my first park and will always be my best park. You taught me what being a team really meant. We have grown together and accomplished more in three years than anyone ever expected. I love you all and will miss you." Then I gave each employee and guest a copy of my book, *The Last Frontier: A History of the Yukon River of Canada and Alaska,* individually inscribed. Emotionally wrought up, I hated to leave. I felt warm, loved, and special.

My three years at LBJ were the best years of my career. I had a responsive park staff who strove for the goals I enumerated. We flowed together as one entity. There were no divisions between locals and career employees nor seasonal versus permanent staff. For the first time in my life, I felt a success.

Of course, Cook ensured my success. He not only supported me, he took the political heat when I screwed up. Although I developed the rapport with Congressman Pickle, I could never have secured the approval and funding for the visitor center without Cook's aid. Occasionally I mouthed off, and more than once I suffered his notorious tongue-lashings. Yet it was a surprise when he told me that he was not ready for me to leave LBJ, that he still had work for me to do. Marks had apparently made a unilateral decision that I should move on without discussing it with him. How differently things might have turned out.

Bob and I enjoyed Texas and Texans. They were the friendliest people we had ever known. Drivers wave even when they don't know each other. While every other state establishes criteria for inclusion, Texas takes new residents and makes them full Texans as soon as they arrive. Of course, it helps if you are white and non-Hispanic. The most disturbing underlying quality about Texas was racism. Nearly everyone we met exhibited some element of it.

We had a Hispanic male who lived in a marginal apartment in our barn. In exchange for rent, he kept our one-acre lawn mowed. We trusted him implicitly, and he never betrayed us. One day he told me that the townspeople were blaming him for the disappearance of some goats. He went to the sheriff's office for a polygraph test to prove his innocence. The deputy sheriff called him every sort of name, accused him of various unsolved crimes, and threatened to put him in jail. Suddenly the deputy said, "You can go now." After he had endured that humiliating experience, the goat owner learned that his own son was selling the goats for drug money.

Repeatedly we saw how illegal Mexican aliens were abused and over-worked. Desperate to earn money for their poverty-stricken families in Mexico, these men often lived six and eight to a room and earned far less than the minimum wage. Complainers were simply turned over to the Immigration and Naturalization Service and became a lesson for others to keep their mouths shut and their heads down.

On the other hand, I saw strong values well developed among Texans. They worked hard and took pride in their work. Seldom was a job done "good enough"; it was done as perfectly as could be. Children were reared to respect their elders and always used "ma'am" and "sir." Education, how-ever, seemed to take a second place to sports, especially football. Only the State of Texas itself was more important than football. Texans loved their state with nationalistic pride and loyalty. Where else could the phrase "Don't mess with Texas" prevent littering?

Texas proclaims itself a macho state, where men are men and women cherished and protected. Contrary to that image, the men at LBJ willingly accepted my leadership. They all worked hard to please me and sought my approval in everything they did. I had expected resistance but found none. They proved a big contrast to those in Wyoming—the first state to grant women the right to vote.

Texas was an experience positive enough for us to consider returning for our retirement years. Yet it was Lyndon B. Johnson National Historical Park that bound us. I loved the park, its staff, and all that it stood for. None-theless, I watched the numbers of visitors decline each year. When Robert Caro published his second derogatory book, *The Years of Lyndon Johnson: Means of Ascent,* I railed against his dishonesty and hyperbole. Then Oliver Stone's movie *JFK* infuriated me with his impossible fabrications of LBJ's role in the assassination. LBJ deserved better. Usually, twenty years after a president's term, historians revise and reevaluate contributions against liabilities. Probably because of the Vietnam War, LBJ had not received proper credit for his domestic program, especially civil rights and Medicare. Instead, he was underappreciated and poorly understood by historians and by the American people.

Shortly after leaving LBJ, I tried to do my part in revising LBJ's image. I researched LBJ's personal role in establishing forty-seven new park areas encompassing fifteen million acres—the best conservation record of any president. To critical acclaim, I delivered the paper at a scholarly conference and later published it in a book, *Frontier and Region: Essays in Honor of Martin Ridge*, released in 1997 by the University of New Mexico Press. I also enumerated LBJ's contributions to the West in an article for the *Journal of the West*.

The irony of a child of the Sixties and a hater of LBJ defending the president and his policies didn't escape me. In large part I credited my perceptual change to the park and its resources. Seeing the environmental, cultural, and personal forces that shaped the man gave me a different perspective than I had during the Vietnam War. More extensive and objective reading also reminded me of all his contributions on the domestic side of his administration. But getting to know Mrs. Johnson colored my emotions more than all the Vietnam teach-ins and protest marches ever did. I became an unabashed Johnson supporter.

Thus, a couple of years after I left LBJ, I received a personal and professional blow. The ABC network decided to do an exposé on the LBJ visitor center for the "It's Your Money" segment of the nightly news. The television crews ignored the fact that it was a construction priority of the National Park Service and focused only on Jake Pickle's affiliation with LBJ. The story tried to make it a political payoff to a failed president by a loyal friend. Comparing visitation figures between LBJ and Yellowstone, the news story tried to prove the incongruity of an elaborate visitor center in a rinky-dink town when the vastness of Yellowstone lacked such a structure. The reporters made no effort to gather facts or to present them objectively, and the producers wanted to shock, not inform. They probably succeeded.

In September 1992 we felt deep sadness as we left LBJ's Hill Country and *my* park. While the challenges of Grand Teton excited me, they also scared me and brought out my insecurities. Although we both looked forward to living in a national park and fully experiencing a big natural park, I knew deep in my heart that I would never have another park like LBJ.

# Grand Teton Ordeals

Although it was only September when Bob and I drove into Grand Teton, it seemed like late fall. Heavy winds and low temperatures had stripped the trees of their autumn colors. My beautiful mountains hid behind a bank of clouds, and visitation had dropped nearly to zero. The park staff had closed and winterized most of the facilities north of park headquarters in Moose. Winter felt near.

Only a month earlier Superintendent Jack Neckels had insisted that I come for a two-week orientation. He knew that if I hadn't seen the park's busy season, I would make erroneous assumptions based on my observations of the slow season. With great delight I rode horses with the maintenance supervisors into the mountain wilderness to assess whether a historic ranger cabin could be replaced with a new, more usable structure. Later, with the search-and-rescue rangers, I observed helicopter-rescue techniques developed at Grand Teton. Then, on a hot August day, Neckels and I floated the Snake River, where I learned about eroded boat landings, protecting bald eagles, and conflicts between large scenic-float tours and smaller guided-fishing operations. It had been an exciting and overwhelming two weeks.

Now my real work would begin. Unlike at LBJ, where the superintendent handled both public relations and park operations, at Grand

Teton the superintendent handled community and external issues and the assistant superintendent managed park operations. But what a park! Instead of two units of the same park as I had at LBJ, here I had two separate national parks with different legislative purposes: Grand Teton National Park with 110,000 acres and John D. Rockefeller, Jr., Memorial Parkway, a recreational area joining Yellowstone and Teton, with 24,000 acres. Grand Teton's budget tripled LBJ's—six million to two. But the permanent staff was only twice LBJ's. On the other hand, Grand Teton hosted more than three million visitors, almost all in the summer, compared to LBJ's mere two hundred thousand spread throughout the year. To cope with so many people, Grand Teton fielded more than two hundred seasonal employees each summer. LBJ had only eight.

The two parks differed vastly in the host of complex issues that confounded Grand Teton's managers. These included long-standing problems with the Jackson Hole Airport within the boundaries of the park, brucellosis in bison, grizzly bears eating cattle, too many elk, and dwindling park budgets. For assistance in these, I assumed that because most of the division chiefs had been there more than ten years, they could help me handle them. Although Jack had been superintendent only a year, ten years earlier he had held my job and confronted the same troubling issues.

First of all, Bob and I had to get moved into "Quarters No. 1," also known as the Superintendent's House. From his first interview with me, Jack made it plain that one of us needed to live in the park, and he had already bought a house in town. We welcomed the opportunity to live in the park. In 1933 the Civilian Conservation Corps had built the large two-story log house in the Beaver Creek area at the foot of the mountains. Recently the maintenance staff had modernized the kitchen and bathrooms. A huge living room with walls of exposed log and a viga ceiling focused on an immense stone fireplace recently adapted to accommodate a wood stove. At first, the fireplace conversion appeared to be a sacrilege, but the subzero winters made us appreciate it. All in all, the house thrilled us.

As we struggled to get settled, Jack Neckels drove up to welcome us to the park. In the eight years since he had left Santa Fe, his broad-shouldered, football-player physique had added more than fifty pounds in middle-age bulge. His square, lean face had grown puffy, and his straight brown hair was sprinkled with gray. Yet his eyes still twinkled as he hugged me and said, "I'm glad you are here. We are going to have lots of fun."

As we chatted, I asked him about the park staff, which I had met only briefly the previous month. "As you saw, they are talented, hard-working, and accustomed to having their own way," he said. "I've told them repeatedly that they don't have to like each other, but they do have to work together. Because squad meetings had become catfights, the previous assistant superintendent stopped holding them. I have reinstituted them—not once a week but three times a week. They will work as a team if I have to drag each one into harness."

Remembering my own successes in developing a team at LBJ, I said, "If you have never been part of a team, it is hard to give up individuality and personal identity. But once you have experienced the joy and camaraderie of teamwork, you will never regret the move." Jack agreed wholeheartedly.

The next morning at my first squad meeting I renewed acquaintance with the six division chiefs and the public information officer. I liked Linda Olson, whose long, brown hair and youthful face belied her nearly twenty years as an interpreter. Remembering and admiring her from his tenure as assistant superintendent in the 1970s, Jack had appointed her public information officer. Her sparkling personality, skill with words, and ability to relate to people made her a natural for the job.

The other woman in the room, Edna Good, also welcomed me warmly. Edna, ten years my senior, had worked her way up the ladder the hard way—without a college degree. She had moved from secretary to administrative assistant to budget assistant to concession specialist. Once in concessions management, she hit her stride and became one of the best in the service. Involved in nearly every major park decision, she provided indispensable history, context, and perspective to Jack and his predecessor. Because none of the division chiefs trusted the judgment of the assistant superintendents, she became the de-facto assistant and often served as acting superintendent.

The five male division chiefs were more subdued in their welcome. Dick McMullen, the administrative officer, slumped sullenly in his chair. Short and overweight, his one vanity was long silver-blond hair, which capped a pudgy and mottled face. He did not look happy or positive.

Seated next to him was his physical opposite. Bill Swift, chief of interpretation, was tall and thin with a receding hairline. Thoughtful, intellectual, and often reticent, his aloofness had alienated much of his staff. Jack had told me that Bill had been slapped with an Equal Opportunity complaint and was still vibrating with feelings of injustice.

Jack Peay, chief of maintenance, was a likeable man with an engaging sense of humor. Although he had spent time in parks, most of his latter years had been in the Western regional office. Thus he focused on getting money rather than providing leadership. With his background, Neckels had expected him to develop a maintenance program. Instead, the park jerked along from one year to the next without long-term maintenance planning.

The chief ranger, Doug Bernard, looked stronger than he had a month earlier when he was recovering from pneumonia. Still thin from his battles with cancer and chemotherapy, he projected a forceful presence. I had heard that he was good, and he exuded self-assurance. With a bluff, hearty welcome, he seemed to accept me. He told me later, "You know, when I announced your appointment to my rangers, I got a shitpot of grief. Then I circulated your application to a few of the more vociferous, and they shut up. Your experiences in Alaska and with the fire department gave you a credibility that your doctorate didn't."

Marshall Gingery intrigued me. Ten years earlier the park had established a second assistant superintendency, and he took a downgrade to fill the position. When Neckels decided to merge the two assistants into one, Marshall gracefully agreed not to contest the move so long as he could compete for the job. When Marshall failed to qualify as one of the top three candidates, Neckels asked his counsel in making the selection. I was Marshall's choice. Subsequently, he became the division chief for resource management and reported directly to me. A man of medium height with thinning blond hair, he looked preoccupied and withdrawn, not participating in the introductory comments. Yet when his turn came to greet me, he turned charming and welcoming.

From the beginning I picked up a sense of Jack's strong leadership. No one questioned who made the decisions. In fact, many of the mid-level managers, especially Rande Simon in maintenance, complained good-naturedly about their loss of authority.

I soon discovered that Jack and I differed on management styles. I believed in using park committees to involve all the staff in decision-making. Jack firmly believed that the division chiefs had to be held accountable. He had learned that if a committee made a recommendation, the division chiefs refused to accept responsibility. Therefore, after discussion in squad, he made the decisions.

After a month, I still felt overwhelmed. Never one to equivocate on decisions, however, I reacted quickly to most questions. Then Jack would patiently talk me through the issue and show me that my decision was based on incomplete information. Always questioning, probing, analyzing, he was always right. At LBJ I had learned to trust the instincts and judgments of my staff, but at Grand Teton Jack taught me over and over that I could not base decisions on staff briefings or recommendations. Slowly I began to feel like Rande Simon and lost some of my LBJ self-esteem. Meanwhile, Dick McMullen kept counseling me, "Nothing is as simple as it looks. There is always background to every problem. Don't move so fast."

His advice hit home in a meeting with Rande and his foremen. Rande, among the best-liked and most respected supervisors in the park, had moved from contracting officer to maintenance manager without working up the labor ladder, yet his hard work, good judgment, and appealing personality won over the skeptics. With winter coming, he sought direction on which roads should be plowed with what priority. After an hour's briefing on the significance of the major roads, I began to assign the highest priority to certain roads.

As we talked, Jack stuck his head into the conference room. Learning the topic, he came in and sat to one side. Observing my approach to the problem, he suggested that we work geographically through the park rather than arbitrarily assign priority levels. Sure enough, his tactic was more systematic, rational, and effective. As he took over the meeting, I could only marvel at his problem-solving techniques. From that day on, I recognized Jack as a strong operations manager who wanted to be involved in most decisions. My ego felt a bit bruised, and my feelings of inadequacy stronger. But I realized that I could grow and learn more from him than from my own foolish mistakes, which, if not for him, I might never recognize as mistakes.

In addition to operations, Jack excelled in personnel issues. "As deputy regional director," he said, "I never saw a personnel issue until it became so messy and screwed up that it was almost impossible to salvage." Unlike park operations, I thought I had a feel for resolving personnel problems. During my eighteen years of management, I had never faced a grievance or an Equal Opportunity complaint. I felt strongly that most grievances and complaints arose from failed communications.

Within my first month I tested my theory. A longtime seasonal filed an EO complaint against her new supervisor. As a Native American, she complained that his criticism of her interpretive talks reflected racism. He told her, for example, that young bears should be called bear cubs, not baby bears, which she apparently regarded as patronizing. What really triggered the complaint, however, was a lower performance rating than she had received in previous years. I met with her and her supervisor, listening hard to find a nonpersonal perspective to address. Eventually, I brought both parties to agree on the need for more Equal Opportunity and cultural-diversity training. She did not get her performance rating changed, but we softened some of its language. I felt good about resolving my first complaint. Only later did I learn that the supervisor believed that I had not properly supported him.

I did not realize that this first EO complaint was only the beginning. I quickly learned that my two-week orientation to park issues hadn't prepared me for my real job. I had expected to handle all aspects of park operations. Instead, I spent most of my time on personnel issues. This included trying to improve attitudes and morale and to resolve complaints. The relationship between management and employees contrasted greatly with that of my LBJ team. I detected a sense of distrust of management among everyone. I missed the easy camaraderie I had enjoyed at LBJ. Here, they always seemed suspicious of management overtures and cynical of Jack's fine phrases and enthusiasm.

I began to see one EO complaint after another. Every disgruntled employee filed a complaint, often thinly documented. Someone seemed to be advising them to file EO complaints rather than grievances. The latter were resolved within the park or region. EO complaints, on the other hand, went to Washington and eventually to the Equal Employment Opportunity Commission. Many of the complainants were white males over the age of forty, claiming age discrimination. Initially, I took each complaint seriously and tried to resolve it through open communication. Then I learned that often the complainant's only acceptable resolution was the removal of the supervisor. I resolved few of the complaints. Most were appealed to Washington. Nonetheless, as the complaints, grievances, and performance appeals stacked up, I began to understand what John Cook had faced in Santa Fe.

With the largest number of complaints emerging from Bill Swift's interpretation division, I believed there must be serious supervisory problems there. When I personally audited him and his two subordinate supervisors, however, I found one of the best-managed divisions I had ever seen. The trouble arose from Bill's strict accounting of time and money. Previous supervisors had allowed employees to set their own costly schedules, drive their own cars with government reimbursement, and accumulate hundreds of hours of undocumented compensatory time. Bill not only cut costs, he changed lifestyles, and that made him very unpopular. After my management review, I had less sympathy with vindictive employees.

Several months into my tenure, I held a position-management meeting. As dreadful as it sounded, position management determines what new positions could be added during a period of severe budget constraints. These meetings usually pitted division chiefs against each other, as each tried to get limited positions and money. This time, however, all chiefs agreed on one explosive concept: Jack's micro-management. I was taken by surprise and tried to refocus the meeting without avail. Everyone wanted to expound, except Bill Swift, who simply said, "Jack provides strong direction as a good manager should. He tells me where he wants me to be, and I decide how to get there." No one else except me agreed with him.

Next morning, I briefed Jack. He was as surprised as I. Although their comments undoubtedly hurt him personally and professionally, he decided to address their unhappiness. "Wait a minute," I said. "This park has had three superintendents with a hands-off management style for a total of twenty years. The division chiefs want to do as they please without any oversight or accountability. You are involved in everything they do, and you hold them strictly accountable. They admire and like you, but they are uncomfortable with their feet held to the fire. The worst thing you could do would be to back off now." Eventually he agreed and held firm to his management style. Over time, the division chiefs learned to accommodate to Jack's and my leadership.

Although we often tired of trying to get the park and its staff going in the proper direction, neither Jack nor I acknowledged even to each other the strain we felt. I would be at work by seven each morning, and Jack would arrive a half hour later, greeting me with "another beautiful day in paradise." I would always respond equally enthusiastically, appearing as happy to start the day as he. I knew I was role-playing. If I acted the way I felt, I would drop the morale of the staff even further. I learned early in my supervisory career to pretend to be eager and excited regardless of my true emotions. I had no doubt that Jack role-played too.

My job grew even more distasteful as I tackled its most unpleasant aspects. Not only did all personnel problems fall to me, but I was also responsible for ensuring that all employees did a satisfactory job. When anyone stopped performing or performed poorly, I began to "keep book" on them. For each poor performer, I required the supervisor to define the tasks clearly in writing, with due dates fixed and criteria specified for performance evaluation. As deadlines approached, written reminders had to be sent, asking if help were needed. When employees failed to meet the deadline or measure up to the evaluative criteria, their supervisor or I would counsel them and document the meeting. Sometimes we found training courses to assist such people. Other times we spent supervisory time coaching them through the task. Since Grand Teton employees had not been held accountable for so many years, the workload was immense. Some responded, others resisted, and still others filed lawsuits alleging hostile work environment.

Because it is essentially impossible to fire a federal employee, "keeping book" served only to pressure and cause discomfort to the employee. Regardless of the assistance we offered, rarely did nonperformers return to full-performance level. The best we could hope for would be that they would quit, retire, or move on.

In addition to performance problems, I also disciplined employees for insubordination. In some divisions there was a tug-of-war between employees and supervisors over how and when the work would be done. Often I mediated, but seldom succeeded. In contrast to my superintendency of LBJ, this job was not fun.

Jack and I worked hard to improve morale. We attended divisional meetings and tried to address employee concerns. Once a week one of us tried to visit all work sites to "show the flag" and let them know we cared. When employees went the extra mile, we sent handwritten notes of appreciation. These notes had gone over big at LBJ but didn't help a bit at Grand Teton. While LBJ employees clamored for high-profile special assignments, at Grand Teton these often went begging, or employees had to be cajoled into taking them. We also gave honor and monetary awards freely. Just as at LBJ, Bob and I gave dinner parties, and we annually hosted a Christmas open house for park employees and town leaders. The townspeople always expressed their appreciation. I rarely heard from the park staff.

Seasonal employees also had monthly meetings with me, and I followed up on their long list of valid complaints to improve the quality of their lives. Unlike permanent employees, seasonals lived in marginal quarters. Most occupied forty-year-old trailers—some rat-infested, others leaking, and one even with a bathtub that fell through the floor.

No matter how hard we tried to make life better, unhappy employees streamed into my office to complain about many things, usually housing. Most large natural parks have housing for some employees. Although the town of Jackson was only twelve miles away, early park planners designed and constructed park housing. As town rents skyrocketed in the 1970s and 1980s, park housing became a premium. The house in Jackson that rented for $1,200 rented in the park for about $350. Ironically, most of the highest paid employees lived in the park, and the lower paid tried to live in Jackson. This inequity was always an issue. Other issues included maintenance, improvements to one house but not others, and general dissatisfaction with the lack of housing amenities.

In addition to employee issues, I tried to track the 185 priority issues that Jack wanted done in 1992–93. Because they had not been completed in more than twenty years, the probability that they'd be done in one year was next to nil, but I kept the pressure on the division chiefs. With all the work to be done, my eleven-hour days were not long enough. Often I spent the weekend writing proposals, policy positions, and performance evaluations. No longer had I time to write for professional journals or to travel with Bob.

Bob, however, was having the time of his life. He loved living in the park and being married to the assistant superintendent. His biography of Sitting Bull had paid off its advance in the first month, and he was happily at work on his next book, about mountain men. Although his small study was cramped, he looked out on the mountains in all their splendor. While he knew that I had to do a lot of dirty tasks, he thought that I loved my job as I had at LBJ.

But I was not happy. Fortunately for my well-being, Dick McMullen became an unexpected ally. Strange, moody, but loyal, he offered sound counsel and tried hard to deliver whatever I asked of him. Despite his negative reputation, I found him more positive and team-oriented than most of his peers. Bill Swift, under siege by insubordinate employees, tried to be as responsive. Without those men, my first two years at Grand Teton would have been one horrid mess after another.

Despite the disgruntlement, complaints, and nonperformers, I was not ready to give up on the staff as a whole. I suggested to Jack that we celebrate the fiftieth anniversary of Jackson Hole National Monument with two goals in mind. First, use the anniversary as a team-building experience as I had with LBJ's twentieth anniversary and the fiftieth anniversary of the Santa Fe regional office building. Second, use the occasion to improve relations with the community of Jackson, which had opposed the formation of the Jackson Hole National Monument. Jack thought it was a great idea.

The controversy over the Jackson Hole National Monument began in the 1920s. John D. Rockefeller, Jr., observed how the curio shops and dance halls cluttering the valley floor desecrated the panorama of the Teton mountains. To ensure that no one knew his involvement, he formed the Snake River Land Company to purchase land at fair, even elevated, market prices. For years ranchers and business owners, delighted to get out of debt, sold their land. Then someone discovered Rockefeller's role. Suddenly embitterment replaced joy, and everyone felt cheated out of their land. When Rockefeller tried to donate the land to Grand Teton National Park, Congress, led by the Wyoming delegation, refused to sanction the gift. Frustrated, Rockefeller turned to President Roosevelt and told him that he would have to sell the land soon. In 1943 Roosevelt stretched his authority under the Antiquities Act of 1906 and established Jackson Hole National Monument.

Feeling twice betrayed, the citizens of Jackson Hole howled. One photogenic county commissioner, Clifford Hansen, enlisted the support of actor Wallace Beery. Together with some fellow ranchers armed with rifles and handguns, they drove a herd of cattle onto the lands of Jackson Hole National Monument and into the pages of *Time* magazine. Time, death, and skillful placation won over most of the park's vociferous opponents. Cliff Hansen, who had gone on to the governor's mansion and the U.S. Senate, even became one of the park's strongest supporters. Yet some animosity over the way the park had been established survived. The year 1993 offered an opportunity to revisit the monument and heal buried sores.

I hoped to involve everyone in the celebration and held several brainstorming sessions. Although everyone in the park was invited, just twenty attended the meetings. Eventually, only a few supervisors demonstrated any interest or enthusiasm. Marshall Gingery, with his ties to the University of Wyoming, enlisted its sponsorship of an academic seminar assessing Jackson Hole National Monument fifty years later. Rande Simon held a cowboy-culture day with a luncheon address by Cliff Hanson, now in retirement, a beloved citizen of Jackson. Other supervisors constructed a float for the Old West Days parade in Jackson. Linda Olson and Jack Neckels planned the program for the culminating ceremony, held in elegant Jackson Lake Lodge.

Community leaders and park supporters enjoyed the opportunity to commemorate the park. Even Rockefeller's son, Laurance, traveled from New York to help us celebrate. Few employees, however, attended any of the functions, and only supervisors participated. My efforts to pull the park together in planning and executing a major celebration failed, but we succeeded in securing closer ties with the community and former adversaries.

When I was trying to generate enthusiasm for the fiftieth anniversary, I discovered several maintenance men ridiculing my efforts. They had little use for a woman in management, especially me. When I attended their maintenance meetings, I often sensed a discomfort and awkwardness. I didn't know their business, and they didn't want to share it with me. They also resented my efforts to create a smoke-free work environment and mumbled that I ought to leave well enough alone. Ironically, in the macho world of the rangers I had better rapport and found them more responsive to my overtures.

In the midst of planning for the fiftieth anniversary celebration, we got hit with our most surprising, enduring, and puzzling EO complaint. One of the most popular interpreters claimed discrimination because of a learning disability and his age (he was forty-two). Because we did not know that he had a learning disability or what we could do to accommodate it, I offered to pay for a professional assessment to guide us. He refused and demanded that management find him another job in the park until his supervisor and Bill Swift left.

While I was trying to open channels of communication, the interpreter arrived at the park with a three-page essay entitled "The Death of a Ranger." He distributed it widely among the staff. I suspected at once that it had not been written by someone with a learning disability but by a disgruntled former employee who now lived in Jackson and spent much effort stirring up trouble for park management.

"I have been told that when the spirit leaves the body, death has occurred," the essay began. "I am writing this now as a dead man, for I no longer have a spirit.... I would like to share with you how my death came to be, but please have patience with me, for I have been told that I am an illiterate man and cannot spell or write well." He went on to describe the joys of being a ranger in the National Park Service and how he had spent eighteen years learning the secrets of his park. "Think of how I felt when I first met and talked to a new park administrator, and one of the first questions *she* [italics added, obviously referring to me] asked me was how long I had been here. I said proudly, '18 years,' and her reply was, 'Well, it's about time for you to move on.' I was taken aback, as if she had asked me how long I had been married and said, 'Well, it's about time to get a divorce.'" Most of the essay railed against the Park Service's preference for supervisors with a wide variety of experiences in numerous parks. This man wanted to stay at Grand Teton, become a supervisor, and get promoted up the ladder. His essay hit close to home for a number of employees and raised problems with the community when the local newspaper printed it as an op-ed piece.

Knowing we had done no harm to this man, Jack Neckels tried his hand at resolving the complaint. We met twice with the ranger and his personal representative, a retired businessman. Each time we thought we had the issues worked out, but each time he took the resolution home and returned opposed to all he had tentatively agreed to. Finally, when he demanded $600,000 in damages and a noncompetitive promotion, Jack threw up his hands in frustration. At the end of the meeting, the employee's own personal representative kept repeating, "I thought we were so close the last time we met. What happened? What happened?" The ranger never answered, but we had little doubt of the instigator behind his obstinacy.

Over the next two and a half years, the case continued to fester. Although the EO complaint process has definite deadlines, few of the formal complaints that went to Washington met their timetables. As a result, the tension and stress of unresolved issues ate up both the employee and his supervisor. Eventually, the employee decided his job wasn't worth the pressure and resigned, but he continued his complaint. After I left the park, Jack succumbed to pressure from the Interior Department's attorneys and settled out of court.

As the ranger's EO complaint went to Washington, my second year at Grand Teton came to an end—the hardest two years of my career. Although I had made little headway in building a team, I saw hope on the horizon. Doug and Edna moved on with promotions to other parks. Dick, Jack Peay, and Marshall accepted the government's incentive of $25,000 for their retirements. Although I was saddled with the load of five divisions without chiefs, I looked forward to building a new team.

My biggest concern, however, was a nagging feeling that Jack Neckels was unhappy with me. Although I worked longer hours than I had at LBJ, I did not feel that I used the same level of imagination and initiative in solving problems. My job did get easier over the two years, but I still found myself bogged down in personnel issues and employee problems. I did not believe I was giving Jack the managerial support he needed. Instead of acting like an assistant superintendent, I often felt that I was simply a glorified administrative assistant.

As Jack and I sat down for my performance appraisal, I leveled with him. "I know that my decision-making ability is not as good as yours and you can't trust me with park operations," I started out. "So I think it would be a good idea if I moved on and let you find someone with more operational experience, whom you can trust." Jack was astounded. He immediately contradicted all my doubts. He was giving me the highest performance evaluation possible—a rare occurrence for him. He said that he could count on the fingers of one hand the number of times that he had given that high an evaluation. Now I was speechless.

Over the next five hours we had the most remarkable conversation that I ever had with a supervisor. We were both open, candid, and appreciative. "You executed the changes I proposed, but you suffered the criticism and resistance that change brings," his evaluation read. "Moreover, you had the stamina to follow through on a number of personnel issues that others of us should have tackled earlier and that lesser people would not have succeeded in. You have been good for Grand Teton." Then he too admitted that the last three years had been the hardest of his career. For the first time in two years I did not feel a failure. The barriers of role-playing had blinded us to our emotional needs. We were two managers, both feeling besieged and overwhelmed, but neither able to own up to those needs.

When I moaned about the chronic complainers and unreachable employees that Grand Teton had bred, Jack shook his head. "I think you will find employees like that in every big natural park," he said. I was surprised and disappointed. I wanted to work with my employees to build a better park, not do it despite them. For the first time I began to have doubts about my chosen career goal—to be a big-park superintendent.

Even at the time I knew there were more good and supportive people at Grand Teton than ungrateful and demanding ones. I also knew that nearly all park managers contended with employee problems. Unfortunately for me, the negative employees overwhelmed my idealism. While I had handled such employees in the past, their sheer numbers at Grand Teton, coupled with their attitudes, played havoc with my own morale and well-being. They contrasted greatly with my employees in Alaska, Santa Fe, and LBJ, where hard work, commitment, and enthusiasm reflected love for their job.

Many of Teton's problems arose directly from the change of leadership. Jack and I brought a totally different approach to management, a style that disrupted comfortable patterns and traditional ways of doing things. Not only were new goals and directions forced on them, but intense methods of following up also ensured painful accountability. Work stopped being fun and a financial boon. Performance ratings and awards had to be earned rather than given automatically to maintain morale. Slowly we removed one "perk" after another—undocumented compensatory time, excessive use of privately owned cars, free books from the park's bookstore, eight-hour work days that included lunch, and drinking beer after work in park facilities. Perhaps worst of all, we assigned work that did not always accord with the employee's wishes. Consequently, we paid the price with plummeting morale, increased complaints, and distrustful apprehension over where the next blow would fall.

One other change that distressed many Grand Teton veterans was Jack's desire to bring in new blood. New blood helped break old patterns and powerful cliques and fostered a sense of loyalty. But new blood became an employee issue when it involved the selection of supervisors. Previous park management often chose the best worker who qualified from the park, a known quantity. As a result, there were few surprises for the employees, the status quo continued, and they could anticipate a potential promotion themselves. When Jack arrived, he turned the selection process on its head.

The mobility issue reached a frenzied peak with "The Death of a Ranger." Jack felt compelled to explain his philosophy to the staff, the community, and even his own regional office. Although he came to Grand Teton after experiencing a wide variety of positions that allowed him to see management from a number of perspectives, he did not expect everyone to move on to different parks and central offices. He stated emphatically his belief that each park needed a strong mix of long-term employees who knew the intricacies of the park and newer employees who had broad experiences and new ideas. "Mobility is a personal decision," he concluded, "and accepting the implications of the decision to move or not is the individual's responsibility." In other words, one could remain at Grand Teton for years but could not count on promotions.

While I had many employees at LBJ who had been hired locally, I did not find the same problems that arose with "homesteading" at Grand Teton. Long-term employees coupled with little change in management created complacent workplaces with tremendous resistance to change. The locals at LBJ had the same dedication to their one park that Grand Teton's home-steaders did, but because management changed every three to five years, they rolled easily with new directions. Their goal, occasionally independent of the superintendent's, was to ensure the quality of the park for the visitor and, probably more important, for Mrs. Lyndon Johnson. Thus, when I first arrived at Grand Teton, my experience with long-term employees had been positive, and I argued with Jack about his emphasis on new blood. As usual, he was right.

Resistance to change manifested itself in employee grievances and

EO complaints. Dissatisfaction with new supervisors and their different ways of conducting business sparked nearly every EO complaint I saw. As a strong feminist, I came to Grand Teton believing in the EO process. Although I had never faced blatant sexual harassment in the workplace, I knew it existed. Initially, I took each employee complaint at face value, but soon realized that each one had the same ulterior motive: get the supervisor and make him pay. In all the EO complaints I processed, not one had merit as the law had intended.

Unfortunately, the media has focused only on supervisory abuse of employees. Thus, most people are unaware of how employees abuse the EO complaint process. This abuse occurs in all parks, other agencies, and probably corporations. Most complainants claim age discrimination because, being white males, they have no other basis. Not surprisingly, I found complaints often followed performance evaluations. One employee even tried to claim a physical handicap because he had lost weight and couldn't wear a uniform properly, which didn't explain why it was unironed and sloppy and his hair uncombed.

Complaints also seemed to have become part of the application process. After a supervisor has selected a new employee for a position, an unhappy applicant over the age of forty slaps the supervisor with an age-discrimination complaint. I found it impossible to resolve EO complaints filed by people I didn't know.

Unfortunately for both managers and employees, government attorneys and administrative judges force the parties to settle out of court. Although supposedly a win-win solution where no one "loses," settlement usually means management pays some quantity of cash in exchange for the employee's dropping charges. In the eyes of anyone except the legal profession, management has lost. Consequently, the number of meritless complaints has ballooned, overwhelming the administrative processes. More important, while settlement may be perceived as the least costly alternative to the government, it undermines management's ability to manage. It also feeds the impulse of the malcontent for revenge against an unpopular but accountable supervisor.

In addition to Grand Teton's resistance to change, I observed numerous differences between large parks and smaller parks that I do not believe were unique to Grand Teton and LBJ or even to the National Park Service, but probably can be applied to corporations and universities as well. Job assignments in large parks are more prestigious, have greater profile, and attract more applicants. Usually employees in large parks have come from other large parks. Selecting officials try to find applicants who will do the best job with the least "start-up time." Thus, they often choose candidates from other big parks who have a background and experience similar to the position being advertised. The applicant from a small park may have had wider responsibility, handling many more and different assignments, but lack experience in the detailed complexity of a large park. As a result, employees from large parks gravitate to other large parks, and employees from small parks stay with small parks.

This division between small and large parks has essentially created two National Park Services, with different traditions, goals, and motivations. Most top managers have recognized that there are two National Park Services geographically—one in the East and one in the West. Few have conceded the more fundamental division: The eastern parks are mostly small and the western parks mostly large. Small-park employees feel they are part of a team. Large-park employees seldom understand or appreciate the concept of team. If they do, it is usually at the division level. Most large parks have rivalries among the divisions over funds, philosophical orientation, and workloads. These rivalries result in "us" versus "them" confrontations, antagonisms that often expand to include top management. More specialized training and experience make them less willing and able for cross-divisional training. Being less well-rounded promotes a dependence on traditional structure with an unwillingness to change or to volunteer for new assignments.

Small-park employees, on the other hand, work closely with management on a daily basis and share a common goal. Thus they are easier to build into teams, willing to help other divisions through cross-training, and receptive to new assignments. In many ways small parks reflect the idealism of the mythic old-line parks of the 1930s, before specialization and unique assignments compartmentalized employees in large parks.

Much of my adjustment to Grand Teton came from the dichotomy between large and small parks. I had expected park employees to be more or less alike regardless of the size of the park. Subsequently I learned that each has its own culture. Seldom are employees comfortable in both. A manager, moreover, cannot change a large-park culture into a small-park culture. Each has evolved to fulfill its own concept of mission. The dynamic of size is the primary determinant of that culture.

Personally, I found adapting to the large-park culture difficult and unrewarding. My job and the employees contrasted so intensely with my experiences at LBJ that I was in a state of shock for the first several months. Not only did I drop in status and authority from being the boss to being "number two," but more crucially I missed the team experience. As do all assistant superintendents, I had to "pay my dues" by handling the dirty jobs until I, too, earned the right to be the boss again. Reflecting back, I see how naive I was in moving into a large-park culture and expecting employees to respond to my overtures as enthusiastically as my smaller park had. I was totally unprepared for back-stabbers, whistle-blowers, EO complaints, and other means of petty harassment.

I was glad to have my first two years behind me. I lost my naiveté but I probably became a better manager without the rose-colored glasses. I had to admit, however, that I missed the joy that comes from working with loyal employees. Nonetheless, those two years tempered me for the issues to come.

Even though intimidated by Alaska's male-dominated bureaucratic environment, I welcomed the opportunity to work in this huge land of mountains, lakes, and glaciers. It allowed me to act out my tomboy youth as an adult. This picture was taken at Lake Clark National Park in 1978.
*Courtesy of M. Woodbridge Williams/National Park Service, Harpers Ferry Center.*

As much a maverick as his name, Zorro Bradley transferred to Alaska in the early 1970s to develop a contractual program with the University of Alaska, Fairbanks. When the Alaska Native Claims Settlement Act offered new programs, he jumped to expand knowledge of historic and archeological sites and subsistence and cultural lifeways. He patiently taught me program management, interagency cooperation, and supervisory techniques. Throughout my adjustment to the bureaucratic culture, he supported my abilities with sound counsel and a judicious sense of humor. *Courtesy of Robert Belous.*

In 1976 trapper Dave Evans walked into my office at the University of Alaska, wanting to know the history of the Nation River, a tributary of the Yukon River. Later he agreed to serve as my guide as I tried to inventory the historic sites of a proposed park called Yukon-Charley National Rivers. During our three months on the Yukon, using his canoe and nine-horsepower engine, we found more than four hundred sites. *Courtesy of Dave Evans.*

In 1980 Bob Utley retired from the President's Advisory Council on Historic Preservation and left Washington, D.C., to join me in Santa Fe, New Mexico. We purchased a passive-solar, pueblo-style house with two kiva fireplaces. After waiting seven years for the perfect opportunity to meld our two lives, Bob began researching and writing history full time, and I became the Southwest Regional Historian.

From 1980 to 1986, Bob and I were members of the Eldorado Volunteer Fire Department. I advanced to assistant chief before resigning to protest the removal of our chief. *Courtesy of Carolyn Wright.*

In May 1984 I received my doctorate in American history from the University of New Mexico. At commencement the university president honored me with a prestigious award for the best dissertation in a three-year period. The dissertation became my first book, *The Last Frontier: A History of the Yukon Basin of Canada and Alaska.*

In 1989 I chaired the fiftieth anniversary of the Southwest Regional Office Building in Santa Fe. Following my brief speech welcoming the public to the celebration, the National Park Service director, James Ridenour, announced my appointment as superintendent of Lyndon B. Johnson National Historical Park, Texas.

For most of my superintendency, Johnson City fell within the district of the highly popular congressman J. J. (Jake) Pickle. With his leadership in Congress, we acquired a beautiful abandoned hospital to rehabilitate as a visitor center and more than $6 million to rehabilitate it. Here he poses with me, his wife, Beryl, and the first lady of Texas, Rita Clements, on the far right.

When I was named assistant superintendent of Grand Teton National Park in 1992, the LBJ park staff threw a grand farewell party in the ranch show barn. Regional Director John Cook and Mrs. Johnson shared the barbeque and subsequent skits and speeches. Without the support of both, my superintendency would never have succeeded as well as it did.

Barely a month after I arrived at Grand Teton National Park in 1992, Angus Thuermer, reporter for the *Jackson Hole News,* wrote a feature story about me and took one of the few good photos of me in a uniform.
*Courtesy of Angus M. Thuermer, Jr.*

Because Superintendent Jack Neckels had purchased a home in Jackson, Bob and I had the privilege of living in Quarters No. 1, the big log superintendent's house built in 1933 by the Civilian Conservation Corps. Nestled at the base of the Teton Range, it received more snow than the visitor center, but Bob's study commanded an inspirational view of the mountains.

On August 25, 1994, I reached the summit of the Grand Teton, 13,770 feet high. A grueling summer of long hikes, practice climbs, and extended exercise workouts prepared me for the awe-inspiring experience.

Jack Neckels awarding me my twenty-year pin. I respected and loved Jack for his patience, warmth, and ability to articulate every decision logically and clearly. Day after day he talked me through one complicated issue after another, grooming me for the time I would have my own big park. When I retired instead, he cheered me for acting on the right priorities.

In 1995 President Bill Clinton, Hillary, and Chelsea vacationed for seventeen days in Jackson Hole. On the seventy-fifth anniversary of woman suffrage, the president gave a speech behind the Jackson Lake Lodge in front of the most spectacular facade of mountains in America. Afterward, he had his photograph taken with me and expressed his appreciation for all our hard work.
*Courtesy of the White House.*

During my last days at Grand Teton, I wanted a memorable photograph of my beloved mountains. Joan Anzelmo, former communications director for the National Park Service, took the picture on a sparkling clear day. I never stopped loving the mountains. *Courtesy of Joan Anzelmo.*

Although retired, I still keep current of National Park Service issues through my role on the board of directors of the Eastern National cooperating association. Through the sale of books and other interpretive materials in 132 eastern national parks and other public trusts, the nonprofit organization donates its profits to interpretive funding, publications, research, and services. *Courtesy of Eastern National.*

# Mountains

During my first eighteen months at Grand Teton, I hardly saw the mountains. The first summer was cool and damp. Most of the time, clouds hid the mountains. When they did peek out, ice and snow encased them with an occasional sunbeam reflecting off their glistening cliffs. So cold was it that mountain climbing was reserved for winter mountaineers, even during the summer. I forgot my careless boast that I would climb the Grand Teton, the park's highest peak. Instead, I dug into the personnel issues and doggedly tried to build a team.

Even during the first half of 1994, I found myself buried in paperwork. I toiled diligently through the personnel processes to recruit and hire five division chiefs, a management assistant, and a secretary for the superintendent. The spring of 1994, however, differed vastly from 1993. Warm temperatures began to melt the heavy snowfields and loosen winter's hold on the mountains. Daily, as I processed applications, the mountains stood before me brilliantly, reminding me how lucky I was.

Watching the sun move across the mountains one morning, I realized how little my job had to do with the purpose of the park. The mountains, their plants and animals, and even the visitors hardly entered my consciousness. Personnel issues had imprisoned me. No wonder I was unhappy.

I decided to follow through on my boast to climb the Grand. First, I had to get in good physical shape. Although Bob and I had faithfully exercised an hour a day since our years in Santa Fe, I was pretty sure that I needed more strenuous workouts to develop stamina and flexibility. I added ten minutes to my aerobics workout, began lifting free weights, and started stretching muscles as recommended in rock-climbing books. After the first month of this regime, I found myself worn out by the time I reached the office.

As spring rains melted the valley snow, park trails became accessible. Each day of the weekend, Bob and I explored a new trail. Although the guidebooks listed the valley trails as "easy," we found they tested our strength and endurance. The first few weeks we had many sore muscles. More discouraging to me, on hikes more than five miles long, my boots rubbed painful and debilitating blisters. Seeking the best gear for narrow feet, I invested a couple of hundred dollars in boots that fit like gloves.

Slowly our muscles shaped up, and we moved to more difficult trails—those that climbed into the mountains. These trails ascended steeply and continued longer than our legs willingly carried us. After one grueling eight-mile hike, Bob decided that he was not in training for climbing the Grand and had no desire to exhaust himself on such rigorous hikes. For me, I knew that the climb through Garnet Canyon and up to the Lower Saddle of the Grand Teton would make most trails seem easy. As a compromise, on one day of the weekend I agreed to hike a valley trail with Bob, and the other day I would push myself alone on more difficult and longer trails.

Our weekend jaunts gave us a familiarity with the park and helped us develop a repertoire of favorite hikes. Occasionally we took interpretive tours and audited the seasonal interpreters. Seldom did they recognize us until after the hike, when we introduced ourselves. The more we hiked, the more we saw park employees enjoying their proximity to 250 miles of hiking trails. Slowly the word came back to headquarters of our excursions— always with a positive accent of surprise.

The acting chief ranger, Colin Campbell, concluded that I was serious about climbing the Grand. He charged the park's best climber, Renny Jackson, with the responsibility for ensuring that I made it safely to the summit. Slight but wiry, Renny was in his early forties and married to the first woman guide to work for the park's concession, Exum Mountain Guides. I knew that Renny would accept me as a person, not as the weaker sex. Quietly he asked me what experience I had in rock climbing or mountain climbing. Embarrassed, I told him of the three mountains climbed in Outward Bound and the rappelling done during college. Diffidently, he suggested that we spend a couple of days testing my skills at what the climbers called "Exum's Rocks." Here the park's concessioner trained clients for an ascent of the Grand—usually a four-day package.

Renny made sure that we did not conflict with the Exum climbers. Then he introduced me to the technology that replaced the old Goldline slings and ropes I had used with Tucson's search-and-rescue team. Now nylon slings and harnesses cradled the pelvis more comfortably. He also demonstrated the use of hex nuts, cams, and bolts as opposed to the steel pitons that we used in Outward Bound. The biggest difference was the lightweight yet powerful synthetic multistrand ropes that replaced the old heavy hemp or nylon Goldline ropes. To protect against falling rocks or even actual falls, Renny also insisted that we wear helmets.

Although the Exum Ridge route, which we would take to the summit of the Grand, and the Owen-Spalding route for descent were at the lowest level of technical rock climbing, Renny wanted me to have the basic skills. "You never know what you might need," he said. "The weather can destroy the best-laid climbing strategies, and individual abilities also require different techniques. It is best to have a variety of skills to use as necessary."

From the top of the practice rocks, Renny showed me how to tie bowline and figure-eight knots. These two knots would be our primary focus, but he also taught me five or six others whose names I promptly forgot. Using the bowline, Renny tied into a tree to set up a belay station. Then cautiously, almost gently, he explained rappelling to me. Considering how recklessly I had rappelled during college—kicking myself off rocks and going as fast as I could—I gained new respect for Renny's safety consciousness. "Remember," he cautioned, "more people die in descent than in ascent, mostly from carelessness. Rappelling can be terribly dangerous."

After I slowly and carefully rappelled to the bottom of the rocks, I began to climb back up. Unfortunately, I had forgotten to yell the time-honored command "climbing." When Renny noticed the slackness in the rope, he got upset—I was climbing without a belay. Not only was I a woman but also his assistant superintendent, of whose skills he was completely ignorant. If I had fallen and hurt myself, he would have been held responsible. When I quickly clambered to the top, he lectured me sternly on the proper commands.

Renny tested me on two other easy pitches. Since childhood, climbing rocks had come easy. I had breezed through Outward Bound's climbing classes and threatened the nineteen-year-olds who found the experience daunting. Yet when Renny told me to slow down and enjoy the climb, I found that my instinctive climbing ability failed and intellectualizing took over. Climbing slowly was difficult and frustrating. On the other hand, I needed the various techniques Renny had taught me just in case my gut instinct failed. It was good training, but I did not enjoy the climbs as much.

One more day on the practice rocks convinced Renny that I could climb the Grand. He even allowed me to rappel a seventy-five-foot free fall. As I remembered to take it slowly and carefully, he rewarded me with a rare smile.

Renny had set the first week of August as a target date for our climb. Because Bill Swift had climbed Mount Rainier nine times, I asked him to join us. Rainier had snow and ice, but Teton had sheer granite cliffs. The contrast would be exciting for him. Already running more than two miles a day and hiking as much as I, Swift was in good shape. It hadn't occurred to me that Renny would see my invitation to Bill as added responsibility for him. When I realized my presumption, I apologized, and he gracefully accepted.

As the big day approached, I lengthened my hikes. To test my stamina, I climbed Garnet Canyon as far as the Meadows, where I lost the trail. It was a haul, but I felt that I could survive the rest of the hike to the Lower

Saddle. One of the resource managers suggested a hike to Static Peak, which was comparable to the Lower Saddle in length, difficulty, and elevation. Because my boots had rubbed a hot spot during my hike to Garnet Canyon, I made sure that blister-preventive moleskin covered my ankle. By the time I reached the summit of Static Peak, however, I feared that I had a full-fledged blister. As I took off my boot to examine my foot, I didn't notice that the sock had stuck to the moleskin. When I pulled the sock off, the moleskin came off too. Now, I had not only a blister but a bloody sore. I hobbled down the trail, kicking myself for my carelessness. I knew that I could not climb the Grand until it healed.

After months of preparation and training, I feared that I would not be able to climb the Grand in 1994. August was the last month of stable weather. I had also made plans to have my seventy-eight-year-old mother visit, hopefully after I had conquered the Grand. Bill Swift reminded me that he had a couple of commemorative occasions to attend. Time was running out.

The blister took more than a week to heal sufficiently to wear shoes. My mother came and enjoyed the mountains, the cool air, and our lifestyle. Meanwhile the weather held. Renny, Bill, and I once again set a date for the climb, August 24—the day Mother planned to leave. Because I could not hike, I worried about staying in shape. I started running up and down the two sets of stairs at our house. In some ways the stairs gave me more of a workout than hiking had.

The morning of August 24, 1994, was cool and crisp. Because Renny was not a morning person, we didn't plan to leave until nine o'clock. Bob drove my mother and me to the Lupine Meadow parking lot, the trailhead for Garnet Canyon. After he saw us off on our trek, he would take my mother to the airport. My blister had not totally healed, but Renny had advised me to try a product called Second Skin. Its cool gel covered by moleskin felt soothing to my heel. But I did not attempt to wear hiking boots. Instead I decided to hike in my Reebok walking shoes and to reserve my boots for the actual climb.

My eagerness showed—we were the first to arrive. We had to wait another fifteen minutes for Swift and his wife, Sue, who would climb with us only to the Lower Saddle, then still another fifteen minutes before Renny arrived. Meanwhile I shivered in my shorts and wanted to get started. Four recent deaths in the Tetons, three on the Grand, grimly reminded me that the climb exacted its toll from the unwary or overconfident. Just before we started up the trail, Bob excitedly took photographs of the four of us on our memorable trek.

Although I had already climbed halfway to the Lower Saddle, Renny pointed out the trail on a U.S. Geological Survey topographical map. "The route follows a well-maintained trail for half the distance," he said. "Then it ends at a huge pile of boulders the size of houses. We will scramble over these to the Meadows. Here we can refill our water bottles from the falls, before the last hard climb to the Lower Saddle—our destination for the night. We should be there by five this afternoon. Tomorrow we rise early to climb the Grand." I calculated that he had allowed eight hours to hike seven miles with a 4,800-foot elevation gain.

As we hiked, many other hikers and climbers passed us. The popular trail, ablaze with wild flowers, wove in and out of forested areas as it rose ever higher. When we reached the boulders, the trail ended. For the next hour we clambered from one granite boulder to another and from one stone cairn marking the "trail" to another. At last we reached the Meadows. Here a small meadow with a stream and grass offered relief. About twenty or thirty climbers had made camp. Although they tried to avoid walking on the fragile vegetation, their very numbers caused erosion, loss of vegetation, and sanitation dilemmas.

Beyond the Meadows the trail grew rugged. Every eight to ten steps I stopped to rest and breathe heavily. As Renny and Sue Swift ambled nearly one-fourth mile ahead, Bill Swift stayed behind with me. "You are killing yourself," he said. "Do the 'rest step.' You place one foot in front of you, lean forward with your weight, resting the rear foot. Then move it forward in the same manner. This way you move continuously without tiring." It worked. After that, I made reasonably good time but still couldn't keep pace with Renny and Sue.

When we refilled our water bottles at the falls, Sue came up to me as

I rested in the shade of a huge rock. "I know how important this climb is for you," she said. "Since I am carrying only a small daypack, I would be happy to lighten your load. That is, if it wouldn't insult you to have help." Gratefully I handed over my heavy hiking boots and a few other items. Then off we went again.

Finally we reached the Moraine. The receding glacier, which formed the Moraine, first dropped the huge granite boulders that we had crawled over prior to the Meadows. Then smaller and smaller stones fell as the glacier melted until only gravel or glacial moraine remained. The Moraine consisted of a series of fairly level gravel benches. These too sprouted tents everywhere. The mountain wind tore at our unprotected legs and arms. In the shelter of a boulder we pulled on our Polarguard pants and jacket. Instantly I warmed up twenty degrees. I found the new synthetic fabric as remarkable as everyone claimed.

Finally, as the day neared its end, we straggled into our camp at the Lower Saddle. The hike had been as hard as I had expected. Although my aging muscles and bones complained, they had not failed me. Unlike all other climbers except Exum clients, we had the luxury of a hut with a board floor, table, and bunks. Every few days the Jenny Lake rangers rotated shifts at the Lower Saddle. Here they monitored use, answered questions, and provided immediate emergency assistance. We shared the hut with the two rangers on duty. After resting a bit, Sue Swift left to return home by dark.

Following a spaghetti supper, carried and cooked by Renny, we relaxed on the step of the hut. Slowly the skies changed color and cast their haunting aspen glow of pinks and purples over the mountains. Watching the changing colors, I realized how Teton mountaineering could get under one's skin.

The next morning we left the hut at four o'clock. We climbed past the Black Dike along the Needle to the Eye of the Needle. Here, we roped up as we squeezed through a tunnel under a huge boulder. Renny warned that the ledge beyond was often slippery and dangerous. Safely over that hurdle, we confronted Wall Street—the first frightening chasm.

We followed the Wall Street ledge until it stopped precipitously at a twenty-foot gap. In climbers' lingo, the "exposure" dropped five thousand feet and commanded one of the best views of the climb—straight down. Renny attached a rope to a permanent anchor. "We put these here to limit the number of pitons hammered in and removed," he informed us. "It minimizes erosion." Without much more fuss, he belayed us across the gap. If we slipped while traversing the gap, he and the belay rope would catch us before we fell to our deaths. Wall Street tested both our climbing skill and our stomach for heights. It was exhilarating. In 1931 Glenn Exum, the first to climb this route, jumped the gap. I couldn't imagine such a frightening leap.

From there, we moved at a steady pace, passing several parties. Each pitch had permanent belay anchors and colorful and graphic names: Golden Stairs, Wind Tunnel, and Open Book. Some of the more experienced climbers disdained ropes, helmets, or even established routes. They passed us quickly in seemingly effortless movements. Only one pitch stumped me. Called Friction Pitch, it afforded no handholds or toeholds. It seemed impossible, yet no one had marred the climb with assistive devices such as pitons or bolts. I made it, but I still don't know how.

As we neared the top, the wind picked up. The Open Book pitch, shaded by overhanging rocks, was so cold and windy that I had to stop twice to warm my hands before continuing. By this time, I was getting tired and winded. The Final Problem was almost one too many. Bill and I were fatigued but determined.

The last hundred yards to the Summit proved almost anticlimactic. It required no last burst of strength or endurance. It just took extra deep gasps for breath as the air had thinned noticeably. Our stay on the top of the Grand, at 13,770 feet, lasted only twenty minutes, but they were thrilling and rewarding minutes. We could see for miles and we had succeeded. Renny radioed park dispatch: "I'm calling from the Grand's summit. I have a couple of desk jockeys here." With that announcement, monitored on receivers all over the park, everyone knew we had made it.

The descent along the Owen-Spalding route, despite a 125-foot free-fall rappel, was uneventful. Nonetheless, Renny took extra care. He reminded us again that more falls occur on the descent than on the ascent. The route included many areas of loose rocks where carelessness could bring instant death or serious injury. I could also see multiple trails winding off the main one, causing more erosion than one single trail and bewilderment to a novice climber. At the Lower Saddle hut, Bill Swift hurried on down to handle a special event, but I stayed another day to observe visitor use and ranger activities.

Because of increasing use, sanitation in the mountains continued to be a problem. A few years earlier, our Public Health sanitarian had found the human bacteria *E. coli* in the natural springs that everyone used for drinking and cooking. To minimize contamination, the park built a toilet for climbers' use. First, self-composting toilets were tried, but the cold temperatures limited the growth of composting bacteria. Then the rangers backpacked bags of human waste down Garnet Canyon Trail, but the quantity of waste and distastefulness of the experience ruled it out. Even pack mules proved unsuccessful because they could only travel half the trail before boulders blocked the way. Finally the park resorted to flying waste out by helicopter. Because most of Garnet Canyon Trail and all of the Lower Saddle lie within proposed wilderness, helicopters on anything but life-threatening missions were frowned on. When I saw that more than a hundred climbers a day used the outdoor toilet, I knew that we could not retreat to a latrine system. Within existing technology, there seemed no solution except the helicopter. To minimize the use of helicopters, during the summer of 2002 Grand Teton rangers asked climbers to bag and pack out their solid waste—a practice already used in Grand Canyon, Zion, and Mount Rainer national parks.

Next morning I headed down on my own. I nursed three blisters, aching muscles, and scraped fingertips. As I limped into Lupine Meadows parking lot, Bob met me. He was as thrilled as I was tired. Dispatch had called him the previous day with news of our successful ascent and had relieved his anxieties. After showering, I called my mother and told her I had returned without injury. She had worried much more than Bob and said, "I still can't understand why you wanted to climb that mountain in the first place."

In many ways climbing the Grand was the high point of my Teton career. For one thing, I had succeeded at a difficult task. I had no comparable feeling of achievement in handling employee problems. For another, everyone in the park, the Jackson community, and the National Park Service appreciated my dedication and success. Even the most skeptical ranger admitted grudging respect for my efforts. But mostly my intangible feelings of self-esteem, coupled with my love for the mountains, raised the climbing experience above all others. For the first time since I had moved to Teton, I was happy.

Mountain climbing is probably Grand Teton's most glamorous recreation. In 1994 nearly 70 percent of the climbers who attempted to climb the Grand succeeded. But as the mountains attracted more and more climbers, the human toll grew alarmingly. First, fewer of the climbers were as well trained as in previous years. More started coming from sport-climbing backgrounds, which include climbing gyms and climbing rocks near urban areas. They were not trained for mountains, high altitude, long hikes, or severe environmental conditions. In addition, rock falls and snowfields, coupled with difficult-to-follow routes, had caused greater numbers of accidents and fatalities. An average of four people died on the mountains each year. Some years the fatality rate rose to six or seven.

Another price for inexperienced climbers is the cost of rescue. The average cost during the early 1990s was $18,000. These rescues, approximately ten per year, usually required expensive helicopter time. The cost for the rescue is not paid by the rescued climber, but by the National Park Service. In addition, the cost of the rescue does not include the hundreds of hours spent in training for that rescue. Again the National Park Service, most specifically the park, bears the brunt of helicopter costs. Consequently, the search-and-rescue program was the most expensive single item in Grand Teton's budget. At Denali National Park in Alaska, the mountaineering program for 1998 soared to a million dollars.

At Mount Rainier and Denali national parks, managers have reviewed ways to recover rescue costs. They explored requiring climbers to post bonds or carry insurance. In 1995 Mount Rainier started charging $15 per climber while Denali charged $150, which contributed to the training costs of the rangers but not to recovery costs of rescues. Managers fear that the less experienced climbers may perceive the fee as "rescue insurance," which many European countries have.

The climbing community, on the other hand, has resisted bonds, insurance, and fees. Most climbers have little disposable income, move from one climbing area to another, and climb on a shoestring. They say that they climb at their own risk and will find their own way out of any predicament. Some even believe that search-and-rescue programs foster a false sense of security. Yet both managers and climbers recognize the riskiness of the activity and seek solutions to the dilemma.

For perspective, in 2001 the Park Service spent three million dollars on 3,619 search-and-rescue incidents. Only 202 involved climbers, but 1,270 applied to hikers, 780 to swimmers, and 495 to boaters. Although the cost and drama of rescues seem high, the cost per visitor is only about a penny.

# Fire

The hot, dry weather that allowed my climb of the Grand began to raise concerns among firefighters. Tall, thick grass from many spring rains had cured to dry tinder. Dry lightning filled the sky each afternoon, and wildland fire crews increased their patrols. With each small strike, anxiety intensified.

The weather pattern for 1994 resembled that of 1988—the year Yellowstone burned. In 1988 heavy spring rains brought lush growth to the meadows and hills. Then the rains stopped, and hot summer winds dried out the woodlands. Then dry lightning sparked small fires. In 1988, however, the firefighters put out only those fires that endangered developed areas, such as around Old Faithful, Mammoth, and Grant Village. Following the National Park Service's fire policy at that time, they allowed small fires in wilderness areas to burn. Fire ecologists preached that small fires burned off the underbrush without creating so much heat that it killed large trees or sterilized the soil. A series of small fires improved the ecosystem by adding nutrients back to the soil, allowing new species of plants to grow and creating a variety of habitats for wildlife.

Unfortunately, the summer of 1988 was hotter and drier than fire managers had realized. The small fires boomed into infernos in the course of a few days. What had been controllable became threats to everything in their way. The few fires multiplied as lightning, without accompanying rain, continued to strike. Immediately the park tried to suppress the flames, calling aircraft to drop fire retardant and helicopters to dump water. High, hot winds simply pushed the flames, sparks, and embers around and over the retardant. What had been quenched with water dried quickly and burned fiercely.

Following the fires in the nightly news from Santa Fe, I watched in horror as the "mother park" burned. One of our best superintendents, Bob Barbee, handled the media and the politicians better than anyone, but he was besieged. Everyone found fault with everything the park did. Newspapers called him "Barbee-cue Bob," and politicians wanted him charged with arson. Even sister agencies fought among themselves. The Forest Service blamed the Park Service for not fighting the fires sooner, and the Park Service decried the heavy-handed methods of the Forest Service. Nothing that anyone did seemed to make a difference. The fires appeared unstoppable, and they burned throughout the Yellowstone ecosystem. Even Grand Teton had more than forty strikes that summer.

Despite 25,000 firefighters and 117 aircraft, the fires raged. Firefighters came from around the nation. Although other areas of the West faced the same conditions, Yellowstone became a national priority. In a desperate last-ditch effort, President Ronald Reagan sent in the U.S. Army. Although unskilled in firefighting, they offered relief to the exhausted and numbed professionals. Even the huge numbers on the fire line made no difference to the relentless fires.

Fires approached Old Faithful Inn, a national historic landmark and icon of rustic architecture. Only vast quantities of water, backlit fires, thousands of firefighters, and a lucky shift in wind direction saved the old hotel. The park evacuated visitors from one area after another, but at no time was the entire park closed.

Meanwhile an astonished nation watched its favorite park burn. Television caught the roar of the fire and the fears of the people. Newspapers examined the "Let It Burn" policy, excoriating Bob Barbee and his staff. Local communities complained of smoke and loss of business. Then, as fires lapped at the edge of towns, anger turned to panic. Nothing suppressed the fires. If firefighters contained one area, another became worse. Thousands of acres burned and still the fires ravaged park, forest, community, and private home. Estimates of burned area soared to more than a million acres.

Finally, in late September, rains assisted the weary firefighters. But not until the first snows fell did the nation breathe freely. Slowly the firefighters withdrew from the fire lines. The army left first, then the special teams. By late October, as snow deepened, even park employees returned to their offices. In the end, the fire cost nearly $120 million, required more than 25,000 firefighters, used ten million gallons of water, and burned nearly half of Yellowstone National Park.

The fires of 1988 created a legacy that everyone in the National Park Service lived with. Misinformation, hyperbole, and distortion colored a disastrous situation and made it one of flawed principles, mismanagement, and bad judgment. Instead of seeing Bob Barbee as a courageous and conscientious superintendent, the public blamed him for the cataclysm. Few knew enough to comprehend the complexities, but everyone had opinions. Fires were bad and should be suppressed. The National Park Service became the scapegoat for the summer's catastrophes.

Meanwhile, Yellowstone's political pressure reverberated throughout the Service. Sarcasm ridiculed basic ecological principles. The concept of natural fire became "Let it burn"—a political inaccuracy impossible to defend. Reason disappeared as politicians played to constituents, and local communities complained of lost revenues despite millions of dollars flooding the area from fire programs.

In those emotionally heightened days, I tried to explain the value of fire to my environmentalist mother. She could not accept the loss of all the beautiful trees as a valid principle. "It may take a hundred years for Yellowstone to be as spectacular as it was. It is not fair to those who were not lucky enough to see it before the fires," she argued. "And what about all the animals without homes?" I tried to clarify how fire returned nutrients to the soil, varied the habitat so other species of animals had homes, and reduced the fuel load. She never accepted my argument.

My mother and the public at large had been effectively brainwashed by one of the most compelling programs any government agency ever initiated. Just after the Second World War the U.S. Forest Service created the graphic image of Smokey the Bear (ironically in a National Park Service ranger hat). He instilled in adults as well as children beliefs such as "Only YOU can prevent forest fires" and "Stomp out forest fires." Forest fires were bad—they burned trees and killed animals; sometimes they burned homes and killed people.

Nevertheless, by putting out small fires, the fuel load within the forest increased. With each year the grass grew thicker, brush got heavier, and dead or fallen logs multiplied. Then, during a hot, dry summer, a lightning strike would cause a fire that humans couldn't squash.

Until the 1960s and the Leopold Report, the National Park Service accepted the Forest Service dictum. Slowly, with the increase in the number of scientists, ecology became better understood. The value of fire, especially controlled fires, became preferred doctrine. Top management also recognized that the Forest Service, unlike the Park Service, had a monetary reason to fight fires. The timber saved from fire could be sold to lumber companies. More fires meant less income.

During August 1994, I looked at the baking landscape with worried eyes. Everywhere I hiked, I saw thousands of fallen lodgepole pines and thick underbrush. The sagebrush alone was nearly fifty years old, and some grew as high as my chest. In the two years I had been there, we had tried several controlled fires, now called prescribed fires, ones that we specifically set to eliminate dangerous deadfall and aging sagebrush. Bad weather prevented us from burning as much as we had hoped.

Then one Sunday afternoon in late August, only a few days after my climb (I was still nursing my blisters), the feared lightning strike came— not in a forest but in the sagebrush. When it struck, I felt it, saw it, and heard it. From our house we could see across the sagebrush plain to Mormon Row, a series of historic houses dating from the 1920s. Here Bob and I saw the flash that exploded the sagebrush into fire.

One of the park's fire crews, patrolling only a couple of miles away, rushed to the scene. The fire blazed brightly only half a mile from Mormon Row Road. Although first-year firefighters, they set out to drive into the high brush and head off the fire. "Wait," radioed an older, more experienced supervisor. "Don't drive out into the sagebrush. Fight it from the road until I get help." The high winds quickly took the flames beyond the crew's small pickup. Meanwhile, from our home nearly three miles away, we saw the fire flare several stories high. I knew this was the fire of the summer.

Even before dispatch called me, I called Jack Neckels. He, like Bob Barbee, would be on the hot seat. He needed to know about the fire before the press called him. "Well, we've been expecting this," he said. "I'm comfortable with you and Colin handling it." From a regional office in 1988, he had supported Bob Barbee in the same way—morally, physically, and emotionally.

Several times over the afternoon and evening I thought we had the fire under control. Then new winds would fan the embers and away it would go. It moved fast, several acres per hour. Finally, by nine that night the winds died, and the crews got the fire under control. Several fire crews remained to clean up and put out hot spots.

At dawn the next morning, I drove out to spend some time with the weary crews. Covered with soot and sweat, they preferred eating to talking. The fire had been frightening, but they had beaten it. The toll included a couple of hundred charred acres and several burned historic cabins. I drove out along the edge and talked with a crew putting out hot spots. They stated how sorry they felt about losing the old Pfeiffer Homestead, but the fire had moved too fast to do anything but chase it. I told them that I was relieved to have lost so little. I saw a couple of places where the fire had even jumped the paved road. There seemed a lot of blackened earth, but it could have been much worse. After seeing most of the fire scene by road, I returned to the office.

By nine o'clock the winds began again. Jack and I turned on the park radio and learned that the fire had blown up, even worse than before. The park called all available units from town, county, and national forest. Still the winds got higher. Colin called in air support to drop flame retardant on the northern edge of the fire. The fire just moved around it. It burned the power poles carrying electricity to the northern half of the county. Still it moved on.

Private homes in the woods beyond the sagebrush stood in its path. Colin sent firefighters to set backfires to protect them. A shift of the wind turned the fire on them. Only a few feet of burned earth saved them. Encircled by flames, the firefighters could not be rescued. Jack and I could not sit still any longer. Into the field we went, aware that our presence would add pressure to Colin and his fire crews.

Winds howled at more than forty miles per hour. They swirled and twirled, and we never knew which way they would push the fire. Nearly the entire road crew ran their bulldozers, front-end loaders, and other heavy equipment in front of the flames, trying to create a firebreak. Time and again the wind simply blew embers across the break or circled around behind the equipment. Concerned for their safety, Colin pulled them out.

With no end in sight, Colin yelled to us above the roar of the winds and the flames, "I'm going to call a Type I Team. Our crews are worn out, we've exhausted our resources, and we may lose more property and even lives if I don't." Firefighting teams come from various federal agencies all over the United States. Once called, the team takes over the fire; local management signs a delegation of authority to the team. Because of the loss of historic structures and potential loss of private homes, we would receive a Type I Incident Management Team of more than five hundred firefighters, due to arrive within the next two days.

Meanwhile, we decided to use our largest campground, Cottonwood, for the team and asked all visitors to leave. Before the end of the day, the Forest Service sent several large trailers to serve as team offices. A large trailer outfitted with showers came from Montana. The shortest and fastest route was through Yellowstone. Because Yellowstone did not allow tractor-trailers, we had to obtain special dispensation. We rented school buses to meet each plane and bring in the firefighters. Our procurement specialists hustled to meet demands for food, radios, supplies, and equipment.

That night the fire burned on. It turned from burning northeast to erupt and blow toward the southeast, racing across Brush Creek and moving toward Teton Science School, a nonprofit summer environmental education school for children ages eight to eighteen. As a precaution, the park evacuated the children and instructors. Swirling winds prevented backfires. Instead, a rocky ridge overlooking the school served as anchor for a fire line. Here all the resources available struggled to hold the fire. By midnight they knew they had won. Nonetheless, the fire came within yards of the school.

Jack and I stayed at the command center until 10:30 that night. From my bedroom window I watched the fire burn and burn. Throughout a sleepless night I brooded. Jack and I had planned to travel the next day to Yellowstone for Bob Barbee's farewell party—he was moving to Alaska as regional director. While I liked and admired Bob, I believed that my job was at the park, even though the fire would be in the hands of the Type I Team. Early the next morning I called Jack and told him to pass on my regrets to Bob. I could tell that Jack, too, was torn. Bob Barbee was one of his best friends, and he needed to be there. He also wanted to reinforce his confidence in Colin, who was new to the job of chief ranger, by not being underfoot or second-guessing him.

That morning I attended a management briefing on the fire. Exhausted representatives from the city, county, and national forest could hardly talk. Most had battled to save the Teton Science School and then fought rear-guard fires all night. Still the fire raged on. Now it burned largely to the east of the park in the Bridger-Teton National Forest, but hot spots still glowed in the sagebrush. We discussed several tactics, including bulldozing a firebreak around the northern edge of the sagebrush. The resource-management staff hated to see that much resource damage unless the fire reignited to the north. The last thing I wanted, however, was the fire to move back into the fast-burning sagebrush. I could live with a few scars if they stopped the fire.

Colin said he expected the leadership of the Type I Team for a noon briefing at the Kelly School, not far from Cottonwood Campground. Their plane arrived late, but I was impressed with the professionalism of the group. The incident commander, a man in his late fifties with many fires behind him, came from the Bureau of Indian Affairs in southern Arizona. His leadership staff came from several agencies, including the National Park Service.

Because the fire burned in both the park and the forest, we decided to have a Dual-Agency Delegation of Authority. The Bridger-Teton forest supervisor had recently retired, so Deputy Supervisor Ben Worthington signed for the forest, as I did for the park. Coincidentally, in January 1993, Ben and I together had attended a course on fire management for administrators. There we learned how a Type I team should work with agency officials. In addition, the fire coordinators from our agencies worked exceptionally well together. Bureaucratically, we moved as one coordinated unit with no egos requiring stroking.

As quickly as the firefighters arrived, the incident commander sent them out on the lines to relieve the fatigued locals. Meanwhile his planners and logistics experts worked out fire plans and needs. At the evening briefing, I was astonished at how much they had done. The incident commander even had an estimated cost—two million dollars. "That is shocking!" I choked. "We've got to do it for less." He responded that it depended on how much air support and helicopters we needed and whether the winds eased or not.

Twice a day for a week, Ben and I attended briefings. With five hundred firefighters and decreasing winds, the fire was largely out. But the huge camp and how it operated fascinated me. The crews rotated through three shifts. It seemed that the cooks were constantly cooking, and some crew was always eating. The shower trailer proved the most popular of all. Regarded as a luxury and limited to only the largest fires, showers helped morale more than all the pep talks of management.

I felt I needed to show my appreciation for the team's presence. They had all given up their jobs to come and help us. I ate several meals with them, circulated among them, and attended some evening programs. The incident commander admitted that he had never worked with a woman administrator before and found the experience enjoyable.

The closeout was a lovefest. No one had any complaint. There had been no accidents or injuries—unusual for a fire and camp of this size. The costs came in considerably lower than two million. The final total was just over a million dollars. Ben and I expressed our appreciation for how well everyone had worked together. The incident commander remarked that in all the fires he had fought, he had never seen two agencies get along better. He credited Ben and me with setting the example. Maybe because we were both deputies and by definition not allowed egos, we didn't know anything different.

Fighting the fire was only half the battle. The community, which typically split on any issue, proved as big a problem. Many people owned radio scanners and listened to park and sheriff radio traffic all day. The day lightning struck the sagebrush on Mormon Row, a scanner addict heard the fire supervisor say, "Don't drive out into the sagebrush. Fight it from the road until I get help." He assumed that it was the Yellowstone fires all over again, that the supervisor did not want to harm the precious sagebrush—"the resource." He stirred up his friends, and they got the newspapers involved.

A reporter called to get my side of the story. I told him that the primary reason was safety. The firefighters were inexperienced. They drove a simple four-wheel-drive pickup inappropriate for sagebrush as high as that on Mormon Row. The supervisor feared that in attempting to wheel around the fire, they would overturn the truck and wind up in the path of the fire. Lives were more important than a few acres of sagebrush.

Local armchair firefighters hooted at my explanation. They continued to complain that the Park Service didn't want to fight fire—just like Yellowstone in 1988. They praised the other firefighters but labeled the park scared to fight fire. For more than a week they belittled the park's efforts and claimed we worried too much about the park's natural resources. "There is nothing valuable about sagebrush," one man said. "Hell, I burn it, drive over it, and try to get rid of it every chance I get." Few accepted the safety concerns for an inexperienced crew.

Another letter writer claimed he had gone out to Mormon Row on the morning following the start of the fire: "The park thought it had the fire out and didn't even bother to keep a fire crew patrolling the perimeter." Well, I had been out there that morning too, and I knew we had crews patrolling the perimeters. I saw them and talked with them.

These overblown accounts upset one business owner. He faxed a handwritten letter to Interior Secretary Bruce Babbitt, blasting the park for mismanaging the fire. "Because of their incompetency the American people lost valuable and beloved historic structures," he charged. "Somebody needs to investigate this travesty."

Colin told me that the interagency fire professionals based in Boise, Idaho, always conducted performance audits on large fires. "Everyone can learn from fresh eyes reviewing what happened," he said. "The high cost of fires demands accountability, but it also teaches us how to be better fire managers. In any event, I think our actions can stand up to any objective scrutiny."

The Tuesday following the fire, I attended the Jackson Hole Rotary Club. After lunch and before the scheduled speaker, the club allowed any member to speak on any subject at the cost of one dollar. The club used the money for charitable projects. "I missed Rotary for the last two weeks," I said, paying two dollars. "The first week I climbed the Grand. Last week I was with my staff and that of the city, county, and national forest fighting a fire that burned 2,200 acres. Despite the Monday-morning quarterbacks, I want to say how proud I am of all the firefighters. No lives were lost. No homes were burned. To ensure that we did our best, I have requested an independent, interagency review of our actions."

Afterward, several members came up and thanked me for my comments. They had heard the gossip and thought we had mismanaged the fire again. But my words made sense and put things into perspective—no lives were lost and no homes were burned. Those were the things that mattered.

A couple of months later the interagency team from Boise arrived for the performance audit. I asked them to pay particular attention to our handling of the initial attack. Were we overly cautious? Did we have the proper equipment? Were our crews adequately trained? The audit concluded that we handled the fire appropriately. Other fire supervisors would have made the same call, given the crew's level of experience and the type of equipment. We all felt vindicated.

Of course I released the results to the media. But even an independent investigation did not silence the naysayers. For several months after the fire, periodic criticism appeared in the newspapers. Several people insisted that we wanted the fire to burn and refused to fight it.

We even received a letter from the state historic preservation officer lamenting the loss of Pfeiffer Homestead. Because the park and the state had disagreed over its significance, the letter implied that we had deliberately allowed the structures to burn. I remembered the regret the fire crew had expressed the morning after the fire had started and realized again how unfair and ignorant people could be.

The next spring the value of fire became apparent to everyone. The former sagebrush flat flourished with phenomenal flowers, grasses, sedges, and other nutritional browse. Wildlife of all kinds found new homes in the burned area. Bison in particular had roamed throughout the park. Now in 1995 they spent nearly the entire summer among the tall grass. Wild flower enthusiasts almost outnumbered the bison. Nowhere else could more varieties or greater quantities be found. For the next several years the Mormon Row burn supported greater numbers and diversities of species than ever before. The naysayers finally held their peace.

Yellowstone's recovery from the fires of 1988 was not as quickly recognized. But within eight years new forests rose among the charred stumps of the lodgepole pines. Animals of all kinds enjoyed the diverse habitat. Scientists flooded the park to study the effects of fire. Even areas sterilized with fires above four thousand degrees had knee-high Douglas firs and a myriad of wild flowers. Contrary to the practice after other forest fires, no trees or seeds were planted. Nature had grown a better forest than millions in recovery money could have done. As the media and politicians watched the remarkable greening of Yellowstone, they stood amazed and even somewhat humbled.

The National Park Service used the regrowth of Yellowstone to educate the public on the values of fire. But the fires of Yellowstone also educated the Park Service. Fire managers learned to plan for future fires with criteria that considered fuel load, temperatures, humidity, rainfall, and wind direction. Previously, parks were simply divided into zones where fires were suppressed or allowed to burn, depending on the level of development.

Because of the lessons of Yellowstone, we developed comprehensive fire-management plans. Under these plans, the conditions of August 1994 required instant suppression, especially the Mormon Row fire, because it was in a zone of historic structures. Yet we also suffered from the political fallout of the Yellowstone fires. Our prescribed burns, those that we set ourselves, were too carefully timed, too cautious, too small, and thus ineffective. Controlled natural fires were kept small and burned only small areas far removed from human activity. By 1996 I firmly believed that Grand Teton had to become more aggressive in its prescribed and controlled fires, or it would suffer the fate of Yellowstone.

Then, in October 1999, a small controlled natural fire, carefully watched for six weeks, flared up. Burning rapidly through the backcountry, it hit the highly popular String Lake picnic and hiking area. Without pausing, it jumped the lake and burned toward Jenny Lake Lodge, an elite concession on one of the most beautiful small lakes in Grand Teton National Park. Fortunately, two years previously Colin Campbell had concentrated his fire-management crew on thinning the trees and removing the brush and deadfall from around the lodge. This mechanical clearing slowed the fire and allowed the fire crews to suppress it before it harmed the lodge.

As I followed the flames, I realized how fickle fire could be. Grand Teton's fire crew had watched the smoldering fire for weeks as it conformed to "prescription." Then, without warning, it roared into a wildfire that demanded suppression. Because the park crew had used an expensive alternative to prescribed fire, mechanical thinning, they stopped the fire before it became catastrophic. I now realized that my concepts of caution versus aggression were irrelevant.

Another more dramatic example of the unpredictable nature of fire occurred in May 2000. Bandelier National Monument, located among the forests, ridges, and valleys of north-central New Mexico, had suppressed lightning-caused fires since the late 1800s. As a result, the park contained huge quantities of tall grass, ponderosa pine, mixed conifer, and deadfall consisting of leaves, needles, branches, and logs. In 1993, in a thousand-acre area about five air miles from the city of Los Alamos and its associated nuclear laboratory, the park had attempted to burn the hazardous fuels. Because of inherent moisture among the fuels and insufficient wind, the fire did not burn well.

Seven years later the park tried again. A prescribed-fire plan, completed on April 19, 2000, defined the area to be burned; described the pattern and phases for the burn; included records of prevailing winds and precipitation; completed a complex computer model that evaluated moisture content of the fuels, relative humidity, air temperature, and wind speed; and assessed the complexity of the burn with a worksheet that determined the number, experience, and training levels for the fire crew and burn boss. Then, before ignition could occur, three snowstorms swept through the area, dumping more than sixteen inches of snow on the site. The wet conditions and excessive winds forced postponement of the burn.

The superintendent, Roy Weaver, was a thirty-three-year veteran of the National Park Service. He had served in numerous national parks, including as superintendent at Edison and Nez Perce national historical areas. Since 1990 he had been at Bandelier. I knew him when I was regional historian and he was struggling to slow the erosion of the park's prehistoric pueblos. When I became a fellow superintendent, we often shared staff and commiserated on budget shortfalls. During his ten years at Bandelier he won several awards. One was the coveted "Superintendent of the Year Award for Natural Resource Stewardship." His sensitivity and concern for park resources made him a strong contender for that award and others each year. He was a kind, caring, thoughtful manager, unafraid to tackle difficult issues. I liked him very much.

Following a positive weather forecast on May 3, 2000, Roy approved the prescribed burn for the next day. When the burn boss notified the Santa Fe Zone dispatcher of the prescribed burn, however, the dispatcher expressed concerns about giving mixed messages to the public. Apparently because conditions were dry and windy, the adjoining national forests had suspended prescribed-fire activities and were even fighting wildfires, yet Bandelier was proceeding with a prescribed burn. Nonetheless, the burn boss notified appropriate agencies and individuals of the prescribed burn; fire policy did not require concurrence, only notification.

At 7:30 P.M. on May 4, the prescribed burn began. The test fire showed that the fire behavior fell within expected parameters, allowing the burn to continue. During the early morning hours, the burn boss sent part of his fire crew down the mountain to get some sleep. Meanwhile, he tried to order additional crew and a helicopter to give the park staff relief. A misunderstanding occurred between the Santa Fe Zone dispatcher and the burn boss, and the extra resources were not ordered and did not arrive for nearly ten hours. As a result, the Bandelier crew worked nearly a thirty-five-hour shift.

Just as the additional crew arrived, an unexpected wind arose and the fire flared. By noon on May 5, the wind and heat had become so intense that flames leaped into the forest canopy, causing a raging crown fire that jumped from tree to tree. The burn boss declared it a wildland fire—known as the Cerro Grande fire.

During the next two days, fire crews battled the flames. Still the winds increased. Roy, with his peers from other agencies, decided to close highways and begin evacuations of nearby housing areas. Backfires set to protect Los Alamos National Laboratory and the town of Los Alamos suddenly blew out of control and tore toward the town. An hour later, the multiple agencies involved called for a Type I Incident Management Team with more than 1,200 firefighters.

From May 8 to May 18 the fire, fed by winds over fifty miles an hour, roared through nearly 50,000 acres. It engulfed Los Alamos, forced the evacuation of 25,000 people, eventually destroyed 235 structures or 405 housing units, and cost more than a billion dollars in damages. Fortunately it caused little damage to the national laboratory, where nuclear weapons are stored, and no lives were lost. Nonetheless, firefighters reported flames and wind spewing burning chunks of wood thousands of feet into the air and more than a mile distant, starting new fires.

Once again the press, Congress, and the public vilified the National Park Service in general and Roy Weaver in particular. The new regional director, who had succeeded John Cook, suspended Roy. Public-relations experts within the Interior Department struggled to provide perspective on prescribed fires. They pointed out that in the last twenty years the National Park Service had set 3,783 prescribed fires and had only 38 escapes, or less than 1 percent. To respond to congressional demands for accountability, Interior Secretary Bruce Babbitt ordered an immediate investigation.

While the fires burned, the investigative team worked around the clock. Its forty-one members included representatives from four federal departments, six different agencies, three county governments, and two Indian pueblos. Within a week the team delivered its conclusions to Secretary Babbitt. While the Interior Department and the National Park Service accepted responsibility for the disaster, the team described in excruciating detail all of Bandelier officials' mistakes, poor judgment, inadequate planning, lax oversight, and bad decisions.

On May 18, at a press conference, Secretary Babbitt read portions of the investigative report: "This prescribed fire was based upon a flawed plan and required fire management policies were not followed." Planners miscalculated the complexity of the project, and managers approved the plan without scrutinizing it carefully. "In all decision-making," Babbitt added, "the higher up you go, the more tendency there is for busy supervisory personnel with many other responsibilities to simply rubber-stamp decisions that are basically made by technical people at the field level."

The day after Babbitt's press conference, I downloaded the document from the Internet. The report was devastating to Roy and the park's fire program, but claimed that the Federal Wildland Fire Policy (completed in 1995 in response to the Yellowstone fires) was sound. My heart ached for Roy. Too often, at LBJ and Grand Teton, I followed my staff's recommendation without carefully assessing the situation. Jack hammered into me the need to ask questions, keep a distant perspective, and independently work to a final decision. If it hadn't been for Jack's caution, I too would have "rubber-stamped" numerous fire plans.

A month later Roy retired nearly a year earlier than he had planned. In an interview, he claimed that he had not rubber-stamped the fire plan, but had carefully reviewed it not once, but seven different times. Moreover, he stood by his decision to burn. The conditions were right but high winds hit the fire unexpectedly and whipped it out of control. "I think we did everything right," he reiterated, "It was just unfortunate." Surprisingly, he said that he had received nearly two hundred encouraging cards, letters, and email messages from people in the Los Alamos community, some saying that the fire was inevitable one way or another. The community support helped him through a tragic year that included the death of his only child and his wife's health problems as well as the catastrophic fire. Roy admitted that the Park Service had a board of inquiry determining whether disciplinary action was warranted.

On February 26, 2001, the board of inquiry made its report to much less fanfare than that which had greeted the investigative team. The board of inquiry contrasted greatly with the initial investigation. Instead of forty-one committee members, the board had six members plus an attorney from Interior's Office of the Solicitor. While the investigative team reported in one week, the board interviewed twenty-six people, sifted through 1,600 pages of transcript, reviewed the investigative report and Bandelier's fire plans, compared actions to specific policies and standards, and spent seven months thoroughly analyzing the data and writing the report.

Although the board carefully and diplomatically couched its language, it concluded that the investigative team had worked too fast, embraced many factual errors, and inappropriately measured performance against policy requirements not yet adopted. In short, the board refuted nearly every damning detail of the first report. Roy and his staff had been sacrificial scapegoats on the altar of public opinion and congressional outrage.

Both the investigative team and the board agreed that Bandelier's staff had underestimated the complexity of the burn. In fact, the worksheet used the wrong numeric values (that is, 1, 2, 3 instead of 1, 3, 5) to rate the fire as low complexity, instead of high when the correct values were used. The investigative team had blamed the burn boss and demonstrated that he would not have had the experience required to manage the burn if the complexity rating had been calculated properly. The board, however, dug more deeply into the issue and discovered that the complexity form posted on the National Park Service's Internet website had the wrong values. Moreover, whereas the team believed that the wrong complexity rating led to insufficient personnel and inadequate backup resources, the board showed that no policy requirement tied staffing to complexity level. In short, Bandelier's staff proved less at fault than the failure of the National Park Service and other federal agencies to standardize complexity-rating systems.

In summary, the board exonerated Roy Weaver and found that he had fulfilled his responsibilities. Although the board found no violations of policy on the part of individuals, they did find that the burn boss exercised questionable judgment. Most critically, he failed to maintain adequate staffing, which resulted in the spread of the fire.

Unfortunately for Roy, the public and media had left the Bandelier fire and moved to other issues. Few people understood the enormous differences between the investigative report and the board of inquiry. Whereas the investigative report needed to establish accountability quickly, if inaccurately, for political reasons, the board of inquiry recognized a more basic problem: The interagency fire policy of 1995 had not been widely or uniformly adopted by individual federal wildland-fire-management agencies.

Until all land-managing agencies accept this policy and adopt uniform standards, there will be backbiting and bad-mouthing among and within the different agencies. Equally important in light of the Bandelier disaster, the public must understand and appreciate the value of fire. While the regrowth of Yellowstone and Grand Teton have helped in that education process, we still have the consequences of the Bandelier fire and fifty years of Smokey the Bear mythology to overcome. Local communities, in particular, resist the concept of natural fires. Until they can be enlisted to support basic ecological processes, politicians will crucify the Bob Barbees and Roy Weavers of the world.

# Bison

My next crisis involved the symbol of the National Park Service: the bison, or as most people know it, the buffalo. On the shoulder patch and badge of the ranger uniform, the bison represents the protection of all wildlife. As North America's largest land animal, the bison roamed the West in giant herds totaling more than sixty million animals. By the 1890s, however, Indians and white hide hunters had annihilated all but a thousand survivors. Twenty-five bison sought refuge in Yellowstone National Park. Because most of the subsequent bison herds came from this stock, park protection of bison became a great success story.

With few predators, the Yellowstone bison herd increased. Then, in 1917, the park documented brucellosis among the bison. This disease under certain circumstances can cause abortions in cattle. Ironically, the herd probably contracted brucellosis from the park's own dairy herd. Until the 1950s, Yellowstone managed the bison much like cattle. They roamed freely in the summer, and in the winter rangers corralled, fed, and vaccinated them against brucellosis.

Park visitors loved the massive beasts. Because of their seeming passivity, visitors often forgot they were wild animals. Those who came too close learned with a painful goring that bison were not cows, but could move quickly and without warning. While the lone male often posed majestically, herds caused road jams. Unfortunately for the public, during the summer the bison moved into the mountains and largely out of sight.

In 1948, to help visitors view the normally elusive animals, Laurance Rockefeller, the conservationist son of John D. Rockefeller, Jr., established Jackson Hole Wildlife Park. On land destined to become part of Grand Teton National Park, he constructed a fenced enclosure where visitors could view animals such as bison, elk, and deer. The wildlife park managed twenty bison from Yellowstone much like cattle. After the expansion of Grand Teton National Park in 1950, the National Park Service took over the corralling, winter feeding, testing, and vaccinating of the herd. In 1963 the park found brucellosis throughout the herd and killed all adult bison. The following year twelve brucellosis-free bison from Theodore Roosevelt National Park in North Dakota augmented the vaccinated younger animals of the original herd. Then in 1968 the entire brucellosis-free herd escaped from the wildlife park. Following new wildlife policies promoted by the Leopold Report, the Park Service allowed them to roam freely. For the first time, the bison mingled with cattle, which the 1950 Grand Teton act of Congress allowed to graze in the park. Some of these cattle belonged to former governor and U.S. senator Clifford Hansen and his daughter, Mary Mead.

In 1980, the herd discovered the National Elk Refuge, where each winter the U.S. Fish and Wildlife Service feeds part of the Yellowstone and Teton elk herds. To keep the bison from harming the elk in the competition on the food lines, the refuge started overfeeding the bison. With increased food minimizing winter mortality, the Teton herd expanded from only fifteen animals in 1969 to more than 220 in 1995. Of greater concern, because more than a third of the elk tested positive for brucellosis, the Teton bison herd also lost its brucellosis-free status. It had probably contracted the disease from elk.

During the 1980s Grand Teton National Park, the National Elk Refuge, and the Wyoming Department of Game and Fish tried to reduce the size of the herd, first by agency personnel, then by sport hunters. In 1990 the Legal Action for Animals slapped the agencies with a lawsuit, citing lack of environmental processes. All parties settled out of court and agreed to halt bison reductions until the completion of a long-term management plan fulfilled all environmental requirements.

A year later a rancher filed another lawsuit, claiming that Grand Teton bison had given brucellosis to his cattle and to himself. Since he refused to vaccinate his cattle, local cattle associations sided with the park rather than with the rancher. Although the judge ruled that Grand Teton bison did not infect the rancher's herd, he did fault the park for failing to manage its herd.

All this litigation occurred before I arrived. For my first two years, as we wrestled with other concerns, brucellosis fears stayed subdued, and we slowly worked our way through several issues in the Jackson Bison Herd Management Plan.

In one interagency meeting, after I had been there several months, another issue called Jack and Marshall Gingery out of the room. Discussion continued for a while until a wildlife biologist from the Elk Refuge said, "Don't you think we ought to wait until one of Teton's management staff returns?" When his supervisor pointed to me, the biologist blushed and apologized profusely. As the only woman in the room, he had not taken me seriously. Later, after he learned that I had a doctorate, he stopped by to apologize again. He was working on his doctorate and admitted that he felt like a foolish male chauvinist. While I was seldom discriminated against, my management position and skills were often underestimated or ignored—but never by my supervisors.

At the end of 1994 we submitted our bison management plan for public review. Its principal goal was to maintain a free-roaming bison herd in Jackson Hole. We hoped to wean the bison from winter feeding at the National Elk Refuge. The plan, probably unrealistically, called for baiting the bison with a highly desirable food (tasty pellets made from grains, hay, and molasses) to keep them in an area they favored near Mormon Row. The goal was to separate bison and elk and to force the bison to feed naturally during the winter. In addition, cattle drives in the spring would be delayed to allow all evidence of bison calving to disappear, and the route would be different from that taken by the bison herd.

Comments streamed in from livestock associations, environmental groups, and state agencies. The environmentalists wanted a larger bison herd and limited reduction. The livestock groups, as expected, perceived the concept of free-roaming as lack of management and pushed hard for more aggressive control of brucellosis. The sport hunters wanted a bison hunt to reduce the herd.

Suddenly, without warning, in late March 1995 we learned that several western states were considering prohibiting the sale and importation of Wyoming cattle unless they had further expensive tests for brucellosis. Some even contemplated lawsuits, based on the threat of brucellosis existing in the Teton and Yellowstone herds. Wyoming had earned its brucellosis-free status in 1985 and did not want to pay an extra two million dollars per year for testing services to receive the same rights as other brucellosis-free states.

To address the crisis, the Wyoming Livestock Board called a meeting in Cheyenne. Because Jack was out of town, I went. Here I became acquainted with the real bogeymen of the "crisis." The U.S. Department of Agriculture's Animal Plant Health Inspection Services (most commonly known as APHIS) fought brucellosis with focused intensity. The agency rigidly applied its standards for achieving brucellosis-free status, which allows states to market their cattle freely across state lines without additional testing. With arrogance, certitude, and superiority, the agency flaunted its power.

Initially, I thought the meeting concerned the bison of both Grand Teton and Yellowstone. Then awareness dawned: The livestock board targeted solely Grand Teton and its bison management plan. I told the group that we could do nothing with the bison herd until the park had completed the environmental assessment and approved the bison management plan. The last time the park had tried to manage the bison herd, the environmentalists successfully sued us for failing to follow environmental processes. Openly disgusted with my response, the men representing APHIS declared long-term plans a waste of time and demanded short-term action. As a member of Yellowstone's bison management team, APHIS inflexibly held to its standards and refused to compromise or to accommodate any element of risk to cattle. Consequently, Yellowstone's plan ran five years behind schedule. Now the agency pushed to be part of our plan.

As the meeting progressed, I sensed increasing frustration within the governor's office and the cattle industry that we couldn't do more. They knew that the problem with the Teton bison came from cattle either trailing through the park or grazing within the park. To eliminate the mingling of bison with the fifteen cattle herds involved would harm some of the most powerful cattle growers in the state. Hitting that vulnerable point, I said, "Cliff Hansen and Mary Mead have grazed their cattle next to bison for thirty years and have never had a documented case of brucellosis. They vaccinate their cattle." APHIS representatives quickly spoke up, stating they wanted to eliminate cattle vaccines, which were not 100-percent effective and which complicated the testing process. Moreover, the agency had spent more than three billion dollars in the previous sixty-five years trying to eradicate brucellosis in cattle. To allow bison an opportunity to infect cattle would be a waste of taxpayer dollars.

Although the meeting supposedly focused on Grand Teton, the most aggressive and hostile speaker was the state veterinarian of Montana, Clarence Siroky. Young, brash, articulate, and vitriolic, he distorted facts about brucellosis, focused on rare occurrences in humans, and called the disease a public health concern. While other state veterinarians remained professional, he became a demagogue. As his language grew more and more extreme, it occurred to me that he might have instigated the other state vets to threaten Wyoming and Montana with lawsuits to force the respective governors to take action against the national parks. Although I heard that he had a brother who worked for the National Park Service, he certainly acted as though we were evil incarnate.

We recognized that there was little that the cattle industry or state government could do, and the meeting ended with the State of Wyoming agreeing to submit to an independent review of its brucellosis program, which seemed to satisfy the other western state vets. Ironically, everyone at the meeting accepted my conclusion. "Because there has never been a documented case of bison infecting cattle in the field," I said, "all we are dealing with is a perceived threat. Is that worth ending the livelihoods of fifteen Jackson Hole ranchers?" They knew as well as I that if the American people had to choose between bison and cattle in a national park, they would overwhelmingly choose bison.

Following this meeting, the focus shifted from Grand Teton to Yellowstone, with dire consequences. Unlike the governor of Wyoming, Montana Governor Marc Racicot, undoubtedly egged on by state vet Siroky, refused to wait for the resolution of the bison environmental impact statement. Without warning, he filed a lawsuit against the departments of the Interior and Agriculture, alleging that Yellowstone was ignoring the threat to livestock posed by its bison, and APHIS was threatening the state's primary industry by retracting its brucellosis-free status. In addition, Senator Conrad Burns of Montana introduced a bill in the U.S. Senate that required year-round capture of park bison, followed by testing and slaughtering of all bison with positive test results.

Immediately the director of the National Park Service flew to Helena to meet with the Montana governor. Director Roger Kennedy, a published historian, had come to the National Park Service from the Smithsonian Institution's Museum of History and Technology. Somewhat theatrical, he had hosted occasional documentaries on cable television. His egotism, short attention span, inability to listen, and ignorance of national park culture and tradition made him one of the poorest directors in the history of the National Park Service. Refusing to listen to advice from John Cook and the superintendent of Yellowstone, Kennedy had made up his mind that a cooperative relationship with Montana was more important than the last free-roaming herd of bison.

In contrast to Kennedy, Yellowstone Superintendent Mike Finley represented the best of National Park Service leadership. Well trained in many complex and controversial park issues, Finley had served in Grand Teton, Alaska, regional offices, eastern parks, and the Washington office. He had made his name as superintendent of Everglades in a lawsuit against the State of Florida and its successful environmental settlement. Highly competent, articulate, but occasionally arrogant, Finley argued against settling out of court with Montana. The National Park Service's sovereignty in managing wildlife had been tested before and was always sustained in the courts. He believed that caving in to political pressure abrogated the park mission and public trust. Kennedy disagreed, and state and federal lawyers began to work out a settlement.

Lack of a consistent plan for managing bison hampered the National Park Service. Several parks numbered bison among their wildlife, but no coordinated policy guided the parks. Because bison-proof fences are expensive to build, parks smaller than Yellowstone had to maintain brucellosis-free herds or confront chronically angry neighbors and perpetual lawsuits. Thus, Theodore Roosevelt National Park, Wind Cave National Park, and Chickasaw National Recreation Area handled bison like cattle, corralling, vaccinating, and testing them, then slaughtering all positive animals. Only Yellowstone and to a lesser extent Grand Teton tried to justify a free-roaming herd, unconstrained by corrals and ineffective vaccines. APHIS and the State of Montana always pointed to these disparities in policy and management whenever the Park Service resisted treating bison as domesticated animals.

The consent decree that resulted from Director Kennedy's intervention forced Yellowstone National Park to accept previously unacceptable terms. For the first time in the history of the brucellosis dispute, Yellowstone would have a corral within park boundaries. The National Park Service had always insisted that park bison should be safe on park land and had public sentiment to support that stand. The consent decree also required that national park rangers help shoot or ship to slaughter all of Yellowstone's bison that left the park and tested positive for brucellosis.

These terms, during the winter of 1996–97, caused the Great Yellowstone Bison War. Heavy storms during the early months of winter dumped more than four feet of snow in Yellowstone. Then warm chinook winds raised temperatures above freezing, and the snow melted to slush. Suddenly an arctic front dropped temperatures to more than thirty degrees below freezing and created a two-foot-thick layer of ice as hard as concrete between the bison and their forage. No matter how hard the bison scraped or hammered the ice with their sharp hooves, they could not break through to their winter browse.

Unable to find their traditional food in Yellowstone, the bison began to move to lower and warmer areas—outside Yellowstone. The park's groomed snowmobile trails offered them easy traveling to park boundaries. Although rangers tried to haze them back using horses, fireworks, and shooting in the air, nothing worked. The departing bison wound up shot or corralled.

The media captured the drama of the war. Visitors, environmentalists, animal lovers, even President Clinton became upset. The carnage grew so terrible that rangers wore black tape over the bison on their badges in protest of the slaughter. Eventually, 1,083 bison were killed. Another 1,100 died for lack of forage. By spring 1997 only 1,692 bison remained of a herd that had numbered 3,436 only five months earlier. More than half the Yellowstone bison herd had died.

One of Yellowstone's wildlife management specialists captured the crux of the issue. "You might assume that reasonable people could sit down around a table and reach a reasonable alternative to the killing," Wayne Brewster said. "What observers from the outside forget is that this is war. It's an engagement of opposing sides and ideologies whose opinions differ sharply on the real threat of brucellosis." The intransigence of APHIS, the obstinacy of Montana's political leaders, and the weakness of National Park Service leadership created the devastating conditions for the second great bison massacre.

Despite the reality that eradication of brucellosis from wildlife is impossible, APHIS set an equally impossible deadline to achieve it—1998. Moreover, no vaccine exists for wildlife as there does for cattle. And nearly half of Wyoming's twenty-two thousand elk have tested positive for brucellosis. APHIS, however, has not targeted this multimillion-dollar sport-hunting industry. Thus, even if the Park Service eliminated brucellosis from its remaining bison herds, the bison would probably be reinfected through their contact with elk.

One of the horrors of the Great Yellowstone Bison War was that it occurred on public lands. Six national forests surround Yellowstone. The bison leaving Yellowstone moved into national forests, not onto private ranches. But because the U.S. Forest Service had leased its land to cattle ranchers, cattle, not bison, were protected. Even more troubling, at the time the bison moved into the national forests there were no cattle there, nor were any scheduled to graze there for another four to six months.

APHIS and state veterinarian Siroky claimed brucellosis bacteria could remain present in feces and urine for months. Yet the only scientifically accepted method of transmission of the disease is for a cow to be present when an infected bison aborts its fetus and for the cow to then lick the fetus. Because scavengers quickly eat such delicacies and cows seldom overlap in time or space with bison, the risk of transmission is virtually nonexistent. Furthermore, bison seldom abort. In seventy years of observation, Yellowstone rangers have documented only four abortions. But APHIS required zero risk for bison while ignoring the risk from elk, and had the political clout to decimate a bison herd on public lands.

Even though only female animals of reproductive age can transmit the disease, in 1996–97 APHIS demanded that all bison, including males and yearling females too young to reproduce, be shot or slaughtered if they tested positive for brucellosis. A positive brucellosis test, however, only confirms that the animal has been exposed to the disease. It does not prove that the animal is infectious. While more than 50 percent of Yellowstone's herd tested positive, only 4.6 percent actually carried the bacteria. Thus, despite numerous flaws and erroneous assumptions, APHIS requirements dominated the consent decree, the political decisions, and the biological conclusions.

To prevent future bison wars, the judge overseeing the consent decree stipulated several conditions. He set a limit of one hundred bison that could be killed before he would call another court hearing. Although he did not want a repeat of the bison massacre, he refused to block the federal and state agencies from killing the bison, as requested by environmental groups and Indian tribes. The appeals court later upheld his decision. He also suggested that Yellowstone consider closing snowmobile trails and feeding the bison during harsh winters. These latter recommendations brought additional controversy and anger to the volatile issue.

In an attempt to resolve the impasse between wildlife and cattle, Interior Secretary Bruce Babbitt requested the National Academy of Science to study the issue. It concluded that brucellosis cannot easily be eliminated in the wild and should be managed on a risk basis. The authors also stated that brucellosis would have to be eliminated from elk if it were to be eliminated from bison, or reinfection of bison was inevitable. The report called for long-term vaccination studies to control brucellosis in wildlife. Contrary to settling the issue, both sides used the report to justify their actions and planned to continue as they had.

Under the consent decree, officials from Yellowstone, the Forest Service, and the State of Montana continued developing a Yellowstone bison management plan. The draft environmental impact statement had seven alternatives, ranging from killing all bison that left the park to establishing tolerance zones outside park boundaries. Montana representatives insisted that all bison be vaccinated immediately even though no safe or effective vaccine had been found, and refused to allow even bison who tested negative for brucellosis outside the park. By December 16, 1999, the federal government, fed up with the state's recalcitrant position, withdrew from the seven-year planning effort. Federal officials condemned the state's stand as "without scientific foundation" and "unwarranted." Shortly thereafter, a federal judge upheld the federal agencies' withdrawal but asked all parties to try and work out their differences using a court-appointed mediator. Eventually, in December 2000, both the federal agencies and the State of Montana released Final Records of Decision, separate documents but supporting the same plan.

The final Yellowstone Bison Management Plan tolerated bison outside Yellowstone, approximately one hundred along the park's northern and western boundaries. But each spring before cattle would arrive on public lands, the park staff must haze the animals back into the park or capture, test, and hold bison in a facility within the park. The plan also limited the park's bison population to three thousand animals, which would be vaccinated once a safe and effective vaccine became available, expected in 2004 or 2005. APHIS compromised and agreed that the new tolerance of bison would not threaten Montana's brucellosis-free status. In addition, cattle near Yellowstone would be vaccinated.

Amazingly, by summer 2002, only five years after the Great Yellowstone Bison War ended, mild winters had allowed the bison population to balloon to more than 4,000 animals—greater than the population was before the war. As a result of the management plan, all bison that leave the park can be slaughtered without testing. As of March 2003, 231 bison had been slaughtered, the largest number since 1996–97.

Although less complex than Yellowstone's plan, Grand Teton's bison plan did not fare as well. Teton's plan was finally completed in 1997, recommending a herd size of 350–400 animals. To keep the herd within these numbers, the plan authorized sport hunting at certain times when the bison resided on the National Elk Refuge. At once, the Fund for Animals filed a lawsuit, stating that the supplemental winter feeding on the National Elk Refuge provided for a larger herd. The federal judge sided with the Fund for Animals and required an environmental analysis of the impacts of bison feeding before allowing the bison to be hunted on the refuge. Once again the park went back to the planning process. This time, however, the management plan would address both elk and bison: their herd size, disease management, and winter feeding. By this time, moreover, the bison numbered 650 and the elk nearly 14,000.

# Wolves and Grizzly Bears

One answer to the problem of the prolific bison and elk herds was their only natural predator, the wolf. I knew wolves in Alaska, where their forlorn howl still pierces the winter night. As a romantic and a fervent environmentalist, I read what I could about wolves. They lived in packs of ten with only one pair mating for life, but all cared for one another as a family. As a pack, they are the most successful predators in North America. Because of their predatory success, sport hunters lobbied the Alaska legislature and the U.S. Fish and Wildlife Service to reduce the wolf population, leaving more caribou, moose, and deer for their rifles. Joining with others of my ethos, I railed against federal agents' systematically shooting wolves from helicopters. We knew what had happened in the Lower 48 and did not want wolves eradicated.

In the Lower 48 sportsmen and livestock growers eliminated the gray wolf. Wolves were hunted, trapped, and poisoned into extinction. Although the National Park Service did not have a policy of extermination, in its early years it had a list of good animals—elk, moose, deer—and bad animals—wolves, bears, and coyotes. Yellowstone rangers reflected the culture at large and in 1923 destroyed the last wolf den. For the next seventy years, aside from anecdotal evidence of occasional sightings, wolves were no longer part of the Yellowstone ecosystem.

As early as the 1960s the Leopold Report recommended reintroducing extinct native species, especially wolves, but resistance from livestock growers and sportsmen killed any possibility of recovery efforts. In 1985 Director William Penn Mott fell in love with the wolf and wanted to see it back in Yellowstone. He suggested to the Defenders of Wildlife that paying ranchers for wolf depredations might soften their resistance.

Then in 1990 Senator James McClure of Idaho realized that wolves were naturally migrating south from Canada and decided an experimental population that could be managed was the lesser of two evils. Although his bill failed, Congress provided funding for an environmental impact statement with a timetable for a final decision in 1994.

The U.S. Fish and Wildlife Service chose Ed Bangs, a wildlife biologist who led the Montana wolf recovery project, to start collecting data and community concerns for the environmental impact statement. Bangs had tremendous energy coupled with a relaxed sense of humor—two attributes that would serve him well in the next three years. In concert with Yellowstone, he and his team explored the full range of alternatives, from no wolves at all to full protection under the Endangered Species Act. They held twenty-seven hearings to learn the public's interest. Surprisingly, the pro-wolf forces proved better organized than the anti-wolf livestock growers and dominated the hearings. Consequently, the politicians leaned on Bangs to hold additional hearings to ensure that the full spectrum of voices was heard. In total, Bangs held 130 hearings.

In 1993 Bangs distributed the draft plan. He proposed adopting Senator McClure's approach of limited protection for an experimental introduction. If wolves attacked livestock, they could be killed. The goal of wolf introduction in the Greater Yellowstone area was to have thirty breeding packs for three years, when they would be removed from the endangered species list. Once again he held hearings and listened to more than 700 witnesses, of whom nearly 80 percent favored recovery, and received 160,000 written comments, mostly supportive. The public response to the wolf recovery plan was among the greatest in the history of the National Environmental Policy Act.

In 1994, on schedule with congressional deadlines, Bangs submitted the final recovery plan. The Sierra Club and National Audubon Society objected. They opposed killing wolves for any reason. The Wyoming Farm Bureau opposed the introduction of wolves, period.

Yellowstone biologists kept our Teton biologists well informed of the environmental processes. Our staff, in turn, attended the hearings, reviewed the documents, and sent appropriate comments to Bangs. At one point, the wolf recovery team considered establishing a wolf enclosure in Grand Teton's northern wilderness. Instead, the team decided to keep things as simple as possible by dealing with only one park. We all knew that the wolves would migrate to Grand Teton quickly, probably following the elk to their feeding grounds at the National Elk Refuge. Although we had occasional sightings of lone wolves, biologists usually discovered that the sightings were large coyotes or hybrid wolf-dog mixtures released in the wild when they became too hard to handle.

Then, on November 24, 1994, Secretary of the Interior Bruce Babbitt approved the final rules to allow the introduction of an experimental population under the authority of section 10(j) of the Endangered Species Act. Immediately the Canadians began to set traps to collect the wolf packs for shipment to Yellowstone and Idaho. Just as quickly the American Farm Bureau Federation filed for an injunction to stop the introduction. When the government argued that it predicted only one-tenth of one percent predation of livestock and that those losses would be compensated by the Defenders of Wildlife, the judge denied the injunction.

On a cold but glorious day in January 1995, wolves returned to Yellowstone—in steel cages. Secretary Babbitt flew there to greet them, as did hundreds of schoolchildren and the media. Bob and I cheered the historic event on television from our home in Grand Teton. Just before they were to be released, however, Babbitt received word that the Farm Bureau had filed an appeal, and the court ordered the wolves to remain caged for thirty-six hours. Those thirty-six hours traumatized the wolves more than the trapping and air shipment. Because temperatures of thirty degrees below zero prevented artificially watering the animals, biologists feared the wolves would die of dehydration. Some had already hurt themselves gnawing on the steel bars. At last the appeals court denied the appeal.

In Yellowstone Babbitt helped release fourteen wolves into a one-acre enclosure. Here the park fed them roadkill for several weeks. The recovery plan assumed that this "soft release" would acclimatize them to the environment, and that they would remain in the park rather than head back to Canada. For comparison purposes, fifteen other wolves were released in the Frank Church Wilderness of central Idaho without the intermediate step of enclosures. A year later seventeen more wolves came to Yellowstone and twenty to Idaho.

Meanwhile, two organizations sued the Interior Department. Mountain States Legal Foundation, former Interior Secretary Jim Watt's organization, filed on behalf of the American Farm Bureau Federation and questioned the legality of the introduction. The Sierra Club Defense Fund, renamed Earth Justice, filed for the Audubon Society and Sierra Club, which wanted the experimental wolves to have the same protection as naturally migrating wolves. The federal judge joined the two lawsuits. Thus, the pro-wolf and the anti-wolf factions came to sue the government in the same lawsuit.

By December 1997, when Judge William F. Downs made his decision, the wolves had formed eight packs in the park and one outside in a national forest, totaling more than a hundred individuals. The thirty-one wolves had produced about seventy pups and seemed well fed and well adjusted to their environment. Despite worries of livestock growers, only four depredations had occurred. Wolves had killed fifty-six sheep and five calves, but Defenders of Wildlife compensated the ranchers $12,700 for their losses. After being given two chances to stop killing livestock, rogue wolves were shot.

Equally important to their adjustment and growth was the effect of wolves on the ecosystem. For the seventy years that the park lacked wolves, scientists collected data to compare with the advent of the wolves. By the end of 1997, wolves had killed nearly half the coyotes. Coyote numbers dropped from thirteen packs of eighty animals to nine packs of thirty. With the drop in coyotes, the rodent population ballooned and attracted more hawks and bald eagles to the ecosystem. In addition, wolves had killed 124 elk and two bison. Their preference for elk rather than bison surprised the scientists, who hoped they would help control the bison population.

The elk population, however, was also excessive. Wolves forced elk to be more vigilant, causing them to lose weight and to be less able to survive the stresses of winter. In addition, the wolves moved the elk out of the river bottoms, allowing the willows and aspens to recover. Although sport hunters lamented the loss of elk, the managers at the National Elk Refuge in Jackson Hole welcomed the reduction. The refuge had seven thousand too many elk for its forage and feeding budget. Finally, the wolf kills attracted more scavengers, including grizzly bears, which now had better nutrition. Overall, wolves had greatly increased the biodiversity of the region.

Then, on December 13, 1997, federal judge Downes dropped a bombshell. He declared the wolf introduction illegal and ordered biologists to remove the populations in Idaho and Yellowstone, numbering now more than 150 animals. Judge Downes did not accept Ed Bangs's assurance in the environmental impact statement that there was no scientific evidence of existing wolf populations. Bangs and his scientists defined populations as two breeding pairs that raised two sets of young for at least two years. Federal wildlife biologists do not believe that loners or stragglers constitute a population. Moreover, they value populations more than individual wolves.

Judge Downes stated that the Interior Department had violated section 10(j) of the Endangered Species Act. The department, he believed, had established the experimental population where indigenous populations already existed—even if they were mostly loners. More important, Canadian wolves were migrating south and settling in Montana. The wolf recovery plan called for managing these naturally migrating wolves the same as the experimental population if the two groups intermingled. Downes ruled that it was unlawful to provide less protection to naturally occurring wolves than they would otherwise receive if not intermingling with the experimental population.

The debates of the two sides in the lawsuit contributed to the decision. Ranchers, argued the Farm Bureau, would not be able to distinguish between an introduced wolf and a naturally migrating wolf. Thus they would not know if they were free to shoot a wolf killing their livestock. The environmentalists, on the other hand, stated that the introduced wolves should have the same protection as the naturally migrating wolves—no one could kill them for any of their activities.

Given the success of the wolf recovery program, Downes admitted that he made the decision "with the utmost reluctance." "The Court is especially mindful of the concerned efforts of the government and wolf recovery advocates to accommodate the interests of stockgrowers, but the laudable ends aspired to by the wolf recovery plan cannot justify the Secretary's impermissible means."

Response to the judge's decision reverberated throughout the nation. The Farm Bureau said that the decision proved that the Interior Department had "played fast and loose with the law." Environmentalists lamented, "Wolves have been a biological success, an economic success, and a success in terms of people's appreciation of Yellowstone and its ecological processes." Biologists claimed that Yellowstone wolves could not be returned to their original Canadian territory, now reoccupied, because the new resident wolves would kill the returning wolves. The only alternative to captivity was killing them, and Alaskans had shown how expeditiously that could be done from aircraft. The Interior Department filed an appeal, and Judge Downes stayed the removal pending the resolution of the appeal.

Ironically, the ranchers took the very provision that was designed to make the wolf program more acceptable to them and tried to use it to force the total removal of the wolves. Yet when the naturally migrating wolves eventually arrived, the ranchers would not be allowed to manage them. Also, environmentalists have proved that the mortality of wolves was greater where the Endangered Species Act provided full protection than in the experimental population of Yellowstone.

Then, on January 13, 2000, the Tenth Circuit Court of Appeals in Denver voted unanimously to reverse Wyoming's district court decision. In its statement the court said that trying to keep the experimental and the migrating wolves separated "ignores biological reality and misconstrues the larger purpose" of the law. Accepting defeat, the American Farm Bureau Federation decided against appealing to the Supreme Court.

Meanwhile, during the winter of 1998–99, for the first time in more than eighty years, a wolf pack denned in Grand Teton National Park. Even more important, the number of wolves continued to grow. By the end of 2001, wolf populations in the three states of Montana, Idaho, and Wyoming totaled 563 wolves with 34 breeding packs; 218 came from the Yellowstone recovery area (131 in ten packs from Yellowstone National Park, not counting two more packs in Grand Teton National Park). The recovery plan required thirty breeding pairs for three consecutive years before delisting, and 2001 met that criterion for the second year in a row. Consequently, in anticipation of the Interior Department delisting of the wolves in 2003, Wyoming began developing a state management plan.

Livestock predation proved much lower than anticipated. Since introduction, wolves had killed 188 cattle, 494 sheep, and 43 dogs. While the number of sheep killed in 2001 shot up from 30 a year to 138, the number of sheep per wolf actually dropped. As a result of the depredations in 2001, Yellowstone researchers moved 18 wolves and killed 19. Throughout the three-state region, researchers since introduction had moved 98 wolves and killed 97. Thus humans caused more than half the documented wolf deaths—either legally or illegally. The leading natural cause of mortality, however, was wolves killing other wolves. While ecologists had hoped the wolves would feast on bison, their overwhelming choice (87 percent of the time) was elk. In summary, without a doubt, the Gray Wolf Recovery Plan is one of the great success stories of America.

Meanwhile, Grand Teton staff grappled with another animal protected by the Endangered Species Act—the grizzly bear. The wet spring of 1994 followed by the hot, dry summer that caused the Mormon Row fire also produced bumper crops of berries and other bear food. As the summer progressed, black bears became an increasing nuisance. Although there had been no injuries, visitors persisted in treating bears like big dogs—feeding them, photographing them with their children, and trying to run them off the berry patches. Despite interpretive signs and talks, we couldn't seem to educate the visitors. Although we had trapped and removed some panhandling bears, we feared that someone's folly would result in a bear attack, requiring us to kill the bear. During my early morning weekend hikes as I prepared to climb the Grand, I occasionally saw black bears off the trail. I always detoured widely around them. In Alaska, black bears could be more unpredictable than grizzlies and periodically attacked and killed people. In Grand Teton, however, few injuries had warranted much more than some stitches.

On the other hand, Yellowstone, home to the grizzly bear, had two or three maulings a year. Although grizzlies had once spread throughout the West, they had been hunted and poisoned to near extinction. Only in remote pockets of Glacier and Yellowstone national parks did they still reside. Yet not until 1975, when Yellowstone closed the garbage dumps and nearly 140 bears starved, did the Endangered Species Act cover the grizzly bear, and then only as a threatened species, not an endangered one. Following established guidelines, federal land managers designed strategies to protect the bears and their diminishing habitat. Slowly the grizzly population increased, and their range began to encroach on humans. Yellowstone and Glacier confronted the difficult task of managing humans in a grizzly bear environment.

Although Grand Teton National Park lies just south of Yellowstone, few grizzly bears actually den in the park. Never since the park's establishment had a visitor been mauled by a grizzly. The development of Jackson Hole had eliminated habitat and crowded out the space-demanding bear. Nevertheless, the park preserved grizzly bear habitat and each summer tracked the few bears that wandered down from Yellowstone.

One hot July morning, as part of my training for the Grand, I hiked Paintbrush Canyon trail. Because it was a long hike, Bob did not accompany me. Instead, I carried a park radio and monitored park activity. As I enjoyed the profusion of wild flowers that the wet spring and hot summer had brought into bloom, I listened with only half an ear to routine radio traffic. Watching bees and butterflies flutter from one flower to another and smelling the flowery perfume, I felt lazy and ambled along the trail.

On a particularly steep portion of the trail, I caught the phrase "send the helicopter to Emma Matilda Trail." Because of their expense, only serious accidents required helicopters, and these accidents usually occurred in the backcountry, far from access by automobile. Emma Matilda Trail, in the northeast portion of the park, was not typical backcountry. Its trailheads could be reached by car, and the trail itself was fairly flat and easy hiking.

I stopped and pulled the radio out of my daypack. Before I could call dispatch, I heard a ranger request additional help in closing the trail to prevent further bear attacks. Because continuous emergency traffic inhibited me from using the radio to get briefed, I turned around and jogged back to my car. It was unlikely that a black bear would cause injuries requiring a helicopter. Although in previous years grizzlies had been sighted in the Emma Matilda area, this year we had no reports of grizzlies there.

By the time I reached my car, I knew we had a major incident. Driving straight to the dispatch office, I found acting chief ranger Colin Campbell. My first words were, "It's a grizzly, isn't it?" Always the cautious law-enforcement officer, Colin only said that it was a large bear in what appeared to be an unprovoked attack. He asked permission to close the entire area, including all trailheads. Before I could respond, he reminded me that some of the trail was heavily used by guests at Jackson Lake Lodge, including guided horse trips. Until we knew more about the bear, the injured man, and the circumstances leading up to the attack, I felt we had no choice but to close the area.

Limiting access to any area of a national park is an unpopular decision. Even with a bear attack there would be hikers who believed they had the right to hike where they pleased, especially if their trail were more than fifteen miles distant from the bear incident. I expected complaints. Initially, however, most people were shocked and disturbed. They expected to be wary of grizzlies in Yellowstone but not in Grand Teton. The community, concessioner, and visitors responded cooperatively and responsibly.

Meanwhile, I received as complete a briefing as Colin could give me. Apparently the bear's clawed foot had scraped the victim's left leg and missed his femoral artery by less than half an inch. His head looked like it had been in the bear's mouth, and one arm had several serious punctures. The man was lucky to be alive.

Later we learned that he was a journalist from Salt Lake City training for a marathon. For the last several years he and his girlfriend had trained in Grand Teton for ten days each summer. This particular day his friend was nursing a cold, so he went out alone. During the first seven miles of the trail, he sang out loud to alert bears and moose of his presence. But as the trail got steeper and he became winded, he stopped singing. Suddenly, only two miles from the trailhead, something huge charged him. At first, he said, he tried to fight it. Then, as he realized he was losing the battle, he remembered advice to play dead and tried to curl up in a ball. After one last bite on the head that penetrated his sunglasses, the bear stood up on its back legs, snorted, and sprang back into the brush. The runner crawled away as fast as he could. Just as his strength gave out, a couple of hikers found him. While one ran back to call the rangers, the other stayed with him, trying to stop the bleeding. Within fifteen minutes, the park's emergency medical technicians arrived, and just five minutes later a helicopter circled to land.

That afternoon during a management briefing, Steve Cain, the park's longtime wildlife biologist and acting division chief since Marshall Gingery's retirement, said he believed the bear was probably a female grizzly with a cub. "When bears stand up on their hind legs and peer around like that," he said, "it is to see their cubs. As she and her cub were eating berries, she was probably startled by the runner. Protecting her young, she attacked. As long as he fought her, he was an enemy. When he feigned dead, she left him alone. I don't think she is a predatory bear, or she would have continued to eat him."

With Steve's counsel, we decided not to hunt the bear and kill it. Instead, we closed the area until the berries were gone and the bears had moved on. Biologists agreed to monitor the area. Within days they reported seeing a female grizzly with two cubs in the area. These sightings confirmed Steve's savvy advice.

After two surgeries, the runner recovered with only a few scars as reminders. He began to read everything he could on bears and told Linda Olson that he felt a psychic bond with his attacker. When he heard what probably had happened, he was relieved that we had not killed her. His surgeon told him that his sunglasses had saved his eye—a tooth went completely through the glasses and stopped just short of his eye, leaving only a minor scratch. If the hikers hadn't found him when they did, however, he would have been dead in another twenty minutes. All in all, the victim of the first grizzly bear mauling in Grand Teton's history was a lucky, lucky man.

After the excitement died down, people began to pressure us to open the area. The hike was popular and beautiful. Clay James, the manager of Jackson Lake Lodge, could not understand why his guided horse trips could not use a portion of the area. His guests had come from around the world, many waiting years for the experience. They wanted to ride horses, and the best areas were part of the closure.

I asked Colin and Steve for advice. One offered the perspective of visitor safety; the other sought to protect the wildlife. Colin said that he had never heard of a grizzly attacking a horse. Given the pressure that we and the concessioner were under, he believed that horseback riders in groups of four or more would be safe. Steve, however, expressed concern for disrupting the bears. "Last year was nearly a drought, so bears went into hibernation without adequate food," he reflected. "This year the berry crop is great. If we want healthy bears, which will stay out of people's garbage and yards, I think we should allow the bears as much time as they want."

"Since wildlife biologists are monitoring the area, is the entire northeast quadrant being used?" I asked. "Are there berries or other bear food throughout? Can we find some portion that we could open to horseback riders in groups? If we are too restrictive, we lose credibility. On the other hand, if we lose either another visitor or a grizzly we will forsake our mission." Colin and Steve agreed to get together and find a solution, if possible. By day's end, both concurred that the western and northern quarters could be opened to horses. That decision considerably eased the pressure. While hikers lamented the closure, they did not want to push their luck and continued using other parts of the park. We kept the closure for nearly six weeks.

The bear mauling was not the only grizzly issue I confronted. In September 1995, I received a call from a newspaper reporter. He asked me how the park felt about the State of Wyoming's trapping and killing a grizzly on park land. I lamely responded that I hadn't heard about it and gave the party line: Occasionally individual male bears may have to be killed, but we believed in protecting the species as a whole. I then called both Steve and Colin to ask what happened. Steve had been out of town and knew nothing. Colin, however, had been in town and was embarrassed to say he hadn't heard anything either.

Slowly we pieced together the story. Apparently, over the summer, a grizzly bear had killed more than twelve of Cliff Hansen's calves, which legally grazed within the park. He had dutifully reported the depredations to the area ranger and the Wyoming Game and Fish Department, which reimbursed him for his loss, according to the Interagency Grizzly Bear Management Plan. The State decided to trap and move the bear and coordinated with Steve's subordinate, who was in the process of moving to another park. When they caught the bear, neither Steve nor his subordinate was in the park. The State determined that because the bear had already been trapped and moved at least twice, it could not be salvaged and killed it.

The lack of consultation with park management was contrary to the Interagency Grizzly Bear Management Plan and left us in a political hot seat. The plan divided the park into three zones: (1) the most developed areas—campgrounds, motels, and visitor centers—would be managed for people first, and grizzlies would be removed to avoid contact with visitors; (2) the wilderness and proposed wilderness areas would be managed for bears first; and (3) the transition areas would be managed on a case-by-case basis. The cattle depredations occurred in a transition zone.

The State's action outraged environmental groups. They accused the park of protecting cattle, not grizzly bears. "A grizzly is more important to a national park than a few calves," they challenged. The Jackson Hole Alliance, the valley's strongest environmental advocacy group, threatened to sue us for betraying our mission and the Interagency Grizzly Bear Management Plan.

Meanwhile, I was still trying to figure out what had happened and how we had been blindsided by the State. Slowly I collected the facts and found a simple breakdown in communication. The local rangers and biologists had known of the large number of depredations as well as efforts to trap the bear, but had not realized their import to management. Neither Colin's nor Steve's subordinates had passed the information up the chain of command. Wyoming's Game and Fish biologists, having sole authority over management of wildlife in national forests, where most of the cattle depredations had been occurring, didn't stop to remember that Grand Teton was a national park, not a national forest. The cattle industry had pummeled the State and the U.S. Forest Service for tolerating rogue male bears. When a known rogue bear was finally captured—in a park, not a forest—the biologist and his superiors responded to political pressure by removing the bear from the park and killing it.

Once word leaked out that the State of Wyoming had killed a grizzly in a national park, an incensed public voiced its anger. Jackson's two weekly newspapers fanned the flames. Visitors and locals alike accused the park and the State of warped values. "If a grizzly isn't safe in a park, where will it be?" asked one letter to the editor. Knowledgeable environmentalists challenged the biology of the management plan. While male bears contributed to the species only a few times in their lives and had been known to kill their own cubs, the environmentalists believed that each bear lost was a loss to the species and the ecosystem.

After learning that ignorance rather than arrogance caused the brouhaha, I met with the State's wildlife biologist and his supervisors. We discussed the issue over breakfast prior to the annual meeting of the Interagency Grizzly Bear Subcommittee. The biologist apologized and admitted that to him the word "park" meant Yellowstone, not Grand Teton. Because my own staff had kept me in the dark, I couldn't get too upset with him. We agreed that we needed to review the management plan and to ensure that proper consultation occurred in the future.

Tackling the environmental groups was a tougher session. I sat down with the board of the Jackson Hole Alliance and admitted that we had not been in the loop. I felt foolish and incompetent. Somehow my honesty and discomfort made an impression. When the board members learned that park management had not participated in the decision to dispatch the bear, their anger subsided, and they decided to drop the lawsuit against the park.

I met with Steve and Colin to straighten out communication problems. Conscientious and chagrined, Colin told me that he had already "kicked ass" and refused to excuse his staff's failure. Steve accepted responsibility for the communication lapse but remarked that he had only seasonal biologists on duty and couldn't blame them. He pleaded once again for authority and money to hire additional biologists to replace the two who had retired or moved. Steve's constant whining about lack of money and people irritated me, but I admired his knowledge and ability to articulate issues.

The two grizzly bear incidents heightened my awareness of grizzly bears and of how little I knew about them. As I tried to learn more, I found contradictory information. During my first year at Grand Teton, we had a joint management meeting with Yellowstone National Park. One of the issues I vividly remembered. Without consulting the other park, each one had published its own brochure on grizzly bears. The advice on how to protect oneself if attacked by a bear was exactly the opposite in the two brochures. Because most visitors tour both parks, our efforts to educate only caused confusion and may have endangered lives. Yet few bear biologists agree on such advice—much depends on the individual bear just as it depends on the individual person involved.

Because the knowledge about grizzly bears was so inadequate, I was doubly surprised that little research was being done. The focus was largely on habitat. At least 25 percent of the adult bears in the Greater Yellowstone area had been trapped and fitted with a radio collar. This collar allowed Wyoming Game and Fish to track where the bear traveled and what habitat it seemed to like best. When biologists had to kill a bear, they usually tried to collect basic information such as its weight, height, and approximate age; the contents of its stomach; samples of its blood and salvia; and the parasites and diseases it carried.

While the national forests and parks in the Greater Yellowstone area had initiated a comprehensive computer model for grizzly bear habitat, only a few random units—primarily in Yellowstone National Park—had collected all the required information. To most managers the computer model was esoteric and difficult to use. When funding shortfalls hit, managers often couldn't justify the cost.

Aside from the computer model, few scientists conducted long-term research on grizzly bears. Because bears are harder to research than elk or moose, wildlife biologists and university departments can acquire more data and results from working with more easily accessible species.

Despite the lack of hard data and the loss of ten to twenty grizzlies a year, by 1995 most of the federal agencies in the Greater Yellowstone ecosystem believed the bear should be deleted from the list of threatened species. Although less than 1 percent of its historic range still existed, the agencies pointed to an increase of more than four hundred bears since listed in 1975 and an annual rate of growth of nearly 5 percent. Moreover, Wyoming politicians argued that the dispersion of grizzlies, the more frequent conflicts with humans, and the greater numbers of breeding females were proof that the bear had met every recovery criterion for delisting.

Environmentalists, on the other hand, feared that the accumulating effects of eroding habitat would not be detectable until the next century. For illustration, they focused on new residential subdivisions platted in bear habitat at the rate of one per month and on the loss of natural bear food. A blister rust threatened whitebark pine trees, and lake trout endangered the indigenous cutthroat trout—both sources of bear food. They also suggested that a search for food, not increased numbers, caused the dispersal of bears beyond the recovery zone.

In 1995 the Interagency Grizzly Bear Subcommittee, of which Jack and I were members, submitted its conservation strategy for managing grizzly bears once delisted. The Fund for Animals and the National Audubon Society promptly sued. The federal judge agreed with the environmentalists and ordered a rewrite of the plan to define the amount of area a viable population of bears needed and what condition the habitat needed to be in. In March 2000 a revised plan maintained the existing 9,209-square-mile

Grizzly Bear Recovery Area, focused on reducing the number of bear mortalities caused by humans, and required a minimum of fifteen females with cubs or else the bears would be placed back under the protection of the Endangered Species Act. Public comments raised more issues to analyze and resolve. The Interagency Grizzly Bear Committee plans to implement the conservation strategy by 2005.

Bison, wolves, and grizzly bears are the biggest wildlife issues in the National Park Service. I was involved in some measure with all three. I learned how difficult it is to manage controversial species. My biggest frustration was the lack of comprehensive research, especially on bison and grizzlies.

Coming from the resource management field, I could appreciate Steve's appeals for more money. Grand Teton had little research money and even fewer scientists to do research. But during my four years I could never comprehend what our overall wildlife management program was or should be. I left the park nearly as ignorant as I had arrived.

Grand Teton's science program was not unique. The National Park Service has traditionally put its energies and funds into visitor services, not natural and cultural resources. More than 90 percent of the Park Service budget is in maintenance, visitor protection, interpretation, and administration. Roads and visitor centers are especially expensive, both in construction and maintenance. Numerous exposés have brought these facts to public notice. The National Park Service always vows to rearrange priorities, but it always falls back to the traditional pattern of funding development first.

Even as a strong resource manager, I found myself locked in the same mind-set. Visitors vote, write letters of complaint, and involve their congressional delegation. Animals don't. Also, once a park has an extensive road system, it has to be maintained or it becomes a waste of taxpayer dollars. Moreover, local communities make millions off adjacent parks. If parks were wildlife preserves, few visitors would visit them and spend money in the communities. Visitor facilities and activities attract tourists. Local communities know that and want even more of them.

Shortly before I left Santa Fe in 1989, my former supervisor, Richard Sellars, began to research the history of natural resource management in the National Park Service. When he finally completed his study, *Preserving Nature in the National Parks: A History,* it was a damning account. He showed that time and again the Park Service had failed to focus on resource management. Most of the blame he placed on park management.

Although I agreed with much that Sellars related, as a park manager I knew that scientists and resource managers were equally to blame. Most of them want money and people without putting together a program to justify them. The Rocky Mountain regional chief scientist told me that probably only one park in the entire service, Channel Islands National Park, had a comprehensive resource management program in which managers and scientists spelled out what was known and what wasn't, then developed sophisticated research questions to address long-term issues and short-term actions. In addition, I found that most resource managers are not good managers, either of people, funds, or broader research perspectives.

Despite calls for more national park scientists, in 1993 Interior Secretary Babbitt pulled all research scientists out of the National Park Service and placed them in a new agency, the National Biological Survey (later named National Biological Service). Scientists from the U.S. Fish and Wildlife Service and the Bureau of Land Management also joined the new agency. Babbitt wanted this agency to prepare inventories of the nation's biological resources for the formulation of public and private policy. His decision devastated Park Service science and traumatized park scientists. The scientists came together from various institutional cultures of diverse and opposing philosophies with conflicting budgetary procedures. In the next four years science in the parks regressed to a level predating the Leopold Report. At the same time, Congress opposed the new agency and attempted to abolish it. Babbitt salvaged it only by merging it with the U.S. Geological Survey. Unsupported by land managers and misunderstood by Congress and landowners, the agency remained poorly funded and threatened throughout the 1990s.

As a result of the Park Service's own priorities coupled with Babbitt's misguided vision, the Service has failed in half of its dual mission—that of conserving the "scenery and the natural and historic objects and the wild life ... in such manner and by such means as will leave them unimpaired for the enjoyment of future generations." The public, the visitors, Congress, and park employees are just as responsible as park managers for that failure.

Yet the National Park Service has seen what a well-educated and concerned public can do. The recovery of the wolf in Yellowstone won overwhelming public support in large part because of the educational efforts of public and private groups. When the public becomes alarmed, as it did during the Great Yellowstone Bison War of 1996–97, intractable state and federal agencies learn to bend under public outrage. Thus, to keep parks unimpaired for future generations requires a pact between the National Park Service and its public. The agency must keep its public informed and involved in its issues and decision-making. Superintendents must abandon their dictum "I don't need anyone telling me how to run my park" and offer the public more than lip service or condescension to mandated public participation. In turn, the public must assert its will to protect the parks and to prevent irreparable impairment.

# Politics

Most park visitors probably expect the superintendent and certainly the chief operating officer—the assistant superintendent—to spend most of their time handling wildlife or visitors. On the contrary, personnel problems bogged me down, and Superintendent Neckels applied his time to resolving issues with political overtones. When I came to Grand Teton from LBJ, I expected politics to weigh heavily in most issues. I was right.

The thorniest problem, which harassed me from the moment I arrived to the day I left, was the Jackson Hole Airport. The only jet airport within the boundaries of a national park, its presence and expansion rested solely on politics. When Congress in 1950 expanded Grand Teton National Park to include the Jackson Hole National Monument, however, the small gravel airfield with a log cabin for a terminal was anything but controversial. The act does not even mention the airport.

Even though few early visitors arrived by air, I was surprised to learn that early park management supported the airport and limited commercial use. In 1955 the superintendent issued the first twenty-year permit to the town of Jackson to operate the airport. Within the year, the town paved the runway and extended it more than 1,000 feet, to 6,300 feet, without a word of complaint from the park. Then, in 1963, when the Federal Aviation Administration recommended another 2,000-foot expansion to the north, the National Park Service accepted the proposal and began to prepare plans and specifications for funding under the Airports in the Parks Act of 1950. Before submitting the funding request, however, park management finally decided to assess the proposal in terms of its effect on the park. The superintendent realized that a 2,000-foot expansion to the north took away additional park land while an expansion to the south would merely require acquisition of private land. Moreover, a southern expansion would move airport traffic and noise away from the park. This was the beginning of differences between the park, the town, and the Federal Aviation Administration (FAA).

Eventually all parties compromised. In 1975 the town widened and strengthened the runway, but did not lengthen it. In addition, a parallel taxiway was constructed and an instrument-landing system installed on the north end of the runway. But when the Interior Department refused to allow the expansion of the passenger terminal, the airport board filed suit in U.S. District Court. The judge determined that the Interior secretary had a clear right to operate and regulate an airport within a national park. Because his predecessor had given an earlier approval to the terminal, however, he could not withhold final approval.

Then in 1979 Interior Secretary Cecil Andrus shocked valley residents. Following the results of a study of regional transportation in northwestern Wyoming, he determined that the Jackson Hole Airport was no longer essential for operations of the Interior Department, and therefore the airport's lease would not be renewed. The airport board should find another location for its airport. Because Frontier Airlines had phased out most of its propeller planes and had requested authority to fly commercial jets, the decision hurt commercial and development interests in the valley. On the other hand, park management, of which Jack Neckels was then a part, was thrilled.

Within a year, the controversial Wyomingite Jim Watt replaced Cecil Andrus as Interior secretary. Wasting no time, Wyoming's congressional delegation asked him to reconsider the airport decision. After reviewing the issue for nearly two years, Watt made three decisions. First, to allow the airport to exist in a national park, he determined that it was necessary for the "proper performance of the functions of the Department of the Interior." Second, he notified the Jackson Hole Airport Board that it was the "sole proprietor" of the airport. Third, he signed a new management agreement with the airport board that continued operation of the airport for thirty years, with two ten-year renewal options based on satisfactory performance, for a total of fifty years. These decisions dashed any hope that the National Park Service could manage growth and development of the airport within Grand Teton's boundaries.

When I arrived in the fall of 1992, I found the airport undergoing still another master plan for more expansion. Moreover, several scheduled jet aircraft (Boeing 737s and 757s and MD-80s) arrived each day, and the airport had become the busiest in Wyoming, growing nearly 20 percent per year. One of the reasons for the master plan was that once or twice a year an airplane would overrun the runway, usually because of weather or pilot error.

I quickly became enmeshed in the single most complicated issue of my career. The FAA had rules for master plans, rules for noise-abatement plans, and rules for operating airports. In addition, the airport had a history of more than fifty years with accompanying promises, compromises, and expectations. Noise-monitoring methodology was unusually esoteric, overly specialized, and filled with jargon, acronyms, and unreadable charts. Then, both airport and aircraft technology changed radically year to year. Because new technology might offer nonintrusive ways to improve airport safety, we needed to keep abreast of new electronic marvels.

The airport manager arrived in Jackson shortly after I did. A recently retired air force general, George Larson had ended his career working in the massive bureaucracy of the Pentagon in Washington, D.C. Although shorter than most military officers, his close-clipped hair and rigid posture depicted the stereotypical career serviceman. He joined Rotary and threw himself into community activities, demonstrating either tremendous energy or a nondemanding job. Initially, we worked well together, trying to find a win-win position for the airport and the park. He loved the mountains, and his office had a far better view of them than either Jack's or mine. When an airport advocate suggested changing the boundaries of the park to eliminate the airport, Larson countered that this would remove important constraints and potentially damage the park. He preferred to find solutions that benefited both the park and the airport.

The airport board itself seemed less amenable. The chairwoman had been a lawyer with the FAA and knew exactly what the airport needed—a longer runway. She often lost patience with Jack Neckels and occasionally with Larson. Other members included the park's former chief naturalist, who feebly tried to minimize intrusions to the park. One member was a physician, a pathologist and thus allowed more regular hours than most doctors. Another was a developer who had turned river-bottom land northwest of the airport into high-priced suburbia and ironically found the residents opposed to airport expansion. The common denominator among all board members was a private pilot's license.

While I had a private pilot's license, I had not flown in nearly fifteen years. Nonetheless, my knowledge of glide slopes, instrument-landing systems, outer markers, VORTECs, and other aviation minutiae helped to sort necessary intrusions from merely desirable ones. Yet when it came to developing park comments on the airport, my pilot background was useless. I didn't know where to begin. But I had attended all the public meetings and was gratified with the concern for the park that many attendees expressed.

Ever since Watt's devastating blow, however, superintendents had played little role in the airport's plans and operations. Marshall Gingery had tried to influence planning, but was largely ineffective. With his retirement, the entire complicated issue fell in my lap. I realized suddenly that we had only a week to provide comments for the first stage of planning, that of collecting comments, concerns, and issues from the public, airlines, and park. Although we had requested assistance from legal and aviation experts in our central offices in Denver and Washington, none arrived.

I knew that Jack wanted to appear positive and supportive of the master plan process. Yet I could only think of negative things to say, such as "don't expand the runway" and "don't construct more and bigger buildings that would detract from the mountains."

Instead, Jack suggested starting with the concept of park values and the preservation of natural and cultural resources. "Our goal," he said, "is to minimize intrusions on those resources. Park values also involve the right and expectation of park visitors and unborn generations to come and enjoy their national park unimpaired."

After brainstorming for a couple of hours, we developed a seven-page list of comments and issues. Our letter surprised George Larson and the airport board. We charged the master planners to examine park values before recommending further development. Instead of discussing noise, we suggested the concept of quietude—the sound of nature uninterrupted by human-caused noise. Park visitors, we told the planners, seek solitude and inspiration from national parks. They want a minimum of modern-day intrusions to their experience. We reminded the board and its planners that Grand Teton had visitors from around the world. And these visitors had to be considered and even consulted. Finally, we recommended numerous studies to collect data to support a wider range of alternatives, especially operational constraints, than the board wanted.

George Larson tried to dismiss our comments in a follow-up letter. He stated that most of our suggestions were discriminatory and therefore illegal. He and the board did not believe they had any right to impose restrictions on the air carriers, especially regarding scheduling, size, and weight of aircraft. After our letter, Larson seemed less friendly and acted more like an adversary than a colleague.

While our comments dumbfounded the board, the environmentalists cheered. Because we had been on the opposite side on a number of issues, from grazing to snowmobile trails, the environmental community had written us off. Now they perked up and added their supportive comments. In two lawsuits in the 1980s, the Sierra Club had tested Watt's airport management agreement and the FAA's approval of Boeing 737 jet service. In both suits, the court ruled against the Sierra Club. Environmentalists now saw our comments as the basis for holding development to the minimum required to ensure safety.

As the master plan moved toward developing alternatives, we learned that the planning team did not intend to incorporate an alternative on preserving park values. Jack and I submitted an alternative that recommended improving safety with navigational enhancements and operational constraints rather than by lengthening the runway. Despite our efforts, reflected in the concerns of more than half the comments received during the public meetings, the draft master plan did not include our alternative.

By the time the plan reached the streets, Jack and I had help. We had hired a management assistant, Kit Mullen, who focused on the airport issue. Knowing the environmental processes thoroughly from her experience with controversial issues in Alaska and Denver, she kept the planners aware of the constraints of environmental law. Conscientious, hard-working, and thorough, Kit became an aviation expert. She confronted the planners on noise levels, lack of attention to park values, and specific details that Jack and I had no time to digest. Her comments filled thirty single-spaced pages.

Jim Watt, in his 1983 management agreement with the airport board, inadvertently gave the National Park Service two potential weapons to fight development. One was that the runway could not be lengthened without amending the agreement. To amend the agreement would allow a more conservationist Interior secretary, such as Bruce Babbitt, to reverse many of Watt's offensive decisions (just as Watt had done to those of Andrus). The second was requiring a noise-control plan that would keep aircraft noise compatible with the purposes of Grand Teton National Park.

The planning team tried to finesse its alternatives so that the 1983 management agreement would not require amending. Instead of recommending an extension of the runway, the plan explored shifting it to the north and adding paved "stopways." Coincidentally, the combined shift and the stopways added 1,842 feet to the runway. It also allowed airlines to use the entire 8,142 feet to calculate payload, effectively extending the runway without explicitly saying so.

Although Watt had established noise-abatement requirements, he based his limits on the noisy jet technology of the time. In the subsequent ten years, jets had become quieter. As a result, more jets could take off and land and still meet Watt's limits. He did insist that the noise levels be revised as technology changed, but the airport board never complied. The planners also continued to use noise methodology developed for use in urban, not natural, areas. The National Park Service recommended using a new method to assess noise in national parks—measuring quietness, not loudness. Despite the fact that Congress had requested the new methodology and an appeals court had thrown out the use of urban noise standards in national parks, the FAA had not adopted the new methodology. Thus, under the proposed plan, noise comparable to that of an urban area would be tolerated.

Jack tried to challenge the board to justify all development decisions on the basis of safety, but they dismissed his efforts. In frustration he flew to Seattle to meet the regional administrator of the FAA. Here he learned that, to the agency most concerned about safety, the Jackson Hole Airport was safe, with the existing weight-restriction guidelines. He also learned that safety areas, in contrast to stopways, offered the safety margin for aircraft overruns but wouldn't allow increased takeoff weight. The regional administrator even followed up Jack's visit with a letter to the airport board in which he suggested retaining the existing runway location and providing safety areas on both runway ends.

With this ammunition, on March 5, 1996, Jack made his stand. It was a cool, gray day. Because the airport board expected a large turnout for its announcement of a final decision on the airport master plan, the public meeting was held in a poorly lighted and semiheated hangar. After more than four years of public meetings, the public was burned out on the airport issue. Only about fifty people showed up.

"We completely support certain improvements to enhance safety at the airport," Jack began. "These include a tower, radar, paved safety areas, and precision-approach lighting for the south runway." With that said, he then hit the heart of the matter:

Since the airport has been certiWed safe, the current runway's length and position are adequate. Thus, we are unequivocally opposed to extending the runway north farther onto park land. In addition, I don't believe that the plan justiWes the 10,000-square-foot expansion of the terminal, the new two-story building for parking rental cars, and massive new hangars for general aviation. None of these developments improve safety. Instead, they all intrude on park land and park vistas. This is a national park with national values and interests at stake. We must rise above provincial concerns and Wnd the greater good for all.

Despite Jack's plea, the airport board voted in favor of shifting the runway to the north, essentially extending the runway. In addition, the vote approved all proposed development.

Jack and I left the meeting depressed. We had dedicated four years to the battle. Although the board gave lip service to our concerns, the plan incorporated only the issue of noise reduction—primarily because the management agreement and the FAA required it. Since the board had declared its final decision, I thought that the airport's future was decided. Jack, however, did not give up so easily. "I have just begun to fight," he said with a smile. "There is still a lot of time between the 'final decision' and the paving of twenty-seven more acres of park land. They have not seen the stubbornness of this old German."

True to his word, Jack tenaciously fought on. In January 1999, he and the FAA finally agreed to move the runway three hundred feet north to allow the addition of safety areas on both ends without having to acquire private lands. This decision would prevent overruns but have little effect on the park. Essentially, the runway stayed the same length but was made safer—a win-win solution.

By summer 2000, the airport boasted new facilities. A sixty-foot tower used tilted glass, black paint, and a dull finish to prevent glare and blend with its surroundings. New three-hundred-foot paved runoff areas offered safety but could only be used in emergencies. The entire runway was repaved and repainted, eliminating bumps and ripples. All pilots agreed that safety had been improved with minimal loss to park values.

The Jackson Hole Airport was not the only airport causing problems for the National Park Service. Cape Cod National Seashore and Denali National Park have smaller airports also considering expansion, and their managers watched the Teton process with great interest.

In addition, nearly a hundred parks confront the effects of overflights from nearby airports, especially commercial air tours. In 1995, Grand Canyon National Park alone had 140,000 overflights a year, spurring new regulations limiting the number of aircraft but not the number of tours each aircraft could fly. In March 2000 more regulations declared 75 percent of the park as a flight-free zone and capped the number of air tours to protect natural quiet. But before the FAA could implement the regulations, the air-tour operators requested and received an indefinite postponement based on safety concerns—too many tours channeled into too narrow flight patterns.

To assist park superintendents managing the increasing number of air tours, on April 15, 2000, President Clinton signed into law the National Parks Air Tour Management Act. Sponsored by Senator John McCain of Arizona, the law requires air-tour-management plans to mitigate or prevent significant adverse impacts of commercial air tours on the natural and cultural resources and visitor experiences in a national park. The law gave the government considerable latitude in restricting air tours or even prohibiting them altogether. Moreover, in August 2002 the U.S. Court of Appeals for the District of Columbia ordered the FAA to adopt a stricter definition of natural quiet in regulating overflights.

Unfortunately, the new law and legal ruling could not prevent a helicopter company in 2001 from using the airport in Grand Teton National Park. Even though the company flew scenic tours, it claimed it did not fly over the no-flight area of the park. Nonetheless, the helicopter arrived and departed from within the park. Environmentalists enlisted the town, its residents, and even the governor to convince Senator Craig Thomas to introduce a bill banning scenic flights in Grand Teton and Yellowstone national parks. When congressional action failed, the environmentalists filed a lawsuit to prevent helicopter tours over federal lands outside the park. In June 2002 a federal appeals court dismissed the lawsuit because the issues were too abstract.

Politics and tempers became almost as hot over another issue, the Continental Divide Snowmobile Trail. Once again, Jack and I found ourselves in the middle of a controversy that had started years before we came to Grand Teton. In the early days of snowmobiles, the National Park Service had no national policy for their use in national parks. Each park formed its own policy. All but Grand Teton confined snowmobiles to unplowed roads and frozen lakes. At Grand Teton, when snow fell deeply enough to protect the sagebrush, park management allowed snowmobiles to frolic on the vast plains west of the Snake River, an area known as the Potholes. Other years, usually two out of three years, snowmobilers had to content themselves with unplowed roads.

In the 1970s and 1980s snowmobiling became a major winter activity. Thousands of recreationists discovered the excitement and beauty of Yellowstone in winter. Until this "discovery," Yellowstone was essentially closed from Labor Day to Memorial Day. Interestingly, the same superintendent who closed the garbage dumps and thereby decimated the grizzly bears also opened the park to snowmobiles. He could not have predicted the surge of snowmobilers who demanded gas, oil, food, rest rooms, warming huts, and lodging. By the mid-1980s the park concessioners had opened Snow Lodge for the hearty enthusiasts, and the park groomed its unplowed roads to improve the park experience. By 1992 more than a thousand snowmobiles a day buzzed in to Old Faithful.

Unlike parks with plowed roads, Yellowstone had difficulty accommodating the swelling number of visitors. Before heavy snows closed its roads, Yellowstone's employees and concessioners had to ship in all the food and gas needed for the entire winter. Once the gas was consumed, there was no more until spring. Even solid waste had to be stored until the roads were open. To handle emergencies, huge track vehicles, looking much like military tanks, carried fire engines and ambulances. Individual snowmobiles provided transportation between office and home, around the park, and out of the park. In short, logistics became increasingly complicated with the burgeoning winter popularity of the park.

The economically depressed areas of Wyoming, however, envied the profits that Yellowstone's winter wonderland generated. The communities of Lander and Dubois conceived a snowmobile trail that would link them with Yellowstone. Because the trail would crisscross the Continental Divide, they called it the Continental Divide Snowmobile Trail, or just the Snowmobile Trail for ease in usage. These visionaries never doubted that Yellowstone's visitors would love traveling 150 miles in subzero temperatures to reach their communities.

These communities teamed up with one of Wyoming's most vocal lobbying groups—snowmobilers. Together they convinced state government to establish a snowmobile trail with name, logo, and funding. Quickly they hit a major roadblock—Grand Teton National Park. Park management had no interest in the trail and responded with disdain for the concept. Undaunted, the lobbyists found sympathy from their congressional delegation. Senators Malcolm Wallop and Alan Simpson used their political power with the subcommittees that funded and authorized the National Park Service to ensure that their constituents received a proper hearing.

Stubbornly the National Park Service resisted a snowmobile trail in Grand Teton. But political pressure, even coercion, won out. Grand Teton had to address the trail, but park management decided to do it under the broader umbrella of winter use. Regional Director Lorraine Mintzmyer, clearly unhappy with the idea of a trail, stated in a public meeting that when the snowmobile trail through Grand Teton became a reality, the Potholes area would close to snowmobiling. Her quid pro quo raised surprisingly little reaction among the Jackson Hole snowmobilers, who would lose their snowmobiling freedom in exchange for a trail that few of them would use.

Not content with a simple trade-off, National Park Service planners struggled to find the route through the park that would have the fewest environmental consequences. Trail enthusiasts wanted the route to follow the power line, an area already cleared of trees and away from automobile traffic. Instead, park management chose to place the trail within the prism of the road to Yellowstone. The road prism was the distance from the edge of pavement to the drainage ditch, an area averaging only about twenty feet. A trail less than twenty feet wide promised to create safety and construction nightmares—enough that park management hoped the trail would never be built.

When I arrived in late 1992, Senator Alan Simpson was leaning on Jack Neckels to stop stonewalling the trail. As a new superintendent, Jack carried no baggage from earlier battles. He told the senator that he needed funding to hire winter employees, to purchase snow-grooming equipment, and to construct storage sheds and houses for the new employees and equipment. Surprised to get a responsive answer, Simpson added $100,000 to the park's operating base with a promise of more to come.

When I drove the highway to Yellowstone, I could not imagine placing a snowmobile trail so close to the road. First, construction seemed impossible. The road prism often disappeared completely, with talus slopes of mountains coming right down to the roadway. Moreover, there were streams to cross, huge trees obstructing the route, and twenty-foot drop-offs along the way. Second, if constructed, the trail would be unsafe. Elevated above the road and without barriers, snowmobilers could fall off and be hit by highway traffic. In addition, the winding road made head-on collisions a possibility, especially with a trail occasionally narrowing to only ten feet. Third, maintenance would be difficult. The highway's snowplows would throw ice, gravel, even rocks onto the trail. It surely looked as though previous park management had deliberately made the trail an impossibility.

When I expressed my concerns to Jack, he agreed with me. "We've been dealt a hand of cards, and we shall play them," he said. "We may find that it is both impossible and unsafe, but we have to do the best we can to make it happen."

Neither of us could accept the resistance of the environmentalists to the trail. Snowmobiles driving along the side of a road would cause no more environmental damage than highway traffic and snowplows. In many ways, the snowmobile trail appeared less offensive than allowing snowmobiles the use of unplowed roads or frozen lakes. Of course, we both knew that the end goal for the environmentalists was eliminating snowmobiles entirely from national parks.

A more valid concern to us was contributing more snowmobiles to Yellowstone's already stressed environment. To mitigate that additional strain, we worked with the State of Idaho to open and groom the gravel road across the John D. Rockefeller, Jr., Parkway from Flagg Ranch to Ashton, Idaho. This route offered snowmobilers a more natural and less crowded experience than the one to Old Faithful.

Meanwhile park staff worked to make the snowmobile trail operational. First the brush and "dog-hair trees" in the road prism had to be removed. Every tree larger than eight inches in diameter that obstructed the trail required Jack's personal approval to remove. To keep the highway from looking unbalanced and to improve safety, maintenance crews "brushed out" the left side of the highway. Then we investigated renting, leasing, and purchasing special grooming equipment. We finally bit the bullet and purchased our own machines. In addition, we ordered smaller snowmobile speed-limit signs, including a warning light for the Jackson Lake Dam, the only stretch of trail where cars and snowmobiles would mix.

As we worked through a precise on-the-ground trail study, we found the plan forced us to an impasse. The trail could not cross a bridge near the entrance to Jackson Lake Lodge with a safe line-of-sight distance. The only alternative was to follow the lodge's horseback-riding trail under the bridge. If we deviated from the plan, however, we had to complete additional environmental assessments. But we had no choice; the risk was too great. We tied the environmental assessment to the rule change for the trail and addressed public comments on both. No comment stopped our progress.

Following the decision on the Jackson Lake Lodge bridge, our own ranger staff challenged us on the safety of the entire trail. They refused to accept our assurances that we would make the trail safe. Finally I told them that I would send the plan to highway-safety engineers in Denver and to Voyageurs National Park, the park with the largest network of snowmobile trails in the system. When the comments arrived, they confirmed our worst fears. Both entities stated that the trail was unsafe and recommended permanent barriers between the road and trail. Voyageurs suggested finding an old road for the trail to follow. Of course, neither option was viable. We had to prove that the trail was unsafe before environmentalists would allow it to move out of the road prism. Our only hope was that the proof would not require a serious accident.

As we wrestled these technical issues, Senator Simpson continued to add funds to our operating base. Although the division chiefs wanted to mingle the funds with other park accounts, Jack refused and insisted that the funds be used only for winter use. "I want to be accountable for every dollar," he said. "We will show Senator Simpson exactly what the taxpayer received for the money."

Fortunately for us, the winter of 1993–94 was mild with little snowfall. Activating the trail was impossible. We weren't ready either, but we got some good experience in running the trail groomers. We knew that we would have to be ready in 1995. Meanwhile, chief naturalist Bill Swift opened an interpretive contact station at Flagg Ranch, in the John D. Rockefeller, Jr., Parkway just a mile from the Yellowstone border. Here his staff gave winter interpretive talks and even occasional cross-country ski tours.

In late 1994, the first snow fell in October and continued to fall. The maintenance crew began constructing the trail. The great experiment began. In fact, Jack decided to call the first year an experimental year to test the feasibility and safety of the trail. He asked the park planner to develop a monitoring plan with standards and evaluation criteria to determine objectively its success or failure. We even contracted for a noise-monitoring study to assess the increased noise of the trail.

By January 1995, the trail was ready. Jack and I drove along the highway to observe it. I marveled at how the maintenance staff had filled in the drop-offs, crossed creeks with removable bridges, and leveled the trail. Only in two places did the trail invade the highway to avoid talus slopes. Here the crew repainted the center line, moving it to the left to accommodate the trail's dog-leg. I never thought that I would see the trail constructed. We were both tickled pink.

Opening day, January 14, 1995, proved clear and very cold. The temperatures dropped to thirty degrees below zero. Only a few hardy souls ventured out, but enough to test the trail. They took the trail to Flagg Ranch, had lunch, and returned. Although cold, they claimed they enjoyed the trip and commented favorably on the quality of the trail.

It proved to be a short season. By early March the eastern portion of the trail began melting. Jack determined that if any part of the trail became impossible to maintain, the entire trail would close. Although there were complaints from those who wanted to use the trail closer to the mountains where snowfall was heavier, we closed the entire trail. There had not been one accident or safety problem. Our experimental year was a success. I still couldn't believe it.

The following year was anticlimactic. We had done it all before and knew we could do it. The trail carried more traffic but fewer than the predicted fifteen hundred machines. This time we had one or two minor accidents. Also, during a major snowstorm four snowmobilers became lost and suffered considerably before rangers in the trail groomer rescued them. Another time a cow moose took up residence on the trail and refused to leave for several days. We closed the trail until she was ready to move on. This year we also had to give a few tickets for speeding, reckless driving, and using snowmobiles off the trail. Nonetheless, even the loudest naysayers admitted the trail wasn't a big deal. But I don't think many people made the trip from Yellowstone to Dubois and Lander.

For the 1995–96 season Jack announced that the Potholes area was permanently closed to snowmobiling. This time we received considerable complaints from Jackson Holers who had little use for the snowmobile trail. They tried to convince Jack that the plan did not spell out a quid pro quo, but Jack refused to budge. The anachronism of snowmobilers driving wherever they wanted in a national park had ended.

But controversy had not. In May 1997 conservation groups sued the Interior Department for allowing snowmobiles to pollute air and water in Yellowstone and Grand Teton. The National Park Service agreed to settle out of court and complete a three-year, three-million-dollar environmental impact statement on snowmobiles.

Broadening the fight, in February 1999, a coalition of environmental groups called the Bluewater Network petitioned Interior Secretary Bruce

Babbitt to ban snowmobiles altogether from the twenty-eight parks that allowed them. They pointed to the noxious fumes that carry a thousand times the hydrocarbons and nitrous oxides of one modern car. The coalition also asked the Environmental Protection Agency to set air and water pollution rules for snowmobiles and the Occupational Safety and Health Administration to regulate snowmobiles for creating carbon monoxide health risks to workers. The six-billion-dollar snowmobile industry and 2.5 million snowmobilers fought back with an extensive lobbying effort.

Finally, in April 2000, the National Park Service issued a broad ban on the recreational use of snowmobiles in all parks except where authorized by law (Voyageurs and Alaska parks) and Yellowstone and Grand Teton. The ban did not result from new legislation or regulation, but came from a new commitment to laws and rules that had been on the books for years. At last the pollution was clearly documented, and overlooking the law became intolerable.

When I thought that the byzantine world of snowmobiling could not get more bizarre, it did. The final winter use plan, approved November 22, 2000, phased out the use of snowmobiles in Yellowstone and Grand Teton national parks. By the winter of 2003–4, all oversnow travel would be limited to snowcoach. Despite my four years of travail in trying to make the Continental Divide Snowmobile Trail operational, the plan eliminated it. I was thrilled. The safety, expense, and limited use made the trail indefensible except for political reasons.

To avoid future lawsuits, the final winter use plan funded exhaustive studies. For example, it found that the three winter months serviced only 4 percent of Yellowstone's visitors yet consumed nearly a third of its budget. The park spent about five dollars for each summer visitor but thirty-two dollars for each winter visitor. More damaging, the Environmental Protection Agency's pollution studies found that snowmobiles, only one-sixteenth of Yellowstone's vehicular traffic, contributed up to 90 percent of the hydrocarbon emissions and up to 68 percent of the carbon monoxide emissions annually. Economic studies showed that West Yellowstone, the town most affected by a snowmobile ban, received only 30 percent of its annual sales-tax revenues between November and April. Moreover, park roads form only a small part of the hundreds of miles of snowmobile trails that crisscross acreage of the Bureau of Land Management and national forests. Safety concerns also entered the equation. For the past decade in Yellowstone, one to three snowmobilers per year lost their lives and one person per day was injured.

Most important, the National Park Service based its decision not on politics or economics but on the impairment of park resources. Snowmobiles pollute the air and dominate the soundscape. They are used to harass the wildlife and spoil the park experience of nonmotorized visitors. Considering the political environment and local repercussions, the decision took courage and resolution.

Only two weeks after the decision, the International Snowmobile Manufacturers Association brought a lawsuit alleging infractions of the environmental process. The new George W. Bush administration, without involving either Grand Teton or Yellowstone national parks, agreed to settle the lawsuit with still another supplemental environmental impact statement. Primarily the plan would solicit more information from local communities and the International Snowmobile Manufacturers Association. It would also more fully assess the new quieter, cleaner four-stroke snowmobiles.

Once again the political seesaw tipped in favor of a small but vocal group of users. The Bush administration ignored ten years of scientific study, twenty-two public hearings, sixty-five thousand public comments, and an environmental impact study called by the Environmental Protection Agency "among the most thorough and substantial science based" planning documents ever seen.

Moreover, the American public and its representatives reacted vigorously. On September 26, 2001, 102 members of the U.S. House sent a letter to President Bush that concluded: "The National Park Service has chosen to protect their irreplaceable resources and values for this and future generations, rather than allowing damage to the parks to continue. We urge you to stay with the course that gives Yellowstone and Grand Teton the protection they deserve and need as two of America's most special places." Two weeks later eighteen of North America's preeminent wildlife scientists claimed that the scientific findings of the "Final EIS were based on substantial, credible, and the best available scientific evidence." The public overwhelmed the supplemental planning team with 350,000 comments. Although more than 82 percent opposed snowmobiles, Interior Secretary Gale Norton simply replied that the planning process was not a popularity contest and that she was seeking "balance."

In June 2002, the Bush administration decided to allow snowmobiling to continue, but with tight restrictions on numbers and pollution. The new policies established a cap of 1,100 snowmobiles a day in Yellowstone, a 31-percent increase over the current daily average. As of 2003–4, all rented machines will have the quieter, less polluting four-stroke engines and most visitors will be required to travel with a guide. In December 2002 the environmentalists, however, took their turn to sue the Bush administration for failing to preserve national parks in a way that leaves them "unimpaired for the enjoyment of future generations." The battle for America's park lands raged on.

Another national controversy concerned another type of pollution: heavy-metal toxicity. An old gold mine outside Yellowstone led indirectly to immense complications for Grand Teton. In 1989 Crown Butte and other business partners of Noranda Minerals, Inc., a Canadian corporation, announced plans to open a defunct gold mine, the New World Mine, three miles from Yellowstone's northern boundary. Unfortunately, the mine stood at the apex of two streams that feed directly into the park. To prevent contamination of the streams, the mining company planned to construct an experimental "bathtub" covering seventy football fields in area and measuring ten stories deep, filled with toxic tailings. Any leak in that bathtub would wipe out aquatic life in the Yellowstone River and all species dependent on that river. Even before the U.S. Forest Service completed a draft environmental impact statement, the National Park Service opposed the mine.

When I arrived at Grand Teton in 1992, I had little knowledge of the mine. Yet within weeks Jack and I had to reverse established practices to avoid conflicting with the Service's stand on the New World Mine. The issue for us concerned the extraction of gravel, not pollution. For decades, park maintenance staff and contractors took gravel for highway construction from several extensive borrow pits within the park. With the advent of the gold mine, the Washington office did not believe we should continue "mining" gravel. Consequently, we told the Federal Highway Administration, which handled our highway construction contracts, to alert bidders that no gravel sources within the park could be used.

Just as I arrived at the park, the Highway Administration awarded a contract for $3.7 million to the contractor who had just completed an award-winning section of park highway. Unfortunately for all involved, the contract did not make it clear that no gravel could be taken from within the boundaries of the park. Because the contractor had used park sources for his recent contract and had taken gravel from private sources within the park for the airport, he approached the owner of the Moose Head guest ranch, a 120-acre private inholding in Grand Teton. He suggested excavating additional fish ponds in exchange for the extracted gravel.

Even though I was still so new that I wasn't much help to Jack, he bounced the problem off me. "We have an environmental assessment that requires a commercial source for gravel outside the park and we have a land-protection plan that prohibits mining," he mulled. "How can I allow the contractor to mine gravel even on private property within the park and not expect to get sued for failing to protect the park?" Despite my ignorance of the bigger issues and past practices, I did not think we had a choice. We had to prevent the mining of gravel. When we met with the owner and expressed our concerns, she quickly agreed to withdraw from the tentative agreement. She wanted no part of a relationship that made Jack Neckels uncomfortable.

Thwarted, the contractor sought previous sources he had used, all within the park's boundaries. Each time we had to remind him that we could not allow any mining. Frustrated with us, he turned to the Highway Administration, stating that his bid had been based on using in-park sources. He was told to perform or be declared in default. The contractor completed the contract and then sued us and the Federal Highway Administration for

$1.4 million. The National Park Service's interference, he claimed, prevented him from using local sources for gravel and forced him to incur extra costs in acquiring and hauling the gravel.

Since we had simply been following instructions from the Washington and Denver offices, we expected support in our lawsuit. Despite Director Kennedy's strong stand on the New World Mine, he offered us no assistance. We could not even get the Interior Department's own solicitors to counsel and defend us. Instead, we had to rely solely on the solicitors of the Federal Highway Administration, who were more concerned about its reputation.

An administrative judge heard the case in the fall of 1995. He ruled that the contractor deserved $962,000 because the National Park Service did interfere with his efforts to use Moose Head Ranch for his gravel source. The judge also faulted the Highway Administration for failing to inform the bidders that they could not use gravel sources within the boundaries of the park. Although the land-protection plan specifically prohibited mining, the judge referred to the 1872 mining law that did not recognize gravel extraction as mining. He also believed that the park's extensive use of park gravel for construction projects established a double standard—the park could "mine" gravel but private landowners could not. Thus he threw out our defense based on the land-protection plan. It was a professional blow to both Jack and me.

Meanwhile the New World Mine gained the attention of President Bill Clinton and the United Nations. In 1978, the United Nations had designated Yellowstone National Park a World Heritage Site and stated that its preservation was important to all the world's people. In the fall of 1995, just as we went to court with our lawsuit, the United Nations sent a committee to assess the dangers caused by the mine. About the time we heard the judge's verdict, the United Nations voted to designate Yellowstone as a World Heritage Site in Danger. The Clinton administration negotiated with the mining company to buy the mine for $65 million, requiring that $22.5 million would go to clean up historic toxic wastes. Congress authorized the expenditure of funds from the Land and Water Conservation Fund, and Clinton signed it in November 1997. He had averted an environmental catastrophe.

Joining mining as one of the scourges of land use is grazing. Both destroy the native and natural environment, bring powerful political forces to bear in any argument, and prove nearly impossible to extinguish once entrenched in a park. Nonetheless, since its organic act in 1916, the National Park Service has struggled to eliminate these destructive and nonconforming uses. In 1950 the act that established Grand Teton National Park prohibited mining, but allowed grazing on privately owned land within the park. More controversially, it continued grazing leases on park land for the lifetime of the lessee's heirs. Thus, within our lifetimes, we could expect to see an end to grazing on public lands within Grand Teton.

Yet Jack Neckels proposed the unthinkable—extending the grazing leases indefinitely—and created an issue that had not existed. Although Jack grew up on a small ranch in North Dakota and rode a horse to school, he never had any great love for horses or cows. As assistant superintendent of Grand Teton in the 1970s, he looked forward to the end of grazing as decreed by law.

Jack was aware, however, that most of the ranchers in Jackson Hole required grazing leases to supplement their home ranches. In order to grow hay for winter feed, each summer the ranchers drove their cattle north to these grazing leases. When the Jackson Hole National Monument threatened the leases and trailing privileges, Wyoming's congressional delegation ensured that the legislation merging the monument with an expanded Grand Teton National Park preserved trailing rights and grazing leases in the park as long as the ranchers' minority children, at the time of the act, still used the land.

Initially the grazing permits were scattered throughout the park. Cattle strayed into campgrounds and picnic areas, destroying the ambience of a national park. In 1957 the National Park Service suggested that the ranchers consolidate their cattle grazing to the 11,000-acre Elk Ranch in the northeast portion of the park. In exchange, the park would fence and irrigate sufficient pasture. The ranchers of Elk Ranch became known as the Pot Holes Grazing Association.

During Jack's previous tenure in the park, five ranchers used the park.

By 1992, all but two had sold their home ranches to contribute to the developing suburbs of Jackson. In October 1992, I met the two aging ranchers. Small, thin, and somewhat frail, former governor and U.S. senator Cliff Hansen was an eighty-year-old charmer. Physically attractive, with an engaging personality, he was dearly beloved throughout his home state. Although still agile and riding horses, he had turned over most of the day-to-day operations to his daughter, Mary Mead, a former candidate for governor herself. Ralph Gill, the other member of the Pot Holes Grazing Association, was a tall, robust figure with rugged features. As former mayor of Jackson, he too tinkered with politics. Unfortunately, his wife, the holder of the park's grazing lease, was dying of breast cancer. With her death, he faced the loss of the lease and probably the end of his ranching career.

It was a bright fall day when Jack and I met Hansen and Gill to discuss improving the irrigation of Elk Ranch. Although both confronted an end to life as they knew it, they were in good humor, joking and laughing with us and our staff. Cliff Hansen swept me away. "It is a good thing," I told Jack after the meeting, "that you stand between me and Cliff Hansen or I'd give that man anything he wanted." Ironically, what he wanted was what he had fought against so hard in the 1940s and 1950s—to make his ranch part of Grand Teton National Park.

The Hansen ranch and two others comprised an area known as Spring Gulch. These ranches bordered the park on its south and encompassed some of the most scenic land in the nation. A 1970s park boundary study had already determined these lands to be nationally significant, but the old ranchers could not afford to donate them to the park, nor did they want the ranching way of life to end. Yet with estate taxes based on the land's highest-and-best use and the escalating cost of real estate, the aging men and women knew that with their death the ranches would have to be sold and subdivided. One alternative would be extending the boundaries of Grand Teton or the National Elk Refuge and having the government buy them out with money from the Land and Water Conservation Fund.

Cliff had tried for years to find a conservation buyer, a wealthy philanthropist who would buy the land and donate it to a public land trust for a charitable tax deduction. Once Cliff even had one lined up. During the final stages of negotiation, however, the buyer learned that Cliff, like all ranchers in the area, used creosote to preserve his fence posts. Unfortunately for Cliff, in the 1990s creosote had become an environmental hazard and would have to be cleaned out of the soil prior to the sale. Replacing all the fences posts was too expensive an undertaking, and he had to terminate the sale.

Although Ralph Gill's ranch was several miles removed from the park boundary, it was among the last of the valley's private holdings. Only 3 percent of Teton County was privately owned, and most of that had already been subdivided and developed. From Grand Teton through Spring Gulch to South Park and the Porter/Gill ranch, however, was a continuous greenbelt used by the Teton elk herd and other migrating animals. Jack hated to see that lost to development interests.

When Ralph's wife died in the summer of 1994, Jack had a brilliant idea. "What is worse for the park, cattle grazing in Elk Ranch or 150 new houses on Teton's southern border?" he asked. Seen from that perspective, grazing was not the worst evil that could befall a park.

Jack envisioned an indefinite extension of park grazing leases in exchange for some perpetual guarantee of the greenbelt. First, he needed a study to assess ways of preserving the green space in the valley, but he also needed authority to extend Gill's expired lease. To achieve these ends, he had to have legislation. With a plan in mind, he met with Gill and Hansen and won their grateful endorsement. Then he brought in the city and county leaders who wanted to retain the greenbelt. Next, he turned to the strongest local environmental organization, the Jackson Hole Alliance, and convinced its leaders of the greater good for the park and the valley. Only after he had lined up these supporters did he seek congressional assistance.

Wyoming's congressional delegation proved willing to introduce legislation. Senator Malcolm Wallop, the ranking minority member of Interior's subcommittee, attached our proposed bill to his omnibus National Park Service bill. Because of the usual end-of-session machinations, time ran out before he could maneuver the bill through Congress. It was a disappointing blow to all of us in Jackson Hole.

Now Jack confronted a dilemma. Unless he gave Ralph Gill a leasing permit, Gill had no choice but to sell his cattle and then his ranch. If that occurred, Jack's great vision would evaporate. He decided to take a gamble and administratively extended the leasing permit one more year to allow time for Congress to act on the pending legislation.

This time, however, the environmental community turned on him. Having more time to think, the Jackson Hole Alliance determined that ranchers should find grazing leases for their summer pasture on forest instead of park land. The alliance unequivocally opposed cattle in national parks. When it learned of Jack's administrative decision on extending the lease, the alliance threatened a lawsuit, citing lack of environmental processes. Even though Jack extended the leases a total of three years before the Spring Gulch legislation finally passed, the environmental community fought him, but did not take him to court. Finally, on November 13, 1997, President Clinton signed the legislation that officially extended the leases while the Secretary of the Interior studied ways to preserve open space in Jackson Hole. Jack Neckels had won round one.

The National Park Service spent three years preparing the Grazing Use and Open Space Study. This report and one from a group of stakeholders were to be sent to Interior Secretary Gale Norton in 2002. She would make the final recommendation to Congress on whether grazing in Grand Teton should continue. The collaborative Open Space Work Group, comprised of ranchers, environmentalists, and local government representatives, could not agree on the basic premise of grazing in the park. Thus the report to Secretary Norton would probably consist of dissenting opinions.

By September 2001, however, the open-space study seemed almost irrelevant. Several of the ranchers adjoining the park had signed conservation easements, including Cliff Hansen for 181 acres in the southern portion of Spring Gulch. The town of Jackson announced an annexation and development plan for more than 800 acres of Ralph Gill's ranch south of Jackson. The development would construct 1,850 residential units and 475,000 square feet of commercial space, but preserve 520 acres for ranching. Then, in September, Cliff Hansen's family decided to quit ranching in the park altogether and sell most of the cattle herd. Much of Jack's vision had occurred in piecemeal fashion. While there will be some development, it will not be as intrusive as it could have been, not because of governmental action, but because of the personal commitment and altruism of the ranchers themselves.

Although I initially favored grazing in the park rather than suburban development on its southern boundary, the evolution of a patchwork of conservation easements appears a better solution. Because of Teton County's recent comprehensive plan, the heaviest density of housing allowed is one per five acres—a far cry from the five per acre that Jack and I feared. Moreover, with wolves and grizzly bears moving into the park in greater numbers, the potential for conflict with livestock had increased exponentially. With twenty-twenty hindsight, the environmentalists' opposition to extending the grazing leases appears correct—other alternatives for preserving open space developed.

Although most people abhor the role of politics in national parks, politics is a fact of life. As much good as bad comes from politics. While Watt made the Jackson Hole Airport bigger and more intrusive to the park, Andrus had almost eliminated it entirely. Although Senator Simpson forced Grand Teton to consider the Continental Divide Snowmobile Trail, he gave the park badly needed funds to handle a burgeoning winter season.

One powerful congressman, however, can play havoc with the integrity of the National Park System. A ranking minority member of the House appropriations subcommittee for the National Park Service, Congressman Joe McDade of Pennsylvania, foisted a second-rate railroad with third-rate Canadian rolling stock on the system. Without hearings, national significance studies, or even consultation, McDade attached a rider to the National Park Service's appropriation that funded an unknown site in eastern Pennsylvania called Steamtown. Over the next five years he funneled more than $45 million to the area, located in his depressed coal-mining district.

Even without authorizing legislation, the National Park Service dutifully accepted the money and made a tourist attraction out of a rundown town and an insignificant railroad. Several of the major buildings associated with the railroad, such as a spectacular roundhouse, were reconstructed at tremendous cost. Eventually a couple of restored steam locomotives and other rolling stock carried visitors along several miles of reconstructed railroad track. The millions of dollars pumped into the region created a new economy based on tourist trade. Unfortunately for the National Park System, other congressmen began to follow the same unprincipled practice, but none as blatantly as McDade.

Despite my abhorrence of the Steamtown shenanigans, politics had been good to me. It was through politics that I was able to fund a new visitor center for LBJ. It was through politics that Jack was able to study open space in Jackson Hole. In fact, neither of us had suffered a bad political blow. Despite efforts of the airport board to involve the congressional delegation, the master planning process proceeded politically uninhibited.

For me as a park manager, political savvy was more important than uncompromising adherence to park values. Recognition of the power of politics was essential to survival as a manager. I was comfortable with, even stimulated by, the role of politics in national parks. Although diffident about many of my managerial abilities, I knew that I worked well in political situations. As a result, I felt I had something to offer park management.

# The President and Congress

As superintendent of Lyndon B. Johnson National Historical Park, I learned to host important dignitaries. Several times a year Mrs. Johnson entertained members of Congress, former presidents and first ladies, and occasionally television and movie luminaries. Many of these guests spent time at the LBJ Ranch, which President and Mrs. Johnson had donated to the National Park Service. In addition, I worked on a daily basis with the Secret Service officers who guarded the former first lady. My staff and I treated all her festivities with discretion and ensured her and her guests as much privacy as could be gained from a public showplace.

Thus, when Hillary Rodham Clinton's vacation advance team of one person, Kelly Craighead, visited Grand Teton in July 1993, I was excited to think of the park's hosting a sitting president. Kelly's family came from Jackson Hole. For decades, before being alienated by new management theories, Kelly's two uncles, Frank and John Craighead, had studied grizzly bears in Yellowstone. Even though Kelly had spent little time in the valley, she loved it. Confidentially, she admitted being the primary supporter in the White House of a presidential vacation in the Tetons. Although I had only been in the park nine months, I knew we could offer the president what few national parks could: a fantastic scenic experience, isolation, security, and privacy.

A meeting with the park's management staff knocked both Kelly and me off our cloud. Not only was there no enthusiasm, the division chiefs emoted strong negativism. President George H. W. Bush had made a quick stopover during the previous year's campaign, but had spent more time on an earlier visit. "I know how much work is involved with a presidential visit," groused Chief Ranger Doug Bernard. "They are a pain in the butt, if you want to know the truth." His colleagues nodded in agreement.

I disagreed but could not generate any level of excitement. One after another the chiefs laid out problems—staff shortages, visitor needs, additional workloads, unfinished projects, unnecessary distractions, too much profile. I kept shaking my head as Superintendent Jack Neckels listened to the litany. Kelly excused herself and left for Yellowstone.

Later that day, Jack and I were driving to our Rotary lunch in Jackson. "I can't believe that the park is blowing such a fantastic opportunity," I said. "I know how much work these efforts are, but President Clinton has never been to a national park. Just think what we might be able to do for the National Park Service if we host his vacation."

"I'm not opposed to hosting the visit," Jack said. "Did that impression come across to Kelly?"

"I surely thought it did," I responded honestly.

"I agree with all you have said," Jack said. "We need to make sure that Kelly gets the right scoop."

Whether it was too late to reverse her earlier impression or whether the president preferred to vacation on Martha's Vineyard, we never learned. Nonetheless, I was as disappointed as my staff was undoubtedly relieved.

Two years later Jack and I had a nearly new cast of characters among our management staff. All but one of the previous staff had retired or moved on with promotions. Our new division chiefs were almost as green as I had been in 1992. On the other hand, they were much more responsive to political opportunities than their more experienced but jaded predecessors.

One of our major personnel changes came from Washington, D.C., to be our concessions manager. Joan Anzelmo had been the Service's public information officer, reporting directly to Director Kennedy. Her political instincts had been honed to a sharp edge. During the fires of 1988, she was Yellowstone's public information officer and took nearly as much flak as Superintendent Barbee. She actually seemed to enjoy working eighteen-hour days and being hammered constantly by politicians, media, and other agencies. She possessed tremendous vitality and energy. At times her impatience fueled a temper and provoked collisions with her peers. Nonetheless, her charm, hard work, and political savvy made her a great asset, especially if the president were ever to vacation in Grand Teton.

Joan had hardly been on the job six months when one of her contacts in the Interior Department called with a number of vague yet particular questions. She concluded immediately that some highly placed political personality, maybe even the president, was sounding out the park. Responding with considerable imagination and knowledge for so short a tenure, she then reported to Jack and me. This time, Jack and I agreed, the park would welcome any overture from the White House.

Within a couple of days, Chief Ranger Colin Campbell received a more specific call from the Secret Service. The agent wondered what facilities and resources the park had to host the president of the United States. Already briefed by Joan, he described the rustically luxurious Brinkerhoff House, where President Carter had stayed in 1978, and said that he could call in as many rangers in special-event teams as the Secret Service needed. The next day an agent arrived to assess the Brinkerhoff. Its presence on Jackson Lake and near the park's second busiest highway made it too vulnerable. Bombs, automatic weapons, and terrorists had become real possibilities since Carter's administration. With that news our hearts sank.

A couple of weeks later Kelly Craighead called Joan. This time, rather than representing the first lady, she was cochair of the president's vacation advance team. Once again she was promoting Grand Teton National Park. Joan's responsiveness encouraged her, and she urged that Joan serve as White House liaison. Nonetheless, Joan counseled us to keep all information as confidential as possible. Any leaks would send a clear warning that we couldn't be trusted. Only the four of us knew of the White House calls.

The next we heard came from the *Jackson Hole News,* asking us to confirm the rumor that President Clinton would be vacationing in Jackson Hole. Strangely, the White House travel office had reserved more than a hundred motel rooms in its own name. Gently we let our breath out and replied that the White House might be a better source than we could be. Rumor also claimed that he would stay at Laurance Rockefeller's huge mansion at the Jackson Hole Golf and Tennis Club. Apparently Rockefeller had recently sold his place to his Democratic nephew, Senator Jay Rockefeller.

Colin followed up his lead with the Secret Service. Rockefeller's house could be easily secured, with outbuildings providing headquarters for communications and security. In addition, it did not border on a main road, nor was the river too close. Unlike the Brinkerhoff, the Rockefellers had permanent staff to assist the White House. The Secret Service confirmed the newspaper rumor and requested assistance in providing perimeter security. We were so happy we could almost dance.

When Colin tried to call some National Park Service special-event teams, however, he had a rude awakening. Although the Service had spent hundreds of thousands of dollars training these special teams, none of the region's teams wanted to come and help us. I was shocked. I didn't think that teams or even superintendents had the authority to say no. The Service had recently undergone a reorganization, and like all reorganizations chaos reigned and accountability had hit its nadir. Colin had no choice but to call in a national Type I Team.

Type I Teams, similar to those used in fires, are composed of the best specialists in the National Park Service. The incident commander, Jim Northrup, had been the fire-management officer at Grand Teton but left during my first year to become the chief ranger at Big Bend National Park in Texas. Smooth, articulate, and thoughtful, he knew the park, its resources, and the community. His thoroughness led to comprehensive plans; his judgment resulted in sound decisions. He labored hard to minimize the friction between the team and the park staff. Over and over, he repeated that his task was to make ours easier. His competent and effective staff complemented him nicely.

Northrup and his people arrived a week early. They wanted to collect information, develop plans, order forty rangers from other regions, secure motel rooms, and attend to other logistics. With the White House entourage numbering more than three hundred, motel rooms came at a premium. Colin had reserved twenty rooms but had relinquished them to a desperate White House. Each summer Jackson Hole expands from a population of five thousand to more than thirty thousand. The White House insisted that no visitors lose their rooms if the president came to vacation. As a result, some of the rangers wound up in less than standard motel rooms. These rooms lacked all-night desks that would answer phones after midnight. Consequently, we had to lease more cellular phones and pagers than we would have otherwise.

Colin Campbell and Joan Anzelmo served on Northrup's immediate team. Colin represented the park, and Joan functioned as White House liaison. They marched to different drummers. Colin worried about safety and protection while Joan grappled with political and media issues. Occasionally these two opposing pressures blew up, causing Jim, Jack, or me to intercede and find a working compromise. Both employees gave their heart to the project and the team. Long hours filled with tension and anticipation rubbed nerves raw. Northrup's grace salved many wounded egos and kept spirits high.

Northrup broke the team into three branches. The security branch handled perimeter patrol of the Rockefeller estate, managed traffic for the nineteen-car motorcade, and supplemented Secret Service protection of the president and first lady. The park-activities branch planned hikes, bicycle rides, nature walks, horseback riding, and other park-related experiences. The forest-activities branch planned comparable activities in Bridger-Teton National Forest, such as whitewater rafting and camping.

Each branch chose the best location for its activity, determined how many people were needed to assist, how many additional rangers to protect the first family from visitors and potential troublemakers, and what other resources were required. For example, the hiking sub-branch decided that an easy hike around String Lake would require five rangers to assist and another five for protection. The plans also included the lead-time needed as well as time required for the hike. They included such small details as obtaining meals, snacks, sunscreen, and insect repellant. Horseback riding demanded additional logistics, such as acquiring the horses, getting them to the trailhead, and determining how many of the Clinton entourage would ride with the president. These plans were largely completed before the president arrived on August 15.

In the meantime the president's entourage began to filter into the valley. Even for his vacation, more than a hundred of the Washington press pool came with him. Others included White House aides, communication and transportation experts, and the omnipresent Secret Service. While the number three hundred had been tossed around, the size of the party didn't really sink in until we all met in a conference room at the Snow King, Jackson's largest hotel. Here Kelly and her cochair, Mort Engelberg, the Hollywood producer of *Smoky and the Bandits* who was volunteering his services, introduced all the various groups and their functions. One thing I remembered from my days at LBJ was how important communications are to a president. The communication specialists outnumbered all other groups. The president had to be accessible at all times.

On the following day a select number of prominent people from the community met Air Force One. Because Jackson Hole's runway was only six thousand feet long, the usual Boeing 747 could not be used. Instead, it landed in Idaho Falls, twenty minutes away, and the president and first lady transferred to a DC9 to land in Jackson. The mayor, his wife, and his grandchildren were first in line to welcome the president to the valley. Others included the state senator and representatives, leaders of the local Democratic Party, Jackson city councilors, Teton County commissioners, the Bridger-Teton Forest supervisor, and Jack Neckels.

Each member of the welcoming committee had a small message for the president and first lady. Some gave gifts, such as straw hats or ball caps. Everyone without exception commented on the president's ease, grace, and friendliness. Considering that Jackson and Wyoming were predominately Republican, some wondered what political hopes he had for choosing the Tetons for a vacation. Clinton simply said that he was tired and needed to rest, but hoped to hike, horseback ride, and certainly golf. Then he entered a black four-wheel-drive Suburban and joined the first of many nineteen-car processions to drive to his vacation home.

Initially, while the president and first lady (known to the press as POTUS and FLOTUS) waited for their daughter to return from a trip to Alaska, they kept a low profile. Clinton golfed thirty-six holes his first day on the greens. Mrs. Clinton used her time to work on her book *It Takes a Village.*

The day Chelsea arrived, the Clintons moved beyond the country club. Their first stop was a barbeque dinner at Dornans, a private business within the park. The movement of the presidential party was so secretive that the superintendent's office did not learn that the president had been in the park until after he had left. A few rangers, however, did tell their families to have dinner at Dornans without being specific. Dornans had been forewarned, and their staff informed a few of their close friends. Nonetheless, the president's family mixed with visitors and park staff in a low-key way.

After dinner, the advance team asked Joan where the president could go for a private walk. Joan took them to the area behind the visitor center and in the vicinity of the Chapel of Transfiguration and historic Menors Ferry. Here she spent more than twenty minutes walking and talking with the first family. She was so excited when she got home that she called me immediately. I was a bit surprised and disappointed at not being able to welcome the president to the park, but I was glad that so many of the hardworking team members were able to meet him. They certainly deserved any small perk they got.

During the seventeen days of vacation, the Clintons enjoyed Jackson Hole. One evening they went for pizza and walked the wooden boardwalks of the town, exploring various businesses and bars. Another night they went to the rodeo. Still another evening they spent at the Teton Music Festival. Most days Clinton tried to get in at least a few holes of golf.

For his forty-ninth birthday, Mrs. Clinton gave him golf lessons with golfing pro Johnny Miller. Then, at a birthday celebration held at the 135-acre estate of World Bank President Jim Wolfensohn, they all stayed up singing Buddy Holly and Beatles songs. En route to his birthday party, however, he spotted a child's lemonade stand with a handwritten sign: "Ten Cents. Free on your birthday." He stopped the motorcade and received his free lemonade while he joked with the kids. The brief stop made him late for his birthday party but memorialized him with the neighborhood's children.

Next morning, on Sunday, August 20, the Clintons once again sojourned at the park, this time at the Chapel of Transfiguration, a privately owned Episcopal church with one of the most spectacular views of the Tetons. Dressed for hiking, they participated in the church services like all the other visitors and residents.

After church, they wanted a brief hike. Linda Olson, the park's public information officer and most congenial interpreter, agreed to guide them and provide naturalist talks. Linda's knowledge and vibrant personality made her an instant hit with the Clintons. Several stops along the trail offered photo opportunities with the magnificent Tetons as a backdrop—one photo made it to *Time* and another to *Newsweek*. After the brief mile-and-a-half hike, the Clintons dined at Jenny Lake Lodge, the small but elite concession on glacier-dug Jenny Lake.

When we learned that the Clintons had never camped in a wilderness, we proposed several alternatives, including a historic cabin on the west side of Jackson Lake. The Secret Service vetoed all our suggestions. The president, they insisted, had to be accessible within ten minutes anywhere in the world. Moreover, anything that might contribute to security problems, such as the remote potential for grizzly bears, they did not want. They had also told us that any hikes or bike rides should be easy. Regardless of television shots showing the president jogging, they said, he was really in poor physical shape. Linda Olson, however, privately disagreed. "He walks fast and hard," she said. "He can probably hike faster and farther than most of us." Slowly we learned that what the Secret Service wanted was not necessarily what the president wanted, and he usually won.

Thus the Clintons' camping experience was on the historic Rockefeller

JY Ranch within the borders of Grand Teton National Park. It was private, accessible, but removed from visitors. The Rockefeller staff provided horses, fifty-year-old tents, and campfire cooking. Probably unaware of a long-standing war between the park and the JY foreman over the use of pesticides within the park, White House staff complained of mosquitoes. The Clintons, however, had mosquito-proof tents and enjoyed the experience.

The Secret Service also misled the Type I Team on whitewater rafting. They assured us over and over that the president would not go whitewater rafting—it was too dangerous and he would politically shun anything with the word *whitewater*. Well, high on the president's vacation agenda was whitewater rafting. The Forest Service hosted this activity in Snake River Canyon, and the president and Chelsea had a blast. When asked what he thought of whitewater now, he joked, "Better when you have a paddle."

The president had perfect weather for the first ten days. Then, just as he planned to helicopter to Yellowstone for the birthday of the National Park Service, it rained and rained. Cloud levels hovered near treetops. Because Clinton wanted to give an environmental message to commemorate the occasion, Grand Teton spruced up the Menors Ferry area and constructed speaking stands and podiums. For at least one day, I thought that the hyperactive White House advance team wanted my park house for the occasion. It was a historic log home, built in 1933 by the Civilian Conservation Corps, shadowed by the Grand Teton itself. Despite the large log living room, the advance team thought there was not adequate space for the press. All the park's work was for naught, however, because the weather cleared enough for a helicopter flight to Yellowstone.

The new superintendent of Yellowstone, Mike Finley, drove down to Jackson to fly up to the mother park in the same helicopter as the president. As a result, he was able to brief him on the reintroduction of the wolves, Crown Butte's New World gold mine just outside the boundaries of the park, and a meeting with the environmental community.

The weather cleared just long enough for the first family to view Old Faithful. Then, as the president started to give a brief speech, it began to rain.

Bareheaded in the downpour, he championed parks. "I am committed to preserving these parks," he said. He berated the more extreme Republicans in Congress who wanted to force the closure of two hundred parks or sell off "some of our natural treasures to the highest bidder." He also emphasized two of Secretary Babbitt's proposals: keeping park entrance fees in the parks and charging park concessioners higher franchise fees. Never before had a Clinton speech even mentioned national parks. Now he saw their value.

Later that day, in a cleaned-out barn, Clinton met with several of the area's environmental leaders. Here he committed himself to a moratorium on mining around Yellowstone. That decision did not resolve the issue of the Crown Butte mine, which already had leased private land. When questioned about the mine, he expressed concern and interest, but avoided making any commitments. Within a few days of this meeting, Clinton met with several ranchers in Jackson to hear their concerns. He did not want to be accused of playing favorites.

Aside from his brief speech in Yellowstone, Clinton made one other political speech under more formal circumstances. From the beginning of the vacation, the White House told us that Mrs. Clinton planned an address on the seventy-fifth anniversary of the enactment of woman suffrage. Without the usual frantic information gathering and belated decision making, the White House decided to use the back lawn of the Jackson Lake Lodge, overlooking Jackson Lake and the full panorama of mountains, as the location for the speech.

Next, with only three days until the speech, the park's maintenance staff built a stage. What had begun as a modest speech to a small audience mushroomed to a major political event with the president as the primary speaker. Because the president would be speaking, in case of gunshots or terrorist attacks, the Secret Service insisted that the back walls of the stage be bulletproof and far enough from the lodge's terrace wall to allow the president and his bodyguards to kneel behind it. Since the bulletproof walls stood behind the stage, not in front, I wondered about the viability of the expense, but we did whatever the Secret Service wanted. To add refined rusticity, the maintenance crew veneered the stage with logs. They also constructed risers and railings for the press corps.

After three days of rain, the clouds cleared off for a gorgeous suffrage anniversary day. Jackson Lake Lodge set out four hundred chairs for an audience largely of women. Before the speech, Joan told Jack and me that we would meet the president and first lady at the side entrance to the lodge. Then, following the speech, the White House photographer would take our photographs. Even though the park's uniform code prescribed a summer uniform of short sleeves and open collar, for more formality I decided to wear my long-sleeve shirt with cross tie.

Jack and I arrived at Jackson Lake Lodge in plenty of time to review our staff's handiwork. All four hundred guests had to enter the back terrace through an airport-like security gate to check for guns, knives, and other dangerous weapons. Joan showed us our reserved seats among the guests of honor, such as former Democratic Governor Mike Sullivan and his wife, Assistant Secretary of the Interior Robert Armstrong, and local leaders in the Democratic Party. As the seats began to fill, Jack and I walked around to the side entrance, fully aware of the numerous Secret Service agents and park rangers guarding the approach.

Fifteen minutes after the hour, we heard sirens, running late as usual, entering the lodge grounds. First in line was a park patrol car, freshly washed. Colin had told me that the law-enforcement agency into whose jurisdiction the president went led the nineteen-car motorcade. In the middle were several black Chevrolet Suburbans, one of which carried the president, first lady, and former Governor Mike Sullivan. The president wore a gray suit, a red necktie, and alligator-skin cowboy boots. The first lady had on a long brown western shirtwaist dress with an Indian jewelry necklace, concho belt, and western hat.

As they came up to the door to meet us, my first impression was how tired they both looked. This was supposed to be a vacation, but both of them looked worn. Because I was the same age as the Clintons, I could easily see the toll of their jobs. Mrs. Clinton wore very heavy makeup, and the president was badly sunburned, especially his bulbous nose. Yet they were warm, friendly, and even chatty before they were ushered into the lodge. Jack and I returned to our seats for the speeches.

Mrs. Clinton spoke first. I noticed that she was whispering in her husband's ear as she was being introduced. When she stood up to speak she said, "I just whispered to Bill that in all the places of the world that we have been, we have never been to one more scenic than this." The day and views could not have been more spectacular. Jack and I looked at each other, smiled, and felt proud and lucky. The first lady talked about the upcoming United Nations World Conference on Women in Beijing and discussed the roots of woman suffrage in Wyoming, even acknowledged the 1920 all-woman city council of Jackson. Then she introduced her husband. "I always have to introduce him," she said. "If you have never tried to introduce your spouse to an audience, try it sometime. It is difficult. What do you say? Do you refer to the night he walked into our bedroom after I was already in bed and showed off his brand-new, hideous alligator-skin cowboy boots?" It was charmingly handled.

The president spoke for twenty minutes without referring to his speech or notes once. I had seen him on television often, but never in public. He was effective, sincere, and believable. I don't remember much of what he said except some political boasting on what his administration had done for women. It was a political speech, but I liked it and him. Afterward I spoke to several big-name Republican women. "I have to say that I am impressed," one said. "He may not get my vote, but I have changed my opinion of him." Another said that his efforts to minimize the disruption to their lives of his visit went a long way to improve his image. Never once were roads closed for his motorcade. He did not ask for special favors and was an approachable, friendly guy.

Joan came, gathered Jack and me, and escorted us to a remote terrace for our photographs. While we waited, we watched as the president mixed with the admiring crowd of women. He had taken off his coat and tie and rolled up his sleeves. As he started toward the terrace for the photographs, he ran into Joan and Linda Olson, sitting under a tree. He sat down next to them and pulled his wife over on his lap and began joking with Joan and Linda.

Then he caught Jack's eye on the terrace. "Hey, Jack," he called. "I'm going to take these two women back to the White House."

"They are two of my best employees," Jack countered. "You wouldn't want to give me that kind of a handicap, would you?"

"Well, then, give them a promotion or at least some more money," Clinton said.

The two sparred a bit more, then Clinton put on his coat and tie and climbed the stairs to the terrace. As he walked down the line of law-enforcement officers, he shook each one's hand and the White House photographer snapped the shots just as quickly. When he reached me, he took time to put his arm around me and thank me for the hard work. Because Jack had his daughter-in-law and granddaughter with him, his photo required more composition. It all went surprisingly smoothly with little time involved. Then we were invited to a reception. Suddenly the afternoon was over.

I drove home reflecting on the day. I had enjoyed the opportunity to meet the president. It was one of the highlights of my National Park Service career. How often does one meet the president of the United States, especially one whom you liked? I enjoyed the constant state of crisis as we waited for the president to decide what he wanted to do. The long hours, the detailed plans, the logistical arrangements all stimulated my managerial appetite as much as the accolades for a job well done excited my ego.

The following day Clinton told Joan that he wanted a real hike. This time Linda took them into the Tetons along Cascade Canyon Trail. Like thousands of visitors a day, they crossed Jenny Lake on a twenty-minute concessioner boat ride. Then, seemingly without difficulty, he climbed to Inspiration Point, a five-hundred-foot elevation gain in only one mile. With the Secret Service and press sprinting to keep up, he continued briskly along the trail. Here he met hundreds of visitors, startled at running into the president of the United States. Dignitaries in the past had required the trails or roads be closed, but not Clinton. He loved meeting people.

Just as Linda suggested turning back, she saw two moose and pointed them out to him. The president moved forward for a closer look, and the bull moose rose and shook. Immediately the Secret Service drew their guns and prepared to shoot it if it moved any closer. Linda saw the making of a public-relations nightmare with the Secret Service shooting a moose in a national park in front of hundreds of visitors. Fortunately, the day was hot, and the two moose had no interest in Clinton.

Linda's earlier hike with the first family had prepared her for this one. She carried enough water for all of them. When she applied sunblock, she noticed that he didn't seem to have any. "Sir, you really should use sunblock," she reminded him. "You are beginning to look like a peeled lobster." He laughed and agreed that golfing at high altitude had taken its toll on his complexion. To ensure that they kept their strength, she stopped several times and handed out hiker's gorp—a mixture of nuts, dried fruits, and candy. The president was unfamiliar with the mix and ate a lot of it. After hiking five miles in and five miles out, he went back and played eighteen holes of golf, then partied until after midnight. His stamina amazed all of us.

On the president's last day in the valley, he told Joan that he wanted another hike. Linda suggested Taggart Lake. I urged Jack to go and get some quality time with his boss. Jack admitted that he was overweight and out of shape. Instead, he insisted that I go. That made my day. I was scared but excited. Here was the most powerful man in the world, and I would have him as a captive audience for three or four hours. Linda had warned me that he hiked fast and hard, but I thought I could keep up.

Jack drove out to the trailhead with me and would send us off. We got there just as the rangers received word that Clinton was running late again. This time he was more than an hour behind. He had an appointment with the National Wildlife Art Museum first. The Secret Service also reported a rumor that some former hippie was threatening to shoot Clinton. The hour stretched into two and then almost three. Finally we heard that the hike was canceled. The Secret Service did not want him in the open country where some nut could pick him off. My heart and spirits sank as low as they had been in years. My one chance to hike with the president blown because one person mouthed off too much.

Initially, the Clintons had planned to fly out that evening of August 30. Traditionally the Type I Teams celebrate the event with a "Wheels Up Party."

Plans were made and money collected. Then the Clintons changed their minds and decided to stay another day. Gracefully, Colin extended an invitation to them to attend their own Wheels Up Party. It was held at the Jackson Golf and Tennis Club, not far from the vacation home of the Clintons. The manager, Clay James, was also the concession manager of Jackson Lake Lodge. Because of the occasion, he made the party more than what the team had paid for. Typically, it was a class act. Everyone had a grand time, except those who resented the press for not paying their share of the expenses.

At about nine o'clock here came Clinton's ten-golf-cart procession. Both Clintons made small speeches of gratitude, then circulated among the guests. Many park employees got their picture taken with the president or first lady. It was a high point for all of us.

The early-morning departure ended a phenomenal seventeen-day visit to Grand Teton National Park. Then came the bureaucratic hassle of finding funds to pay for the National Park Service's role. The Secret Service paid only ten thousand dollars for part of the security branch costs. We knew from the beginning that the National Park Service would have to fund the special activities branch. We had not counted on the crazy accounting system that allotted overtime to the parks that released their rangers to help us. We sent in their time and attendance and so did their parks. As a result, there was a huge mess of double charges and lack of accountability. Initially, Grand Teton bore the brunt of the visit to the cost of thirty thousand dollars. I made repeated calls to Washington and Denver, trying to figure out what happened and why some parks could charge the account directly while we could not. In the end, the regional office used contingency funds to help us out of the hole. Nevertheless, I could not believe the second-guessing and petty penny-pinching—coffee pots for the press and laundry charges for the rangers could not be reimbursed. Yet during fire season, nearly anything was approved.

Considering the high profile the National Park Service had during the presidential vacation, I could not understand or accept the lack of support from our Washington office. Few of our "leaders" seemed to understand how Clinton's exposure to national parks and our mission would

have long-term benefits. At no other time in the history of the Park Service would such an opportunity take such a low profile. Director Roger
Kennedy's reorganization had left each park to shine or fail independently
of the Service—witness the failure of the regional special-event team to
assist and Washington's resistance to helping fund expenses associated
with the visit. Any other director would have welcomed the visibility of
the National Park Service and would have ensured that the park had all the
resources needed to reflect well on the Service.

During his vacation, Clinton learned exactly how much Americans
valued their national parks—he had seen it firsthand and experienced the
same feelings himself. Never before interested in national parks or environmental issues, he became personally involved in settling the Crown
Butte gold-mining issue, in removing a tract of redwoods from the saws of
lumber companies, and in saving southern Utah from development. I
believe that it was his summer vacation in Grand Teton National Park that
expanded his interests. For me as well, it was a summer to remember.

After his cool mountain vacation, President Clinton returned to a hot,
steamy Washington to confront a hostile Republican Congress. Bristling
with power and intimidation, Congress had repeatedly "rolled" Clinton.
Seeking consensus or compromise, he had lost one program initiative after
another. The most humiliating was the failure of his health-care program
followed immediately by the 1994 congressional elections in which the
Republicans, for the first time in nearly fifty years, swept both houses.

Now, in September 1995, Clinton faced the proverbial showdown.
With less than a month until the new fiscal year, Congress had failed to pass
the necessary acts that would fund his administration. Both sides played to
the public. The Republicans wanted a balanced budget, and Clinton wanted
to ensure that education, the environment, and the poor and elderly did
not lose to the rich. The grandstanding continued throughout the month.
As the new fiscal year opened, Congress passed an emergency extension of
funding for one month only. Both sides were still far apart with no compromise in sight.

Meanwhile, at Grand Teton National Park, Jack and I developed a plan in case the government shut down. Once before, during George H. W. Bush's administration and my tenure at LBJ, a budget impasse had closed government offices over the Columbus Day weekend. Because it was a weekend, the hardest hit were national parks and their visitors. I remembered it as a confused and uncertain time that caused great unhappiness for the visitors.

This time the Washington office sent out more explicit instructions. It authorized only "essential" personnel to work, and no one could volunteer to work. Anyone failing to comply faced serious fines and even jail time. Because we needed to protect the park resources and prevent recreational activities in the park, we deemed most of the rangers as "essential." To keep the water and sewage treatment plants operational and safe, their operators were "essential." Jack made Colin and me "essential" but decided he was not. Only the "essential employees," approximately 20 percent of the staff, would be allowed to work and could be guaranteed a paycheck.

When the first temporary funding allocation expired, Congress extended it one week and then another. Still the executive and legislative branches could not agree on a budget formulation. It looked as though the stalemate would last all winter. The last extension ended with the Veterans Day holiday. Because Bob had an Eastern National board meeting in Branson, Missouri, and we expected another extension, we flew to Missouri.

This time no extension came. The government was out of money, and all nonessential employees were told to stay home. Jack, not I, had to carry out our shutdown plan. I became nonessential. The entire two days of the board meeting I was on pins and needles, momentarily expecting the impasse to be resolved. Instead, the bickering and name-calling in Washington continued. As the shutdown entered its third day, I became increasingly disgusted with the antics of the Republicans in Congress. They held government workers hostage to their revolution. Without hearings or proper legislation, they were trying to change the basic fabric of American culture through the appropriations process. For once, Clinton seemed to be standing firm and refusing to be rolled.

From Branson I called Jack at Grand Teton and heard the latest crisis in the shutdown. As part of the 1950 park legislation, deputy park rangers (that is, sport hunters) helped "reduce" the elk herd as it migrated through the park to its winter feeding grounds at the National Elk Refuge. The elk-reduction program brought hundreds of hunters to the state who in turn spent millions of dollars. If Jack shut down the elk hunt, as he had all other activities in the park, more elk than desired would feed at the elk refuge, but more important the State of Wyoming and every hunter with a permit would be howling at us—not at Congress.

On the third day of the shutdown Bob and I returned to Grand Teton. Although theoretically not allowed to work, I drove the sad and lonely two miles to the visitor center. I passed no cars on the road. When I reached the junction with the visitor center, barricades blocked the road. A ranger seated in his vehicle told me that this was the most onerous job he had ever done for the National Park Service. "It goes contrary to everything I believe in," he said. "It doesn't seem right to keep visitors and taxpayers out of their parks." I asked if there had been any problems. He said that no one blamed the parks, and most people were just disgusted with the politicians in Washington.

Jack and Colin were meeting on the pending crisis over the elk-reduction decision. I listened to their concerns, but couldn't agree. "How can we say that elk reduction is an essential resource-management activity?" I asked. "Hunters only kill about five hundred animals a year, yet the National Elk Refuge has seven thousand more elk than it can feed." Jack agreed. "Until I got here and questioned the practice, the park allowed the killing of bulls," I continued. "Even then Steve Cain told me that there was a surplus of bulls and that the State of Wyoming feared no one would hunt unless enticed here with bulls, which yielded racks of antlers as trophies. Bernard made the decision to kill only cows, and he took a lot of flak because he did it late in the season. Still, it will be a long time before the killing of cows will have an effect on the number of elk feeding at the elk refuge." Neither Jack nor Colin disagreed with my analysis. They were addressing the political aspects of the issue.

As we talked, the telephone began to ring. First, the governor of Wyoming called, followed by a sport-hunting association. Soon I saw the handwriting on the wall. Permits had already been issued, airline tickets purchased, motel reservations confirmed. The park would be overwhelmed with hunters expecting to hunt. If the hunters arrived at the park and were told the hunt was off, angry hunters with loaded rifles would be storming the barricades. It wasn't just politics, it was an explosive environment. Suddenly I saw the problem as clearly as Colin and Jack.

We had only a few options. One, we could close the park to hunting and face the consequences. Two, we could allow the State of Wyoming to take over the hunt and lose our jurisdiction. Despite the 1950 legislation and court cases upholding the authority of the National Park Service to manage wildlife within park boundaries, the State of Wyoming believed it managed all wildlife in the state, including that within the boundaries of Grand Teton National Park. We did not want to create a jurisdictional issue on top of the political crisis of the moment. Three, we could allow the "reduction" as required by law, but prohibit "hunting" as a recreational activity.

This time Washington came to our rescue. The deputy director declared that hunting, where authorized by law, could continue. Because state government managed hunting in other park areas, primarily recreational areas, ours was a unique case. The departmental solicitors determined that elk reduction was a resource-management activity that required a specialized force of deputies (not volunteers) and occurred only once a year. Without that activity the resource would suffer. Thus, the activity became essential. But as far as Jack, Colin, and I were concerned, the decision was made on the basis of safety. It would have been foolhardy to cancel the hunt.

While the decision surprised many local environmentalists, only one person made an issue of it. The local Sierra Club representative expressed outrage that visitors could not enjoy their park, but hunters were able to kill park elk. He confronted the rangers at the barricades and forced them to arrest him. Later the park threw the charges out, but his frustration mirrored that felt by many visitors, including our own staff.

After a full week of shutdown, Congress passed a month's extension. This not only allowed everyone to go back to work, but it paid all employees whether or not they had worked during the shutdown. This inequity caused nearly as many problems as the unfortunate term *essential employees*. All employees believed they were essential. On the other side, those who had worked resented the "free" vacation for those who didn't. The shutdown divided the workforce and hurt morale as well as productivity.

And still the budget impasse loomed over us. As the Christmas holidays approached, so did the end of the funding extension. No one could believe that Congress would shut down the government at Christmas, but it did. Thankfully, the elk-reduction season had ended. Now, however, we had to determine how much snowplowing was essential. We decided to plow the school-bus routes, the main highway, and just enough roads to allow minimal access to our facilities. This time we lowered the ranger presence at the barricades. Those "essential employees" who worked during the last shutdown wanted the holidays off. They figured that Congress would pay the nonworking as well as the working. In some cases, we had to order employees to work. It was an ugly time.

This time the shutdown lasted three weeks. It hurt the National Park Service more than any other agency. Winter concessioners lost nearly one-half of their income. Their biggest season occurred with the Christmas holidays. Motels and restaurants around park areas also lost their winter profits. The nightly news highlighted a different park area each night, detailing the pain of the visitors, the communities, and the employees. Three weeks without a paycheck began to hurt many of our employees. Local banks offered no-interest loans to help out. Several employees even filed for unemployment compensation. Everybody felt like pawns in a political game with no rules.

Daily polls showed the public blamed the Republican Congress for the shutdown. Individual congressmen came across as petty and power-crazy. Still Clinton held tough, refusing to concede to a balanced budget unless Medicare, Medicaid, education, and the environment were protected. Finally the Republican Congress threw in the towel and extended the funding indefinitely until an appropriation bill could be passed.

Everyone went back to work, but without heart or good cheer. Federal employees had suffered through Vice President Al Gore's "Re-engineering Government," which resulted in downsizing and eliminated thousands of jobs and even entire agencies. Earlier, President Reagan had referred to public servants as bullying bureaucrats whom he wanted to "get off the backs of the people." It had been a long time since an administration valued and rewarded its loyal employees. As a result, many of the best and brightest, attracted to government during the Kennedy and Johnson years, left and were replaced with mediocrities. For many in the National Park Service, the shutdown was the low point in their careers, and they decided to leave or retire.

For all, the shutdown created real problems. Government had essentially lost two months of productivity. All programs fell behind. Trying to resolve payroll and leave issues became tremendously complicated. Despite ample snow, we even had to delay the opening of the Continental Divide Snowmobile Trail. Regional Director John Cook recommended time-off awards to help compensate the employees who worked during the shutdown. Those who didn't work resented the awards, saying they couldn't relax or vacation for the uncertainty of when the next paycheck would arrive. Even a welcome-back letter from President Clinton failed to lift the spirits of the employees.

The shutdown marked the lowest point in my career. For the first time, I was not happy being a public servant. At Rotary, I had to defend the indefensible. Business owners couldn't understand why employees didn't work, especially because they would probably get paid in the end. Even when I explained the law, with penalties of fines and jail, they refused to accept the situation. When the employees did get paid, I heard complaints about their tax dollars being spent for nonworking employees. They repeated Reagan's refrain of bureaucrats feeding at the public trough instead of finding real jobs. Some even began to question whether government was needed. "Why not let the state run the parks?" was a frequent rhetorical question.

During the shutdown, Arizona and Philadelphia did fund the Grand Canyon and Independence Hall to keep them open. The Grand Canyon issue became especially explosive. The governor arrived at the park with a fully armed Arizona National Guard unit to take over the park. Rather than fund the opening of the entire park and its staff, the Interior Department only negotiated for funding the highly visible visitor operations. Thus, those employees not funded felt unimportant and undervalued.

The shutdown came on top of a disastrous reorganization of the National Park Service. To meet Gore's requirement of a 30-percent reduction in public employees (which cynically did not include politically appointed positions), Roger Kennedy's National Park Service decided to eliminate central offices and their oversight of park areas. Thus, the brunt of the downsizing occurred at the Washington office, the ten regional offices, and the Denver service center. While parks did not suffer any downsizing, they could not fill vacant positions with anyone but surplus employees from the central offices—many lacking experience or abilities needed in parks. As a result park mobility and promotions stagnated, and morale plummeted even further.

A greater problem arose from the lack of oversight. Suddenly John Cook had more than a hundred superintendents reporting to him, and he had no staff to help hold them accountable for their actions. The reorganization severed the direct relationship between professional staff and line management. No longer, for example, could my successor as regional historian advise the regional director. Rogue superintendents took advantage of the vacuum and undertook initiatives that ran counter to policies and laws. Supposedly the new organization encouraged superintendents to cluster together to provide accountability and support. Although superintendents bond together in a tight brotherhood, they rarely work together to resolve common problems and are uncomfortable assessing the performance of another superintendent. The badly flawed reorganization created chaos, uncertainty, lack of accountability, and devastated morale.

Although senior superintendents had cautioned Director Kennedy against the reorganization, he persevered. He rammed it through a conservative and resisting culture. No matter how hard superintendents and regional directors tried to make it work, their hearts weren't in it. Many of the older and wiser superintendents decided not to fight it any more and retired, opening long-coveted superintendencies. Those employees who played to Kennedy's ego or supported his monstrous reorganization were rewarded with promotions to these high-profile parks. Unfortunately for the good of the Service, the most qualified for these prestigious superintendent positions had alienated the director by opposing him. The unfortunate result was poorly qualified people in highly controversial and publicly visible positions.

My own chances for a big park superintendency would dim considerably until a new director succeeded Kennedy. But mostly I found myself disenchanted with government service, politicians, and leadership. I began to hate the cynic I was becoming. I knew that eventually the reorganization would unravel, that Kennedy would leave, and that the traditional organization that I loved would rebound. All I had to do was practice Jack Neckels's motto: "The courage of patience and the strength of persistence." The good life would return.

# Priorities and Decisions

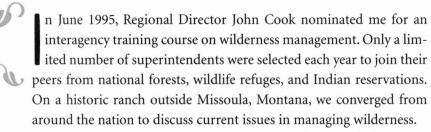

In June 1995, Regional Director John Cook nominated me for an interagency training course on wilderness management. Only a limited number of superintendents were selected each year to join their peers from national forests, wildlife refuges, and Indian reservations. On a historic ranch outside Missoula, Montana, we converged from around the nation to discuss current issues in managing wilderness.

While most of the two-week course involved classwork, the course compelled us to experience the wilderness. We had our choice of hiking, horseback riding, or llama packing. I chose hiking. The course provided the packs, tents, food, and all equipment. Although I planned to hike in my Reebok shoes, just as I had for my hike to the Lower Saddle, I brought along my hiking boots in case of rain.

The guide for our hike came from the National Outdoor Leadership School in Lander, Wyoming. In 1965, a year after the passage of the Wilderness Act, Grand Teton mountaineer Paul Petzoldt had founded the school to train outdoor leaders to serve the increasing number of people using wilderness. Its current thrust instructed people on "Leave No Trace" hiking and camping. Before we packed our backpacks, the instructor insisted that we watch a video on "Leave No Trace." The concept emphasized minimizing human trammeling of the wilderness. Some of the dictums included avoiding camping in the same place twice, scattering the remains of extinguished campfires, keeping hiking trails as narrow as possible, and no bathing in rivers or streams. As our wilderness experience evolved, I found these dictums harder to follow than I expected.

I tried to tell our instructor that I needed to hike in my Reebok shoes instead of boots. He insisted that I wear boots to avoid sprained ankles or falls. I told him that, even using moleskin and Second Skin, I was very susceptible to blisters. To him, blisters meant little compared to serious accidents. When the beautiful blue skies clouded and rain poured, I conceded that my Reeboks would not be appropriate.

Despite a near-drought for the whole summer, it rained the entire three days of our wilderness experience. Sure enough, within two hours of hiking I feared I had a blister. Because the rain had soaked my socks and boots, the moleskin stopped adhering and became an irritant to my ankle. At a rest stop, I pulled off my socks to examine the damage. The irritant had already created a blister. The instructor seemed surprised that my feet were so tender, especially if I had hiked as much as I claimed. When I could not make either the moleskin or Second Skin stick to my dripping feet, he offered me tincture of benzene. This substance established a base to which the moleskin stuck. Gratefully I replaced my soaking socks and boots and continued the hike. Every evening when I took off my socks, no matter how careful I was, part of the moleskin clung to the sock and pulled off with it. With the moleskin came part of my water-tender skin as well. The benzene worked almost too well. What had started as a small blister spread into several immense sores. Yet the tincture of benzene made Second Skin adhere and allowed me to continue the hike.

Hiking was no fun. Again, like Outward Bound, it became a test of endurance. None of my peers seemed to enjoy it much either. The only relief was dinner, when the instructor showed us some of his specialties, even within the constraints of "Leave No Trace." Finally, on the third day we started back, and at last the sun began to shine. Although we knew we should walk in the water and mud in the center of the trail, nearly all of us yielded to selfish interest and walked on the higher and drier edges, widening the trail even further. All we wanted was to get back where we could get dry and clean. Despite my blisters, I was among the first at the trailhead. Here I pulled off my boots and aired my bloody feet. I counted eight blisters or sores on one foot and nine on the other. My fellow hikers were shocked to see what a mess my feet had become.

Back at the wilderness school, my struggles had not ended. I had to hobble half a mile uphill to reach the tent camp. Although we slept on cots, we did have hot showers, in the portable trailers used for forest fires. Following the rains, however, came a significant drop in temperature. The thin sleeping bag failed to hold out the cold, so I piled all the clothes I had brought on top of me and survived the night. The next morning I learned that we had only to ask for extra blankets. Outward Bound had schooled me to cope with limitations. The remaining nights I had several blankets and slept warmly.

I had not had a chance to talk with Bob for nearly five days. I stood in line twenty minutes at the only pay phone before I was able to place my call. When he answered, he sounded weak and drained. I asked him what was happening. "It's been a bad week," he said. "I had a bad episode three days ago and haven't been able to get on top of it. They seem to keep occurring each morning, each with less severity than the last."

What we called "episodes" were characterized by dizziness, disorientation, and mental confusion. Since Bob had had his first episode in 1981 in Santa Fe while responding to a fire call, the doctors had never diagnosed it, but internists still thought it was a migraine variant and treated it with Inderal, a heart medication whose side effects helped prevent migraines. Although the medication didn't stop the episodes, it limited their frequency and intensity. Bob had not had an episode in the three years that we had lived in the Tetons. We had begun to think that the high Rocky Mountain climate was better for his health than anywhere else we had lived.

I thought maybe stress contributed to Bob's episodes. When he started to write his biography of Sitting Bull in 1990, he had an episode while driving into Austin. He forgot where he was going and even wondered if he remembered how to drive a car. Pulling off the road, he waited twenty minutes for his confusion to ease. Then he returned home. Each day for a week he had repeated occurrences with decreasing intensity. Now he was starting his mountain-man book, and the episodes had started again.

When I expressed my theory, Bob denied it vehemently. "I have never been less stressed with a book before," he said. "The writing is going easily and smoothly."

But his brain refused to function as smoothly. He said that following his daily regime of exercising he became dizzy and confused. Then, as he shaved, a jumble of wild unrelated images caused more disorientation. As these faded, he felt physically weakened and had problems reading. The effects continued throughout the day. Now into the third day, he was getting concerned. I insisted that he make an appointment with his internist, who scheduled an MRI, a medical procedure to check for strokes among other problems.

Although we were both sure that his episodes were benign, their intensity and continuation unnerved us. I called him three times that day. Each time he reported having "aftereffects," feeling drained, headachy, and often dizzy. Because he still tried to write each day, the confusion that he experienced especially disturbed him. Throughout the rest of my training, Bob had his episodes, but thankfully they became less severe. When his MRI disclosed nothing abnormal, his doctor slowly weaned him off Inderal and put him on a calcium channel blocker. Nonetheless, for nearly two months he had occasional episodes that undermined our happy equilibrium.

As we worried through each episode, I began to wonder if I had my priorities in order. What if his episodes were a series of minute strokes, not large enough for an MRI to catch? How would I feel if he had a major stroke? All our dreams of retiring together and writing history would be lost.

For the first time since Santa Fe, I considered leaving the National Park Service. Now, Director Roger Kennedy's reorganization encouraged people to retire early, allowing them to claim an immediate retirement annuity. Age and length of service would limit my annuity to only half of what it would be if I stayed another eight years. Financial-planning software, however, helped provide verification that our savings and potential earnings would support our accustomed lifestyle.

As the months passed, I became increasingly disenchanted with big natural parks. No matter what Jack and I tried to do for our employees, it never seemed enough. Although the number of EO complaints had fallen, I still had to handle several a year. When the ingratitude and negativism got to me, Jack reminded me that employees in all big parks believed management was against them. "Some parks, like Yosemite, have an active employee group running counter to management interests," he said. "We have more positive employees than other parks I have seen." His assurances didn't help my exasperation.

While I knew that assistant superintendents shielded most big-park superintendents from employee hassles, I also knew that the superintendent was the ultimate arbiter of employee life. If I wanted to be a big-park superintendent, these kinds of hassles went with the territory.

As I looked at Director Kennedy's recent appointments to major superintendencies, I wasn't sure that I wanted to be part of that politically correct and sycophantic brotherhood. Responding to intense political pressure, he had named a fair share of women and minorities. While earlier directors had groomed employees for higher and higher positions, little mentoring or management training now took place. Kennedy seemed to appoint people loyal to him, regardless of training or experience.

In addition, the Servicewide fund that ensured quality training no longer existed. Training depended on whether a park could afford to send a worthy candidate. Even though at the beginning of each year employees dutifully filled out a training program approved by their supervisors, the need for certain courses seldom coordinated with the courses offered. Employees often grabbed the courses they could get and their superintendent would fund. Specialty training courses proliferated, but there was no longer a basic introductory course that all employees attended. Leadership in Washington, D.C., tried to define a prescribed program for becoming well trained, but limited funds made the program irrelevant.

Thus there was no common foundation on which to build nor a knowledge base that managers could expect all employees to possess.

The employees themselves struggled to keep their lofty idealism that set them apart from other agencies. The reorganization and resultant freeze on all positions depressed morale and enthusiasm. Most employees believed in the mission of the Service even if they may have perceived it differently from their leaders. Although I occasionally became frustrated with employee demands and efforts to undermine my and Jack's leadership, I often had to remind myself that I was no different in rejecting Director Kennedy's misguided reorganization and poor management decisions.

Seasonal employees, especially, are the conscience of the Service. They are usually avid environmentalists untainted with pragmatism. Regardless of their job—whether ranger, interpreter, or maintenance worker—their sole interest is preserving the resources. Many of them would like permanent jobs with the National Park Service, but not at the cost of compromising their values. They accept low wages with no benefits, long hours, and substandard housing to toil among the most beautiful or most significant resources in the nation. While respectful of rank, they are seldom hesitant to question and even challenge park policy. Several times Jack and I met with groups of seasonals to discuss the Continental Divide Snowmobile Trail, concessioner development, and other controversial issues.

Most of them rejected the move to make parks more accessible. They accepted the need for handicapped accessibility for some areas of a park but not necessarily all. But they rightly perceived politics behind other accessibility programs. In the 1980s and 1990s, under the rubric of accessibility, motorized travel became the dominant push. Snowmobilers, scenic-air-tour operators, personal-watercraft users (jet skiers), and motorized rafters all claimed to make parks more accessible to the less physically fit. Because a greater diversity of people (older, overweight, less skilled) could use the park, these special-interest groups boasted that their uses were more egalitarian and less elitist than the more traditional uses of hiking, cross-country skiing, and canoeing.

It did seem that during Republican administrations opening the parks to the greatest number of users was a major focus. Jim Watt, President Reagan's Interior Secretary, believed that limiting Colorado River tours through the Grand Canyon to oar-propelled boats restricted the experience to strong, well-bodied people. He declared that all Americans should have the same opportunity. Consequently, big motorized rafts now carry nearly eighteen thousand people per year, and the industry has ballooned into a $25-million-per-year concession. At popular stopover points, hundreds of people mill around, and portable toilets have to be carried on the rafts. The noise level in the narrow canyon increased by several decibels. Watt also determined, without supporting scientific research, that Alaska's Glacier Bay could handle more cruise ships and a couple of hundred thousand more tourists without harming the endangered humpback whales.

With Watt's emphasis on increasing opportunities to enjoy parks, people reacted with a variety of uses. Some pushed the envelope of appropriateness. Hang-gliding and parachuting off the sheer cliffs of Yosemite were legal during the early 1980s. Then park management determined that the spectacular activities distracted from the scenic wonders of the park and proved unusually dangerous as well. Nonetheless, protesters continued to test management's will. As late as 1999 two groups of protesters parachuted illegally from El Capitan, a 3,200-foot cliff. In June one parachutist drowned in the river and the following October another's chute failed to open. Even at Grand Teton, we had occasional paragliders, who jumped off one of the mountain peaks and paraglided into the valley, where our rangers caught and ticketed them.

Before the advent of snowmobiles, do-it-yourselfers put the fuselage of an airplane on skis and called it a snowplane. While it had difficulty negotiating forest trails, it performed beautifully on frozen lakes. People who enjoyed ice fishing found the snowplane transported them to the best fishing spots, provided a shelter from the wind, and gave them great mobility. During the 1970s, when snowmobiles became more reliable and powerful, Grand Teton managers expected snowplanes to phase out. Instead, they flourished. Snowmobiles could not replace snowplanes on Jackson Lake. They were too heavy for lake ice, ran on a track that froze if driven in even small quantities of water, and lacked a protective enclosure for the sedentary fishers. The fifteen snowplanes of the 1970s had ballooned to more than eighty by the 1990s. The 2000 Winter Use Plan banned snowplanes as well as snowmobiles, but with Secretary Gale Norton's supplemental plan snowplanes wound up back on the negotiating table.

Other new recreationists wanted to use vehicles accepted on other public lands. These included trail bikes, off-road vehicles, hovercraft, and hot-air balloons. While jet skis, also known as personal watercraft, became popular on Jackson Lake, we prohibited them on Jenny Lake. Even so, many visitors complained of their noise, motorboaters grumbled about the safety risks their reckless users caused, and environmentalists claimed their two-stroke engines dumped 30 percent of their oil and gas unburned into the environment. In 2000 the National Park Service, in response to a lawsuit, banned jet skis in national parks and recreational areas unless the industry could prove that the machines did not harm the environment.

Complicating the concept of use, some types of vehicles are not consistently managed throughout the Service. At Grand Teton, we limited trail bikes and bicycles to roads, but some parks allowed them on certain trails. Off-road vehicles, hot-air balloons, and hovercrafts we prohibited. But because some parks allowed these activities, occasional users tested our resolve. In 1999 whitewater recreationists proposed opening Yellowstone's rivers to river running. "Shouldn't there be rivers in some places where whitewater rafting is not allowed?" the assistant superintendent asked, "and shouldn't Yellowstone National Park be one such place?"

With more users came more conflicts among users. Cross-country skiers abhorred the noise and smell of the snowmobiles. Jet skis intimidated swimmers and polluted the water. Motorized rafts brought congestion and noise to the small oar-rowing rafts. Hikers cursed the fouled and damaged trails of horseback riders. Dune buggies destroyed the beach treasures of beachcombers. Each set of users complained to park management and their congressional representatives.

During the 1980s and 1990s, the new theology of use dominated environmental politics. Anti-environmental senators and representatives passed new laws and tried to undermine existing laws. The Endangered Species Act came under intense fire, the Clean Water Act confronted weakening amendments, and Congress used the Land and Water Conservation Fund for balancing the budget. During these years, funds for purchasing park land dwindled to nearly zero.

Alaska's congressional delegation personified this new theology. In 1994, when Republicans won a majority in the House of Representatives, Alaskan Don Young became chair of the House Natural Resources Committee (renamed Resources Committee). Senator Ted Stevens already held the powerful chair of the Appropriations Committee, and Senator Frank Murkowski chaired the Committee on Energy and Natural Resources. Never before in American history had members of Congress from one state controlled the three committees most critical to national parks. They set about to reverse the Alaska National Interest Lands Conservation Act and to "open up" Alaska. They tried to block regulation of commercial fishing in Glacier Bay, force construction of new roads in Denali and Wrangell-St. Elias, and allow unrestricted use of motorized vehicles and helicopters in park wilderness.

The main issue appeared to be: How much use and abuse of national parks would Americans tolerate? They loved their national parks. Since World War II, the number of visitors each year had mushroomed. More and more cars compounded the problems of narrow roads and limited parking lots. Rest rooms, visitor centers, and scenic and historic waysides became crowded and overused. Park budgets stagnated as presidents reduced government services and offered tax cuts instead. Thus, only small sums of money existed to repair worn and rundown facilities. While Americans noted the deteriorating infrastructure, they seemed to prefer a balanced budget, less government spending, and tax cuts. On the other hand, all agencies complained of budget shortfalls, and the National Park Service failed to distinguish its concerns from the general government malaise.

Initially, in the 1980s and 1990s, Americans seemed ambivalent about new and expanded uses for national parks. An attitude seemed to prevail that people ought to enjoy national parks on their own terms. If some wanted to negotiate huge recreational vehicles along narrow winding roads and park in cramped camping sites, they could also use their political power to lobby for wider roads and improved campsites. If others wanted to bring their new technological devices, such as cell phones and computers, parks should accommodate them, even if it meant a transmitting tower or two scarring the scenery—they might save lives.

Just as Americans tolerated all types of park uses as valid until proved destructive, they had no problem with businesses turning parks into profit. Gateway communities especially seemed to believe parks owed them a business. Entrepreneurs devised numerous services to help visitors experience parks with less travail. They offered hiking tours, motorboat excursions, or photography safaris—all for a fee. Because national parks offered these activities free, superintendents often denied such requests. Most businesspeople did not believe that the National Park Service should limit their efforts to make a legal and legitimate profit.

At the same time most Americans saw no harm if movie studios used parks as movie backdrops. They perceived that movies advertised parks and helped the local communities. In reality, park rangers monitored movie companies constantly to keep them from damaging the resources or behaving inappropriately. Unlike the high special-use charges private-land owners billed movie studios for the right to film their land, park managers could charge only overtime and small administrative charges. Moreover, parks seldom benefited from movie production. Instead, they occasionally suffered resource problems, such as the use of detergent in Jackson Lake to create the illusion of rapids and whitewater. They also nearly always confronted staffing problems as they tried to ride herd on the movie production and continue routine operations at the same time.

Park managers also had no authority to review and approve the content of a film. We tried to prevent an advertising agency from superimposing a train passing through the Grand Tetons, but had no legal support. Ironically, only intellectuals became upset with the commercial dishonesty. Earlier, in the 1980s, the producers of the Indiana Jones movies wanted to use a cliff dwelling at Canyon de Chelly. The opening scene showed Boy

Scouts potting an archeological site. Even though the scene actually promoted breaking a federal law in a national park, we could not deny the permit. Instead, the superintendent, a Navajo, told the producers that the movie would offend his people. Fortunately, the studio decided to film the scene on private land rather than upset the largest tribe in the United States.

For a while in the 1980s and 1990s, it seemed national parks were up for sale. As park budgets failed to cover the shortfalls in maintenance and visitor services, park managers became more and more creative in finding funds. Prohibited by law from fundraising, some park managers established special groups, called Friends groups, to do it for them, as John Bezy did at Pecos. Corporations began offering donations for a tax write-off and appropriate park recognition. As the stream of donations became a wave, corporate logos almost rivaled the park arrowhead in visibility. Eventually, the National Park Service minimized the exhibition of corporate logos in parks.

Other park managers used fees to support their programs. Beyond the basic entrance fee, they charged fees to camp in the backcountry, for special interpretive experiences, and for snowmobile and motorboat permits. The superintendent at Glacier Bay proposed a 72-percent increase in the number of cruise ships above those Jim Watt allowed. The fees from the ships were expected to generate one million dollars annually for research on marine wildlife, research that the park could not otherwise afford. Fortunately for the endangered humpback whales, the U.S. Court of Appeals for the Ninth Circuit unanimously ordered the boat traffic to return to 1996 levels and required a full environmental impact statement to assess the proposed increase.

Yellowstone managers also inched into entrepreneurship. They decided to tap the profits of private scientific corporations searching for uses for Yellowstone's microbes, an activity called *bioprospecting*. In 1985 a microorganism from a Yellowstone hot spring contributed to the DNA fingerprinting process and earned the company millions of dollars but nothing for the park. In 1997 the park signed a benefits-sharing agreement with Diversa Corporation of California to ensure that at least half a percent of the profits went toward park resource preservation. A lawsuit tested its legality, and the federal judge declared the agreement legal but required an environmental assessment before Diversa could bioprospect further.

Most business in national parks, however, goes to concessioners. The National Park Service provides monopoly privileges to hotel and food-service operators in exchange for a percentage of the profits. Only recently has the American taxpayer realized that most concession contracts returned less than one percent to the federal treasury. For example, in 1993, prior to a new contract, Yosemite's concession grossed $92 million but returned only $700,000 to the government. Although Congress revised the archaic law in an effort to increase competition for the concession contracts, the new law did not adequately address the method of reimbursement for capital expenditures made by the concessioners, known as *possessory interest.* Consequently, any company wanting to bid on an existing concession contract would still have to pay for the existing concessioner's possessory interests, sometimes totaling several hundred million dollars. Thus the law failed to promote competition, and without competition the concession franchise fees would stay less than 5 percent.

At the same time, concessioners are a powerful lobby. They have been instrumental in the removal of at least one director and several large-park superintendents. Constantly they pressure park management for more costly amenities, such as more and larger accommodations; telephones, television, and spas in the rooms; more showers and RV sites for the campgrounds; and more gas stations and mini-marts. At Teton, two concessioners with formidable Republican connections fought against removing their commercial developments from the fragile river bottoms in accordance with Park Service policy. In the end, Jack succeeded in winning their compliance but only after unrelenting pressure. If he had shown any weakness to compromise, he would have been rolled.

By the mid-1990s, however, the American public refused to accept most of the Republican legislative ploys. The first clear-cut failure of the Republican Congress came as they tried to modify clean-water legislation. Americans demanded safe drinking water. Then, with the success of the

Gray Wolf Reintroduction, Congress defeated damaging amendments to the Endangered Species Act. While Americans might question the need for all extant species in the ecosystem, such as snail darters and rare algae, they had no doubts about the more charismatic species such as wolves, grizzly bears, and bison.

In 1996, after the Republican Congress failed to pass anti-environmental legislation, President Clinton, sparked perhaps by his experiences at Grand Teton National Park, finally realized that Americans wanted environmental protection. Using his executive order authority, Clinton created more than nineteen national monuments and pushed stronger environmental regulations. Before the end of his administration, federal rules for a number of issues appeared. They limited the number of roads in national forests, banned snowmobiles and jet skis in national park areas, and reduced the quantity of arsenic allowed in drinking water.

In early 2001, President George W. Bush tried to reverse some of these regulations. Among the first was Clinton's arsenic limits. The resultant uproar caught Bush's attention. He learned, as his Republican colleagues had earlier, that Americans still wanted safe water, regardless of cost. After this debacle, Secretary Norton's strategy shifted from reversing regulations to encouraging lawsuits against Clinton's regulations. Then, under the auspices of the court, they negotiated settlements that essentially reversed the regulations. By late 2002, this tactic was in the process of modifying nearly all of Clinton's regulations, especially the ban on snowmobiles.

When I arrived at Grand Teton in 1992, I was shocked by how much the park was used. Even though I had been in the National Park Service for nearly twenty years, I was surprisingly ignorant of the pressures on big natural parks. If I hadn't realized how heavily these parks were used, I was almost certain that most Americans didn't know either.

For example, when more than three million visitors in less than four months hit a few favorite trails, the impact became highly visible in trail erosion and deterioration, sanitation problems, litter accumulation, and wildlife habituation to people food. Fewer dollars meant fewer ranger patrols, less trail maintenance, poorer public health, more accidents and injuries, and more polluted streams and groundwater. In short, the individual visitor had a less than satisfactory experience.

Another example was horseback riding, an expected experience in any western national park. Horses, however, tear up trails, pollute streams, and disrupt hikers. When Jack finally convinced the concessioner of Jenny Lake Trail Rides to sell out to the park, neither Congress nor the Service helped the park fund the buyout. Instead, many visitors wrote letters of complaint for the loss of the experience. Still, privately owned horses and outside vendors continued to use park trails around Jenny Lake. Jack could never eliminate all horses from the park. Several concessioners, such as Jackson Lake Lodge and Triangle X Guest Ranch, still provide this popular experience.

While horseback riding is a destructive use of a park, it has a long, continuous history as a desired visitor experience. In contrast, as assistant superintendent I received several requests per week for special permits for some unusual activity in the park. These requests lacked a history of use and usually minimized visitors' experience. Most notorious were fund-raisers who wanted to use the magnificent scenery of the Grand Tetons to market their product. Sometimes charities wanted to sponsor walk marathons or bicycle races. Because safety concerns coupled with national policy prohibited such activities, I was able to resist the political pressure. But when the superintendent of the Black Canyon of the Gunnison National Monument in Colorado tried to eliminate a popular marathon, he wound up with Secretary Babbitt and the whole Colorado congressional delegation pounding him. That could just as easily have happened to me.

I know the feeling of being pressured by an organization that won't take "no" for an answer. My confrontation was with a demanding cellular phone company. To service the visitors to Yellowstone, the company insisted on building a transmitting tower and maintenance road on Steamboat Mountain within a proposed wilderness. When I asked the promoters to provide a less intrusive alternative, they said that they had to have the road, the tower, the power line, and the house-sized structure. When they grew intransigent, I denied the request. Immediately, I began to get calls from the staff of Wyoming's congressional delegation. Once the situation was explained, the staffers backed off and told the company to find another location or an alternative with less environmental impact.

Instead, the company brought in photographs of ongoing construction of a concessioner's long-approved lodge. I carefully explained that the concessioner's construction had gone through extensive environmental processes and public meetings and that it was being done at the insistence of the National Park Service to recover grizzly-bear habitat and minimize conflicts with grizzly bears. Still the company demanded its right to public land. Company officials refused to see any difference between land managed by the U.S. Forest Service, the Bureau of Land Management, and the National Park Service. It was all public land and should be receptive to private enterprise.

After the passage of the 1996 Telecommunications Act, which authorized communication towers in parks, the cell phone company tried again in 2001. This time the Wilderness Society demanded that the agency determine the area's wilderness values before the destructive road and tower nullified its potential wilderness qualifications. Earlier, in 1980, the park had agreed to study whether the Steamboat Mountain area would be eligible for designation as wilderness. Like other controversial and politically unpopular topics, the study was never funded. Now the park could stall no longer.

Another ambitious entrepreneur pressured us repeatedly for a concession on hot-air balloon tours. As a lawyer, he had studied public-land management and environmental policy. He quietly threatened me with illegal discrimination. "You gave the airport a permit and allow commercial air carriers to use park land," he declared. "If you don't allow my hot-air balloons to take off and land within the park, you are discriminating against my type of aircraft." Although I laughed and joked with him, I reminded him that the Interior secretary had determined the airport necessary to park operations and that concession laws required visitor services to be necessary and appropriate. Hot-air balloons did not meet any criteria. Yet every year for the four I served as assistant superintendent, he cajoled, coerced, and threatened us for a permit to use the park.

Some commercial services, such as utility companies, had legal easements across park lands. Nonetheless, these companies cut down trees,

tore up the land, and seldom cleaned up after construction or maintenance. Several times we had to threaten them with injunctions or lawsuits
to get them to use the land more sensitively.

Private land within Grand Teton created its own type of nightmare.
Property rights are sacrosanct. Those who owned land within the park often
had spectacular views, worth nearly a million dollars an acre. Yet houses or,
worse yet, subdivisions conflicted with the purposes of the park. Congress,
responding to private in-holders, required that each park have a land-management plan that spelled out the areas of priority for acquisition. Thus,
people with land listed as low priority for acquisition felt free to build
houses without fear of condemnation. Several locales within the park, such
as Kelly and Poker Flats, had grown into small communities. The high price
of land and the loss of land-acquisition funds brought urban creep into the
park. It no longer stopped at park boundaries.

Even areas of high priority demanded all the ingenuity of Jack's clever
mind to keep them from being developed. He knew that the high price of
Teton land foreclosed access to the tiny pot of land-acquisition funds.
Moreover, he also knew that the will of Congress would probably not support any attempt to condemn a private landowner for simply building a
home. Nonetheless, sometimes just his threat of condemnation discouraged
construction. Other times he sought conservation buyers for marketed land.
For some land he negotiated complicated trades. It was a constant battle to
keep development from marring the breathtaking views of the Teton Range.

Environmental groups try to help the National Park Service fend off
uses and abuses of national parks. Only one organization, however, is solely
dedicated to protecting parks: the National Parks and Conservation
Association. Most groups have broadened their mission so much that park
issues often fall off their radar screen. For example, the Sierra Club worries
about toxic waste, air and water pollution, and urban sprawl. Even the
Yellowstone Coalition focuses primarily on bird-dogging national forests
and usually ignores Grand Teton.

Nonetheless, these groups have become the watchdogs of the parks.
Their dedicated and hardworking but poorly funded staff struggle daily

against wealthy and persuasive developers. Too often, however, these well-meaning idealists fail to see the bigger picture and are rigidly bound by their own traditional view of parks. While we succeeded in turning them around on Alaskan subsistence issues, they could not accept cattle grazing in Grand Teton even to prevent high-density housing on its southern border. In the end, because of the ranch owners' own conservation ethic, the environmental groups may have turned out to be right.

By September 1995, my increased sensitivity to the problems of big natural parks obsessed me. Always an insomniac, I was now lying awake as much as I slept. Everywhere I looked I saw issues that seemed unsolvable. Yet I reminded myself that we had made progress on a number of what seemed to be perpetually futile proposals. I started exploring why some seemingly impossible issues became doable.

The biggest turnaround was the reintroduction of wolves to Yellowstone. In the 1970s Americans, held captive by the livestock associations, believed wolves were dangerous, destructive, and better off dead. No one dared to propose reintroducing wolves to the Yellowstone ecosystem. No one except Director William Penn Mott, a somewhat "spacey" leader with occasional off-the-wall proposals, had the courage to suggest the unthinkable. Not only did he suggest it, he pushed it, and began to win converts. Yet it wasn't one man who changed the paradigm of American thinking— it took a tremendous number of articles, books, films, speeches, lectures, and actual exposure to wolves to educate, sensitize, and inspire the American people. With their consciousness raised, federal public meetings furthered their commitment to the program.

In retrospect it seemed that the turning point came when individuals and nonprofit organizations independently joined the effort. Each one had a different approach. Intellectuals touted the benefits of predators to the ecosystem. Wolf enthusiasts toured schools with wolves on leash, attracting and convincing the youth of their nobility. Environmentalists contrasted the values of livestock and wolves in a wilderness.

The key to success seemed to be engaging the public. The media helped, as did environmental groups, but both had their own agendas. Not until average citizens dedicated their own unique skills and perspectives did the project really catch fire. Ironically, the documents produced by the National Park Service seemed void of passion, too objective and bureaucratic to capture the public's interest. Paradoxically, many people viewed them cautiously, even suspiciously, as propaganda.

As my sleepless nights stretched into weeks, I eventually wrestled through my jumbled anxieties to some conclusions. Success depended on getting the American people behind a park problem. First we had to awaken their consciousness and then focus their concern. The more I brooded about the subject, the more I saw the need for independent articulate spokespeople outside the National Park Service, people who cared and could make others care.

I began to wonder if I could be more effective outside the Park Service than within. There were definite limits to what I could say and do as assistant superintendent or even superintendent. If I took early retirement, I might have more credibility to speak about park issues than I did within the Service. Maybe my observations and experiences could help raise the alarm: "Americans, your parks are being battered and worn. Help save them. Use politics as effectively as those who are abusing your national parks."

After working through this scenario, my insecurities popped up. To capture the attention of the American public, I would have to use journalistic skills that I lacked. Would anyone be aroused by a historian-turned-manager? What if I retired only to find that I couldn't spark interest, let alone concern? The safe approach would be to stay in the Service. I was pretty sure that I could be a good superintendent for a big park, but I wasn't sure that was my best course.

I was also worried about Bob's health. Bob was now sixty-six years old and quietly longing for a permanent home where we could retire together. Although he continued to reassure me that he would go anywhere my career took me, there were places that would constrain his own research and writing career.

As I compared the happiness Bob had given me over the past fifteen

years with the stress and satisfaction I could expect from future superintendencies, I worried that the sixteen-year difference in our ages had caught
up with us. Bob was aging much more quickly than I. Soon I boiled my
internal debate down to one question: What mattered more to me, living
in retirement with Bob for however long he had left, one year or thirty, or
continuing to strive for a big-park superintendency? Phrased in that manner, my priorities became clear.

I suppressed my insecurities and rose to the challenge. I would retire with
Bob and faithfully record my experiences and fears for national parks. I could
only hope that my sincerity would override any journalistic ineptitude.

Then came an even more difficult task: telling Jack Neckels and John
Cook. Both men had invested as much as I had in my career. Each had
groomed me for bigger jobs than Grand Teton's assistant superintendency,
and I dreaded their disappointment. Finally in late October I could stall no
longer. I walked into Jack's office, closed the door, and blurted out: "Jack,
next April, when I turn fifty, I am going to take early retirement." Jack was
even more wonderful than he had been for the previous three years. He
accepted my decision and praised my priorities. Not once did he express
disappointment or reflect on the loss of my potential. I fought back tears
for the entire two-hour conversation. He hugged me as we left, and I knew
how much I loved him.

Next morning we called John Cook. When I told him I was going to
retire, he responded, "You're too young to retire. I know exactly how old
you are." As we talked, three different times he admitted that he was in a
state of shock. Nonetheless, he too was supportive and understanding. "I
have watched you and Bob for years," he said. "I know that you want to
spend more time together." Not once did he hint that I had betrayed his
belief in me.

With the die cast, there was no turning back. The next six months
brought sadness and some second thoughts. As people learned of my pending retirement, they called or wrote, expressing surprise, support, and occasionally disappointment. Although I had never felt completely comfortable
with any group within the Park Service—not historians, superintendents,

or regional office staff—we all had the same common bond that tied us together. I grieved the loss of that community. Doubts about my future career clouded the joy I felt in anticipation of living twenty-four hours a day with Bob. Whereas I knew that I could be a good, but maybe not great, superintendent, I didn't know if I could really reach the public. I was almost as afraid as I was saddened.

Nonetheless, on April 1, 1996, I turned fifty years old. On April 2, I retired from the National Park Service, and on April 3 the moving van arrived. As we pulled out of our driveway and took one last look at our beloved mountains, tears welled in my eyes. It was good-bye to more than a place; it was farewell to a lifestyle, a belief system, and a spiritual commitment. For twenty-two years, nearly a quarter of a century, national parks had shaped my life. Now without them, I had a new life to create.

# Selected Reading

Abbey, Edward Paul. *Desert Solitaire: A Season in the Wilderness.* New York: Random House, 1968.

Albright, Horace Marden, and Robert Cahn. *The Birth of the National Park Service: The Founding Years, 1913–33.* Institute of the American West Books, no. 2, ed. Alvin M. Josephy, Jr. Salt Lake City, Utah: Howe Brothers, 1985.

Albright, Horace Marden, and Marian Albright Schenck. *Creating the National Park Service: The Missing Years.* Norman: University of Oklahoma Press, 1999.

Butler, Mary Ellen. *Prophet of the Parks: The Story of William Penn Mott, Jr.* Asburn, Va.: National Recreation and Park Association, 1999.

Dilsaver, Lary M., ed. *America's National Park System: The Critical Documents.* Lanham, Md.: Rowman & Littlefield, 1994.

Everhart, William C. *The National Park Service.* Westview Library of Federal Departments, Agencies, and Systems Series. Boulder, Colo.: Westview Press, 1983.

———. *Take Down Flag and Feed Horses.* Champaign: University of Illinois Press, 1998.

Foresta, Ronald A. *America's National Parks and Their Keepers.* Baltimore, Md.: Johns Hopkins University Press, 1984.

Freemuth, John Carter. *Islands Under Siege: National Parks and the Politics of External Threats.* Development of Western Resources Series. Lawrence: University Press of Kansas, 1991.

Garrison, Lemuel A. *The Making of a Ranger: 40 Years with the National Parks.* Salt Lake City, Utah: Howe Brothers, 1983.

Hartzog, George B., Jr. *Battling for the National Parks.* Mt. Kisco, N.Y.: Moyer Bell, 1988.

Jones, Courtney Reeder. *Letters from Wupatki.* Edited by Lisa Rappoport. Tucson: University of Arizona Press, 1995.

Kaufman, Polly Welts. *National Parks and the Woman's Voice: A History.* Albuquerque: University of New Mexico Press, 1996.

Rettie, Dwight F. *Our National Park System: Caring for America's Greatest Natural and Historic Treasures.* Urbana: University of Illinois Press, 1995.

Ridenour, James M. *The National Parks Compromised: Pork Barrel Politics and America's Treasures.* Merrillville, Ind.: ICS Books, 1994.

Righter, Robert W. *Crucible for Conservation: The Struggle for Grand Teton National Park.* Boulder: Colorado Associated University Press, 1982.

Rothman, Hal K. *On Rims and Ridges: The Los Alamos Area Since 1880.* Lincoln: University of Nebraska Press, 1992.

—————. *Preserving Different Pasts: The American National Monuments.* Urbana: University of Illinois Press, 1989.

Sellars, Richard West. *Preserving Nature in the National Parks: A History.* New Haven, Conn.: Yale University Press, 1997.

Shankland, Robert. *Steve Mather of the National Parks.* 3d ed. New York: Alfred A. Knopf, 1970.

Skurzynski, Gloria. *Safeguarding the Land: Women at Work in Parks, Forests, and Rangelands.* New York: Harcourt, Brace, Jovanovich, 1981.

Spence, Mark David. *Dispossessing the Wilderness: Indian Removal and the Making of the National Parks.* New York: Oxford University Press, 1999.

Swain, Donald C. *Wilderness Defender: Horace M. Albright and Conservation.* Chicago: University of Chicago Press, 1970.

Wirth, Conrad L. *Parks, Politics, and the People.* Norman: University of Oklahoma Press, 1980.

# Index